Why Stand-up Matters

Also available from Bloomsbury Methuen Drama:

A Philosophy of Comedy on Stage and Screen: You Have to be There
Shaun May
ISBN 978-1-472-58043-6

Performing Live Comedy
Chris Ritchie
ISBN 978-1-408-14643-9

Getting the Joke: The Inner Workings of Stand-Up Comedy
Oliver Double
ISBN 978-1-408-17460-9

Why Stand-up Matters

How Comedians Manipulate and Influence

Sophie Quirk

Bloomsbury Methuen Drama
An imprint of Bloomsbury Publishing Plc

B L O O M S B U R Y
LONDON · NEW DELHI · NEW YORK · SYDNEY

Bloomsbury Methuen Drama
An imprint of Bloomsbury Publishing Plc

Imprint previously known as Methuen Drama

50 Bedford Square
London
WC1B 3DP
UK

1385 Broadway
New York
NY 10018
USA

www.bloomsbury.com

BLOOMSBURY, METHUEN DRAMA and the Diana logo are trademarks of
Bloomsbury Publishing Plc

First published 2015

© Sophie Quirk, 2015

Sophie Quirk has asserted her right under the Copyright, Designs and Patents
Act, 1988, to be identified as author of this work.

British Library Cataloguing-in-Publication Data
A catalogue record for this book is available from the British Library.

ISBN: HB: 978-1-4725-7893-8
PB: 978-1-4725-7892-1
ePDF: 978-1-4725-7895-2
ePub: 978-1-4725-7894-5

Library of Congress Cataloging-in-Publication Data
A catalog record for this book is available from the Library of Congress

Typeset by Deanta Global Publishing Services, Chennai, India

Contents

Acknowledgements

I'd like to say a massive thank you to all the comedians who were kind enough to give me interviews; particularly Dan Atkinson, Dave Bailey, Matthew Crosby, Richard Herring, Stewart Lee, Josie Long, Isy Suttie, Mark Thomas and Joe Wilkinson. To hear their insights and expertise has been a real privilege. I'm also indebted to the many comedians who gave me permission to quote from their stand-up performances in this book, and the agents and others who facilitated this process.

Big thanks are also due to the students I have taught at the University of Kent, and particularly those who studied stand-up. You helped more than you know.

Many people have made this work better by contributing their thoughts, ideas, criticisms and encouragement. Of particular note are Rosie Klich, Robert Shaughnessy, Kevin McCarron, Lawrence E. Mintz, Kevin Wetmore, Lisa Moore, Adam Ainsworth and Mark Dudgeon.

Thank you to all the friends and family members who have been kind enough to get excited about this project, have listened to me patiently, or have been understanding when work encroached on things that should have been more important.

Finally, the really big thank yous go to Oliver Double, a skilled and generous PhD supervisor and guide; my dad, for his uniquely insightful approach to all matters of argument and logic; my mum for her helpful comments, supportive honesty and an outstanding knowledge of the written word, and my sister, Naomi, who sat through an unconscionably long Kevin Bloody Wilson gig because she didn't want me to go on my own. Most importantly to Tom, whose support comes in many forms including love, knowledge and common sense. Thank you.

Notes on the Transcriptions

In all quotations and transcripts, '…' is used to denote a pause. Ellipsis in my quotation is denoted '[…]'.

Interviews

Standard text denotes interviewee's speech.

(Text in italics enclosed in rounded brackets) denotes interviewee's tone, movements, laughter etc.

Comedians in performance

(Text in italics enclosed in rounded brackets) denotes comedian's movements, facial expressions, laughter, etc.

[Standard text in square brackets] denotes audience response.

[Text in italics in square brackets] is used when an audience member speaks.

Where the comedian presents a character, speech attributed to the character is denoted by *text in italics*. For clarity, where the character changes, the speech attributed to the new character starts on a new, indented line of text.

Where the comedian pauses while the audience laughs, '…' precedes the word that breaks the pause.

Where '…' is not included, the comedian speaks through the laugh without pausing.

Occasionally the comedian continues speaking over the laugh, and begins the pause after the laugh has begun. The pause is denoted '…'

Shorter pauses are denoted '(.)'

Introduction

Manipulation, Influence and Stand-up Comedy

Manipulation and influence

Manipulation is usually a pejorative term. When we refer to someone as 'manipulative', we typically mean to imply that they are unscrupulous: a person who plots to control a situation or other people for their own personal benefit. When we refer to ourselves as manipulated, we generally mean to cast ourselves in the role of victim.

This is not what 'manipulation' means; at least, not always. *The Oxford English Dictionary* defines 'manipulation' first as to 'handle or control something skilfully' and second as to 'control or influence someone in a clever *or* underhand way'.[1] A potter may refer to the 'manipulation' of their clay; they would not mean that they deceive it, but that they handle it proficiently in order to craft it. In the medical world, a practitioner 'manipulates' when they skilfully manoeuvre parts of the body in order to treat their patient; when used in this sense, the word may even evoke connotations of care, and of benefit to the person upon whom it is practised. Manipulation is a term that often smacks of deceit and corruption, and whose meaning can encompass the shady motivations of its perpetrator, but it can also mean the simple application of skill to control a situation or outcome: something that every craft requires.

This book reinterprets the craft of stand-up comedy as a series of manipulations. In a few instances, I will suggest that a comedian is consciously manipulating an unwitting audience. These situations are the most recognizable as manipulation in its pejorative sense. There are also instances where the audience is aware that they are being manipulated, and many cases in which the comedian is not cognizant of the manipulative nature of his own actions. The majority of what I will call manipulation, comedians themselves refer to in terms such as 'craft', 'skill' and 'technique'; usually exercised only to ensure that the performer maintains his authority over a rowdy crowd. All of these terms imply the clever use of skill to exercise control. This is manipulation, even when the perpetrator has no darker motivation than to make the audience laugh.

By using the term 'manipulation' instead of more neutral words like 'craft' and 'skill', I aim to highlight some important truths about the nature of stand-up as an interaction. Stand-up is a dialogue: it requires the active participation of its audience, and therefore the comedian has a responsibility to orchestrate and manage those responses. The term also points to the ways in which comedy has impact. I will argue that comedy serves an important prosocial function by testing those ideas that we take for granted, but also that it can coax us into behaving in a way we would not normally countenance. A prolific medium like stand-up can do harm, but it also does important and fundamental good. The important thing is to recognize this, and to be alert to the difference.

'Influence' is the term I will use to signify any ongoing alteration in the beliefs, attitudes or behaviour of audience members that continues after they leave the gig. Influence differs from manipulation in the duration of its effect and in its profundity: where manipulation causes momentary behaviours, such as laughter or applause, influence seeks to have an effect upon the real, internal attitudes and beliefs of the individual: hence it affects the way they interact with the world around them. I will argue that manipulation has an affinity with influence, the one often creating opportunities for the other.

The book is divided into three parts. The first examines the manipulative nature of the joke itself, and those characteristics of comic licence which form a basis for manipulation to translate into influence. Along the way, it provides an introduction to key facets of comic theory; that is, the ways in which various thinkers have tried to describe how and why we find things funny. Part 2 examines some key techniques and conventions in stand-up as tools of manipulation. It exposes some of the subtle tricks of the trade by which comedians tell you when to laugh, or may even assist you to overcome moral objections to their subject matter. I demonstrate that the genius of comic invention is only part of the joke: the way gags and routines are structured are also important components of the joke's creation. Finally, Part 3 discusses the possibilities for influence that arise from this manipulative medium. It examines what the social, political and cultural impact of stand-up comedy might be, and proposes a new way of articulating and demonstrating this efficacy. I ask whether stand-up can influence your attitudes and opinions, and how it might do so.

Stand-up comedy

Stand-up comedy looks uncomplicated. The performance often consists of an individual simply speaking. This does not mean that the interaction taking place and the craft involved are not complex. As Stewart Lee states:

> If you go to, like, a meeting with, like, big-wigs at the National Theatre
> [...] they're always talking about, 'How do we make this immediate?
> How do we connect to all these people? How do we break the fourth
> wall? Wouldn't it be amazing if, in a play, you could have a bit where the
> audience were addressed directly,' and all this sort of thing. Basically
> [...] a lot of highly-educated people spend a lot of time trying to figure
> out, in the world of 'high' art, how to do what the worst Jongleurs
> comic does every night! Of, like, talking directly to people with no
> apparent artifice or interface. It's an amazing thing, and [stand-up's]
> not given the credit.[2]

Stand-up is a complicated interaction. It requires high interpretative competence from an audience who must keep up with a deeply convoluted medium of communication, distinguishing between truth and irony and navigating the grey areas in between. The performer must demonstrate high levels of skill, including exceptional powers of communication and audience management. Stand-up also provides us with one of our most immediate and unmediated sources of feedback upon the world we inhabit. During her show *Kindness and Exuberance*, Josie Long reflects:

> I love stand-up comedy, it's my favourite thing in the world. Erm, and I think it's my favourite thing, at the moment, because of how direct it is. Like, if you want to change what you're doing, you can change it on stage straight away. Like, if you think of an idea in the morning there's no filters, there's nothing to stop you saying it that evening. It's like a really free, pure way of expressing yourself. And I really like the fact that if you wanna run a club, you just book a room above a pub and you start running a club, it's that easy.[3]

Whatever happens in British society, stand-up immediately begins a process of discussing and reinterpreting it. This process necessarily involves more than just an expression of the individual performer's viewpoint. If we find a joke offensive, we protest by not laughing at it. We know that our response to the joke signifies how we feel about the ideas embodied within it and we take our responsibilities as respondents seriously. As we shall see, adherence to this rule can be complicated by circumstances, but by and large it holds true: if we do not agree, we do not laugh. Conversely, then, we understand that when we laugh we are signalling that we agree with – or at least that we permit – the ideas that the joke embodies.

Acknowledging this opens discussion on a range of important ideas about what comedy is and how it works. The practice of joking has been described in many different ways. When we speak of a 'joke' we often think we are simply referring to a text: the actual words said by the joker. However, any joke needs a decent telling, and someone to hear it.[4] Thus the act of performance and the reception of the joke by its hearer are also indispensable elements of any definition. To make matters more complicated, many theorists 'define' the joke not by what it is, but by what it does. Mary Douglas, for example, approaches the joke not only as an exchange between the joker and individual listeners, but also as an exchange between the joker and his society at large.[5] Each theorist is selective, focusing on those features of joking that are most pertinent to his or her own project. These different approaches are discussed further in Chapters 1 and 4. For my purposes, it is important to recognize at the outset that this book treats stand-up comedy as social criticism. When a comedian relates their experiences and opinions, and when an audience responds by laughing, the exchange endorses the comment made as a valid interpretation of their shared world.

An audience will, of course, always consist of a variety of people who differ from one another. The comedian's job is to get this disparate collection of individuals working together: the audience must be bound into a homogenous group which will respond in unison. The comedian, in turn, works in response to that unified reaction, only playing against the responses of individual audience members in relatively unusual circumstances, or when he loses control of the interaction. If the comedian's material is to function as social criticism, the audience's role is to give their affirmation (or otherwise) to the ideas posited. They can agree by supporting the comedian with laughter and cooperation, or disagree by disrupting the exchange with reactions such as silence or heckling.

The comedian can only manipulate if he has successfully taken control of the interaction. This book is, therefore, almost exclusively concerned with successful stand-up performances where a comedian faces a cooperative audience. Naturally, more experienced comedians have better honed their craft and can therefore play most effectively within the control that they exert. This advantage is magnified in the case of better-known comedians, who have the benefit of confronting audiences that are already convinced of their ability to be funny.[6] As Dan Atkinson states:

> When people get to the point where they're becoming famous. [...] They're the easiest gigs because everyone already goes 'I love you

because I've seen you on TV.' And so jokes that you'd previously done when you were just another circuit act – that got nothing – suddenly get huge rounds of applause because people want it to be the case.[7]

For these reasons, most of the examples used here come from established and well-known comedians whose experience and reputation give them the best opportunities for manipulation. This book examines manipulations that are universal within stand-up performances, but it also examines possibilities that are raised by a handful of practitioners. For example, Mark Thomas, Robert Newman, Mark Steel, Stewart Lee and Josie Long represent some fairly unique and specialized practices in the comedy world. They all posit ideas within their work that clash with dominant societal attitudes, but which they hope the audience will award serious consideration. This arguably marks them out from the current mainstream of UK comedy. If they feature more heavily in this book than is representative of the way that the average, pop-culture comedy fan experiences the world of stand-up, this is because their work raises particularly interesting possibilities for manipulation and influence. By examining these overt examples of efficacious stand-up, I hope to provide a model that will allow the more subtle forms of influence found in less overtly political stand-up to be investigated.

Although the book aims to highlight practices and possibilities that may apply to all stand-up comedy, many important questions remain that are beyond its scope. While I would argue that the position and status of the stand-up comedian brings inherent opportunities for manipulation and influence whoever the performer may be, it is likely that these are inflected differently according to the dynamics of power that an individual benefits from, or falls victim to, in the wider society. To take one conspicuous example, women remain strikingly under-represented in the world of stand-up. Indeed, they are so outnumbered by men that many writers – faced with the inevitable confusion that results from using the same pronoun to refer to both comedians and audiences in gender-neutral terms – consider it natural to refer to the comedian as 'he'.[8] I have followed the convention, here, although I consider it far from natural. Generalizations about female comedians abound, including the bizarrely popular notion that women just aren't funny. This background of prejudice surely affects the nature of manipulation and influence in female performance, as it must for members of any minority or marginalized group. By establishing manipulation as a useful framework through which to view stand-up performance, I hope to provide an additional way of understanding how such dynamics of power are expressed in performance. However, such a study is too big a task to be undertaken here.

The methods used

The book focuses on a pool of comedians that may be broadly defined as the current British alternative and DIY comedy scenes. 'Alternative' now seems an inaccurate term for a comic culture that has come to dominate the mainstream, but it is still the term used to describe the style and ethos developed by the alternative comedy revolutionaries of the late 1970s and 1980s. This pool of comedians has its subsections and tensions, with differing ideas about what comedy ought to be. Yet these practitioners are still linked by shared interpersonal networks, experiences, and codes of practice which mark them out as members of the same comedy family. Importantly, they are also subject to the same cultural expectations, particularly as regards conformity to alternative comedy's ethical code. The alternative pool still defines itself partly in opposition to the likes of Roy Chubby Brown and Kevin Bloody Wilson. These comedians are utilized in this book as examples from a separate circuit: they highlight the cohesiveness of our alternative pool by embodying its opposite. A comedian from the alternative pool could expect to be censured for telling a packaged, racist joke (or at least for doing so without the suitable level of irony): Brown and Wilson do not face the same limitation.

Some examples of performances are taken from live shows where it was not possible to obtain recordings. Analysis of these is necessarily less detailed, and the account less precise, than those examples taken from recorded materials such as CD and DVD releases. This live data is nonetheless included because stand-up is, fundamentally, about live exchange: to exclude analysis of stand-up in its natural environment would be to ignore some of its most important and dynamic features. I have attempted to control the imprecision of such material as far as possible by working from detailed notes that were made almost immediately after the live performance. Where direct quotes are attributed to a comedian in live performance they are always taken from the notes made at the time. Live data is balanced with recorded materials which provide the opportunity for more precise analysis. Where recorded material is used, the 'audience' referred to is the audience who saw the show live and whose responses are included on the recording, rather than the audience of the recorded version, unless otherwise stated.

As in other professions, stand-up comedians theorize their work by discussing it among themselves. Backstage, comedians at all levels may be assisting one another with the technicalities of writing, suggesting improvements for specific routines, passing on wisdom from one generation to the next and articulating what general rules they can about what does and does not work. Comedians have a vast body of knowledge about their own craft and, like other professionals and artists, their standards of good and bad practice. I have attempted to capture some of this professional knowledge by conducting semi-structured interviews with practitioners wherever I have had the opportunity to do so. The aim of the interviews was to acquire insight into a craft that is still under-documented; no discussion of it could be complete without some access to this body of professional understanding.

All transcriptions taken from live performance and interviews aim to communicate what happened as accurately as possible, while maintaining clarity and ensuring that they are easy to read. Part of this has been the attempt to distinguish between types of audience laughter.

Determining when a chuckle becomes a laugh, and whether that laugh is 'big', 'small' or just an average 'laugh', is necessarily a subjective process. Yet these subtle variations in the nature of laughter communicate much about how the material has been received, and it is important that they should be noted. What counts as a 'big laugh' in transcriptions of Jason Byrne's radio show, for example, is louder, more raucous and less controlled than what I have cited as a 'big laugh' in Robert Newman's *History of Oil.*[9] The size and quality of laughter in different shows cannot be measured from the same base-rate because the situations are never comparable: Byrne and Newman, for example, are performing to audiences of different size and character, and in shows which have different expectations and intentions attached to them by both the comedian and the audience. I have therefore attempted to transcribe all laughs in a way that accurately communicates their contribution to the exchange in which they occur.

Any scholar who wants to study comedy has, occasionally, to encounter individuals who raise an eyebrow at their choice of subject and see only frivolity in their endeavours. My experience in undertaking this project has been slightly different: often, individuals have retracted their reservations about the usefulness of my research when they discover that I am examining the 'serious' issues of comedy's social and political efficacy. I would guess that they, like many people, instinctively view fun and entertainment as experiences that have little significance beyond their immediate enjoyment, and which certainly do little to advance our social development. This book does indeed look at politically motivated work with 'serious' intentions, but it also examines routines delivered by comedians who have no such motive, to audiences who want no more than an entertaining night out. We should remember that our flippant approach to that strand of comic endeavour which we think of as mere entertainment is a human experience: it is as much a fact of our existence as our serious-minded approach to other material, and is therefore significant. This book will attempt to show that there is no such thing as 'just' being funny.

Part One

Joking is Manipulation

1

Why Comedians Need Manipulation

Control

Stand-up comedy is not a monologue, but a conversation.[1] The primary aim of any stand-up performance is to make the audience laugh. For the performer, stand-up comedy is really about crowd control; causing a group of strangers to behave in a certain way.[2]

The importance of controlling audience responses is demonstrated by the many examples in which the audience reacts 'incorrectly'. In the worst case scenario, the audience does not laugh, or does not laugh often enough, and the comedian has simply 'failed'.[3] Commonly called 'dying', this is a uniquely painful and demoralizing experience, often for the audience as well as the performer. There are other, less dramatic, instances of incorrect responses. On stage at London's Duke of York Theatre, Jack Dee notices an audience member laughing when no joke has been made, and quickly corrects the inappropriate response:

> In itself not actually very funny, but thanks for joining in anyway. [laugh]… Yeah, just try and settle down, try and find your timing, how about that? [laugh] If you could laugh at the right point it would help me an awful fucking lot [laugh]… No I hate it when people laugh at the wrong point, it just kind of, it underlines the pointlessness of what I'm doing up here, you know what I mean? 'You go to a comedy show? You laugh?' 'Yeah but I laugh anyway, I'm mad.' [laugh][4]

Dee's joke at the expense of the audience member gently but forcefully asserts his authority over the audience's behaviour; they are to laugh when, and only when, he wants them to.

In order to be successful, comedians must manipulate and control their audience's responses. Part of this control is orchestrated through performance technique: through the comedian's assertive demeanour or timing, for example. Before the material is performed, though, a more subtle form of manipulation is already taking place through the very selection and arrangement of the comedian's ideas.

What comic theory says: Challenge versus innocent humour

Joking is not merely a frivolous pursuit. On an individual level, the nature of one's sense of humour is considered very important. Lockyer and Pickering point out that to accuse someone of having a deficient sense of humour is a strong personal attack, 'tantamount to declaring us deficient as personalities'.[5] Lash saw the sense of humour as genuinely indicative of the individual personality, saying, 'you can tell a man by the things he laughs at, for in his laughter is reflected the mental company he keeps. Every laugh is a comment, conscious or unconscious.'[6]

On a wider scale, sociologists, anthropologists and philosophers have long regarded joking as an important form of social comment and dispute. As Wertheim states, joking is part of an ongoing negotiation concerning the values, institutions and authorities that control society:

> No human society is a completely integrated entity. In any community there are hidden or overt forms of protest against the prevalent hierarchical structure. In general a more or less dominant set of common values can be discerned – else the society would not have sufficient cohesive power to subsist. But beneath the dominant theme there always exist different sets of values, which are, to a certain degree, adhered to among certain social groups and which function as a counterpoint to the leading melody.
>
> In general those counterpoints only manifest themselves in some veiled form – for example, in tales, jokes and myths, which give expression to the deviant sets of values.[7]

For Wertheim, joking is a 'veil' which allows an ever-present counterculture to express its 'deviant' ideas. Zijderveld builds on this idea, calling joking 'an important means of non-violent resistance'; for Zijderveld, joking can be a weapon.[8]

In her influential article 'Jokes', anthropologist Mary Douglas provides the basis of an explanation for the subversive power of joking. She states that 'the element of challenge' is a vital ingredient of every joke; yet, at the same time, a joke can only work if it is 'permitted' by its audience.[9] In order to laugh at a joke, the audience must both 'perceive' that a joke is being told and 'permit' its content. Jokes are rejected when they trespass on values and authorities that are considered sacred. The comedian must therefore remain, or *be perceived* to remain, within the boundaries of the audience's 'consensus', respecting the standards of 'good taste' that the audience dictates, while also challenging existing authorities.[10] If this is true, then with every joke that a comedian makes he is faced with a difficult and potentially dangerous balancing act. If he cannot persuade his audience to accept the challenge implied within his joke, he will lose the audience's laughter and possibly cause anger among them. If he does not make any challenge at all, he will not be making a joke. Already the comedian must begin to manipulate, as his basic and most necessary task is to persuade the audience that his jokes are dangerous but also permissible.

From one perspective, Douglas' suggestion appears somewhat unconvincing. A lot of comedy articulates our shared experiences and allows us to enjoy what we have in common. We could argue that some of the joy comes from seeing the comedian reflect our own attitudes in this way. Yet Douglas is not only saying that a joke can be funny if it contains the element of challenge, but that it must contain this element in order to be funny at all. If Douglas is correct then every joke must imply an attack upon, or disparagement of, something, be that a person, institution, idea, belief, value or other accepted 'authority'. Audiences must be complicit in this, for the successful challenge will be rewarded with laughter, which signals agreement. There would then be no such thing as an 'inoffensive', 'harmless' or 'safe' joke which was free from social criticism.

For Schopenhauer, there are different types of jokes. He describes two categories of the 'ludicrous' (i.e. 'funny'): 'wit' and 'folly'.[11] Roughly speaking, 'wit' is the joke form in which the joker purposefully links two different objects together through a concept which appears suitable to both objects, only to make his audience laugh when it is shown that, from another point of view, the two objects are unsuited. 'Folly' turns the joke around on us: we carry out actions, make judgements and hold opinions in accordance with theoretical concepts, and laugh at our folly in holding to those concepts when the actions or thoughts that they generate are shown to be inappropriate in a practical situation. We demonstrate 'wit' when we produce a joke intentionally and 'folly' when our own actions are shown to be foolish. Schopenhauer states that 'to conceal wit with the mask of folly is the art of the jester and the clown', implying that our modern comedians form an exception to the rule that all forms of the ludicrous will fall distinctly into one category or the other.[12]

Like many theorists, Schopenhauer identifies a type of joking which he considers superior to others. For him, 'humour' is not a word that should be used to describe all that is funny, but rather a particular brand of commentary upon the world around us:

> Humour depends upon a subjective, yet serious and sublime mood, which is involuntarily in conflict with a common external world very different from itself, which it cannot escape from and to which it will not give itself up: therefore, as an accommodation, it tries to think its own point of view and that external point of view through the same conceptions, and thus a double incongruity arises [...] between these concepts and the realities thought through them. Hence the impression of the intentionally ludicrous, thus of the joke, is produced, behind which, however, the deepest seriousness is concealed and shines through.[13]

According to Schopenhauer, humour is the expression of a conflict between an individual who cannot accept the world as it is and a world that will not adapt to make itself sensible in the eyes of the individual.

The individual tries to reconcile the two, but they are incongruous, and hence funny. Therefore, the best jokes happen when the wit of the joker comments upon a serious folly perceived in the world around him. Mintz expresses this very simply; comedians provide 'a critique of the gap between what is and what we believe should be'.[14] Mintz' theory does, however, differ from Schopenhauer's in that it identifies 'critique' as a universal characteristic of the comedian's art, echoing Douglas' view that all jokes are challenges.

Freud similarly believed that the best jokes served a purpose. He identifies a category of 'tendentious' jokes, which are those that have the purpose of challenging established authorities and thus have the potential to cause offence, but also a category of 'innocent' jokes, being defined as those which 'serve no particular aim', and thus constitute no important criticism.[15] It is not necessarily the case that innocent jokes cannot be funny; rather, they are not usually as funny or satisfying as the tendentious variety:

> The pleasurable effect of innocent jokes is as a rule a moderate one; a clear sense of satisfaction, a slight smile, is as a rule all it can achieve in its hearers. [...] A non-tendentious joke scarcely ever achieves the sudden burst of laughter which makes tendentious ones so irresistible. Since the technique of both can be the same, a suspicion may be aroused in us that tendentious jokes, by virtue of their purpose, must have sources of pleasure at their disposal to which innocent jokes have no access.[16]

Freud here recognizes that humour can be both inoffensive and enjoyable, but states that if a joke is 'innocent' and carries no potential to offend, it has less potential to give pleasure.

Although Schopenhauer and Freud do not go as far as Douglas and Mintz in emphasizing 'challenge' as a vital ingredient of all jokes, they both assert that the best (defined respectively as the noblest or most satisfying) jokes are those which constitute serious social commentary. 'Innocent' jokes have their place, but their value is limited because they offer little satisfaction and do not perform the commendable social function of those which tackle more important or contentious topics. We may, therefore, expect an intensive and largely one-sided joking relationship such as that which exists within stand-up comedy to rely upon meaty, tendentious jokes. A comedian would, by this measure, struggle to craft a lengthy set from material which did not present serious social criticism; such a performance would surely not be satisfactory.

Yet joking, rooted as it is in challenge, is necessarily tricky, and very poor at conforming to rules. Performing on BBC format *Live at the Apollo*, Tim Vine comes on to tumultuous applause and cheering. He lumbers downstage with the microphone stand in one hand, the microphone in the other, and half a football covering the top of his head like a bath cap. Having arrived at the front of the stage he leans on the mic stand and says:

> Good evening! I don't know why, but I keep getting my head kicked in [laugh]… Saw this bloke, he said to me, he said 'Can you tell me your availability to run a football team in Sheffield?' I said, 'I can't manage Wednesday' [laugh]… I saw a football game they came on like that *(Vine hums a tune and dances)* It was Charleston Athletic [laughter and some clapping]… So I watched a football match in Japan, at the end they started doing martial arts. I said to the bloke next to me, I said 'What's going on?' he said 'There's two minutes of Ninjury time' [laugh][17]

These are innocent jokes. They are not designed to serve a tendentious purpose. There is essentially nothing offensive in the silly puns that recognize the dual meaning of the words 'manage', 'Wednesday' and 'Athletic', nor the similarity in sound of 'injury' and the absurd, invented 'Ninjury'. Nor is there any real aggression implied in the wonky interpretation of the phrase 'getting my head kicked in'. Yet these jokes do contain the element of challenge which Douglas identifies as a crucial characteristic of joking. All are puns which emphasize the limits of our language; for example, by highlighting the dual meaning of 'manage' as a senior role within football clubs and as signifying the individual's ability to do something, Vine demonstrates that our language is deficient in providing us with a clear and infallible means of communication. The jokes may similarly expose the limitations of our logic, or shame us for failing to see obvious connections. These are challenges, but they do not seem very important, nor contentious.

A more tendentious element may be detected if we chose to see these as superiority jokes which invite us to laugh at a weak and foolish individual, celebrating our own competence. Vine's gags claim that he is repeatedly kicked and fails to notice that this is due to the football on his head, and that he does not realize the dual meaning of his statement, 'I can't manage Wednesday.' However, this interpretation would be inconsistent with the overall context of Vine's performance. There is no pretence that this is Vine's real life story, but rather an understanding that he is the purveyor of short, packaged jokes which each exist in their own miniature pools of alternative reality. Even if the audience did interpret Vine's persona as a poor soul, they would understand it as Schopenhauer's 'art of the jester and the clown' which 'conceal[s] wit with the mask of folly'.

Altogether, we may conclude that Vine offers a brand of humour which is innocent in as much as it does not aim to serve any social purpose beyond its own funniness, and basically inoffensive, offering no important critique or challenge to authority. Yet Vine does not merely extract the tame responses described by Freud; he gets healthy laughs from his audience, which signifies that his audience find him genuinely funny. This casts doubt upon Freud's theory that non-tendentious jokes are less successful. Despite this, Douglas' idea that jokes must contain challenge is left intact; Vine's gags are not controversial, but neither are they benign.

Joking is always part of an ongoing negotiation through which current thought and practices are challenged and tested. Some challenges are gentle and leave their targets in tact; others are dangerous. Some targets are silly while others are of fundamental importance. Importantly, however, all are challenges.

What comic theory says: Joking and manipulation

Telling a joke is always a manipulative process. The comedian continuously works to manage his audience's perception of his material as both challenging and acceptable. The comedian manipulates further via the skilful selection of the ideas to be expressed in the joke and the structure in which they are presented. Although the process may appear free-flowing, there is nothing random about either of these components. Joking involves an individual using his skill to present material to his audience in a particular way, in order to stimulate a desired response.

Comic theory is commonly divided into three main branches, which identify three basic causes of funniness: superiority, relief and incongruity. Current thought tends to claim incongruity as the most convincing of these theories, because it is appropriate to the whole range of joking behaviours. Superiority and relief theories may help us to provide explanations for particular kinds of joking, but they do not apply universally; we know that it is possible to laugh without feeling superior, and without relieving suppressed thoughts and urges.[18]

As no single theory is universally applicable or able to explain fully the funniness of all jokes, comic theory is best understood as a set of models which help us to interpret the behaviours of joking and laughter through established, universal truths that explain how human beings think and interact with the world around them. Although incongruity, as the broadest of the theories, is easily applied to a large range of jokes, feelings of superiority and the relief of nervous tensions are also useful models through which to understand why a group of people react in unison. Comic theory articulates those processes of the human mind and behaviour which the comedian instinctively understands and manipulates in order to control his audience's behaviour, extracting laughter.

Superiority theory sees joking as an opportunity for participants to assert their own greatness, especially in comparison with outsiders. Thomas Hobbes laid down the following version of superiority theory in the early seventeenth century:

Men laugh often, especially such as are greedy of applause from every thing they do well, at their own actions performed never so little beyond their own expectations; as also at their own jests: and in this case it is manifest, that the passion of laughter proceeds from a sudden conception of some ability in himself that laughs. Also men laugh at the infirmities of others, by comparison wherewith their own abilities are set off and illustrated. [...] I may therefore conclude, that the passion of laughter is nothing else but sudden glory arising from some sudden conception of some eminency in ourselves, by comparison with the infirmity of others, or with our own formerly. [...] It is no wonder therefore that men take heinously to be laughed at or derided, that is, triumphed over.[19]

According to Hobbes, laughing with pleasure at one's own superiority does not necessarily imply the presence of an outside person to whom the joker feels superior; some occurrences of superiority humour arise from the joker's realization that he has bested either his former self or his own opinion of himself. Even so, the superiority theory is a discomforting explanation for the behaviours of laughter and joking. Hobbes' summary is tinged with moral repulsion at the idea of finding amusement in nothing more than our own, arrogant pride. Those who laugh are 'greedy' seekers of self-aggrandizement, and they often have their fun at the expense of others who are 'derided' and 'triumphed over'. As Morreall has highlighted, superiority is not a satisfactory explanation for all instances of funniness.[20] Laughter can and does occur in situations where the superiority of the joker is either absent or comparatively unimportant. There are, however, many jokes in which superiority plays an important part.

Relief Theory supposes that laughter is the release of un-needed energy. According to Herbert Spencer, any excess of emotion or mental energy must be used up by activity of the body, mind or both, and laughter is one way of releasing this energy.[21] Freud refined this idea in reference to his interpretation of human psychology as the battle of the superego to maintain control over the ego in opposition to the id.[22] The joke creates pleasure because it allows an economy of psychological effort. As we have seen, Freud believed that some jokes were more satisfying – that is, funnier – than others. In his theory, the most satisfying jokes are those which save us the effort of policing our thoughts, which we do by blocking uncivilized ideas so that we may not take conscious pleasure in them. Such jokes may prevent the imposition of a new barrier or, most satisfactorily of all, give us a temporary relief from maintaining a barrier which already exists.[23] This is another discomforting way to explain the pleasure we take in laughter, for the implication is that our joy comes from ideas that we would not usually allow ourselves to have: in short, it implies that we take an unconscious pleasure in ideas that are hostile, bigoted or otherwise uncivilized.

Achmed the Dead Terrorist is a popular – and controversial – ventriloquist act performed by American comedian Jeff Dunham.[24] Achmed is a skeleton with a turban and long, plaited beard. He refers to himself as a suicide bomber, and his catch phrase is, 'Silence! I kill you!' In one routine, Dunham is faced with persuading his puppet that he is, indeed, dead. Initially unwilling to accept this, Achmed cheers up when he realizes that it must therefore be time to claim his reward of seventy-two virgins. He scans the audience, saying that he hopes they are not his reward because, if his quota of virgins includes 'a bunch of ugly-ass guys' then he has been 'screwed'. Dunham asks whether it was explicitly stated that all Achmed's virgins would be female. Achmed instantly realizes his mistake, crying 'Holy crap!' The audience delivers a big laugh, accompanied by applause and cheering.[25]

The comments that followed this video on YouTube on 21 April 2010 were divided: some expressed pleasure and admiration at the act's funniness, while others expressed outrage.[26] The debate was heated, with each side launching personal attacks on the other's offensive or deficient sense of humour. Interestingly, a couple of comments bemoaned the extraordinarily high number of views that this video had clocked up, deriding YouTube viewers for giving their time to such fripperies and ignoring websites where they could access important information about the reality of the international political situation. Whether evaluated positively or negatively, it is clear that Dunham's *Achmed the Dead Terrorist* had become an influential and powerful act.

Many people do find Achmed's ranting funny. This may be due, in part, to the incongruity of seeing the terrifying figure of the suicide-bombing terrorist resurrected as a ridiculous and feeble puppet. His suggestion that the audience might be his reward of seventy-two virgins may similarly be interpreted as an incongruity, as might Dunham's pointing out of the potential discrepancy between the suicide bomber's expectations and his actual entitlements under the technically flawed bargain he has entered into.

However, the power of this act is surely more properly understood by reference to the superiority and relief functions that it serves. In an interview with Brian Logan, Dunham recognizes that the act works both by relieving tensions created by fear and by placing the terrorized back on top of the power structure. Dunham is quoted as saying that his intention is to 'make fun of those guys [i.e., suicide bombers] and that mentality that most of us in the free world don't understand' and that one of the reasons for the act's success is that 'we like to laugh at our fears. [...] We're poking our thumb in the eye of something most of us don't want to think about.'[27] Logan notes the 'jingoistic edge' to Achmed that 'some will find unattractive', but also defends Dunham, saying that he is 'an equal-opportunities offender'. He notes that 'another dummy, Bubba J, sends up so-called white trash America; a third, Jose Jalapeno, draws on Latino Clichés'.[28] It is true that Dunham presents several different satirical puppet characters, but it is all the more notable that it was *Achmed the Dead Terrorist*, an act which performs such obvious functions of superiority and relief, which shot Dunham to stardom.

The power of Dunham's act lies in the fact that it allows his audience to indulge feelings of superiority and to express tensions and hostility. They enjoy the assertion of their superiority, as shown in the explosive reaction to Dunham's joke which suggests that suicide bombers may have been duped into a false bargain regarding their seventy-two virgins. This not only mocks the terrorist's folly, but also suggests that the faith which they believed they died to serve was maliciously tricking them rather than looking after them. Thus, the audience are invited to bask in their superior intelligence as well as their comparatively favourable situation; the joke underlines the fact that the audience are alive while the terrorists who attacked and scared them are dead and, according to dominant Western belief, not in the paradise they were promised.

Spencer may have interpreted the laughter as a release of the tension created by an atmosphere of fear about terrorism; the incongruity of Dunham's act shuts down the usual pathways for the expression of anxiety by making the feared object ridiculous, and thus the nervous energy is released by the muscular contortions involved in laughter.[29] Using Freud's model, we see the joke as a way for Dunham and his audience to relieve themselves of the responsibility of censoring their aggressive feelings towards an ideology and a group of people to whom they are opposed.[30] They may temporarily cease their usual self-censorship and release their aggressive feelings by enjoying Achmed's ill fortune. Simultaneously, they are granted reprieve from the unpleasant emotion of fear.

Mass feelings of superiority and hostility require an 'other'; a group of people whom the audience as an in-group considers to be an outsider. In the Achmed act, there are levels of 'other' which are subtly played alongside each other. At its most specific, the act attacks middle-eastern suicide bombers, but the mockery also encompasses wider categories of 'other' including terrorists in general and Muslims. The act is often defended against accusations of racism, and of attacking Islam as a whole, on the basis that Achmed always denies being Muslim. This is a rather spurious defence, given that Achmed references, and Dunham mocks, ideas which are specific to (some interpretations of) Islam, such as the seventy-two virgins. As Allport demonstrates, human beings have a tendency towards 'overcategorisation', where we assume that a characteristic that we recognize in a small number of individuals will be universal among the group to which we ascribe them; this tendency can form the basis of prejudice.[31] In the wake of incidents of terrorist activity by a small group of extremist Muslims, this tendency towards overcategorization led to a disproportionate association of all Muslims with acts of terrorism. Hopefully, most of Dunham's audience would consciously know that this was unfair; yet Freud's theory suggests that they may perhaps enjoy the excuse of the joke, which muddies the ethical waters and disguises this act of religious discrimination and racial hostility, to express an unconscious tension towards Muslims.

Dunham's act is deeply manipulative. Dunham has admitted that Achmed is a response to the post-9/11 climate; indeed, the act could hardly have worked in this form if it were not for the preoccupation with extremist Muslim terrorism that followed the attack on the World Trade Centre.[32] This is to say that Dunham spotted the fear and tension present in his society, and used his act to play skilfully upon it, spinning fear and hatred into laughter. Manipulation is used to home in on a set of uncomfortable emotions and to direct the audience to express them in a very particular way.

The creation of jokes by incongruity is in itself a manipulative process. Critchley states that 'humour is produced by a disjunction between the way things are and the way they are represented in the joke, between expectation and actuality'.[33] Incongruity explains the pleasure received from jokes as the enjoyment of an incongruity between the set of associations or progression of the story which our experience of the world suggests as natural, and a different set of associations or progression provided by the punchline to the joke. Zijderveld builds upon this principle, stating that 'joking is defined as the conscious or unconscious transition from one institutionalised meaning structure to another, without changing much of the original role and behaviour logic'.[34] In incongruity theory, therefore, the success of any joke is dependent upon the joker's ability to set up a particular range of associations in his audience's minds, and then to subvert those expectations by introducing a new set of associations or meanings. Again, the basic technique of the comedian is manipulative; he manipulates his audience into setting up expectations, and then subverts them.

An example of this may be found in the Tim Vine routine transcribed above. The set-up line, 'Saw this bloke, he said to me, "Can you tell me your availability to run a football team in Sheffield,"' takes the form of a question that the audience readily recognizes. They know that the respondent would usually reply by stating their availability, and Vine knows that this expectation will be implied by his question.

The punchline ('I can't manage Wednesday') then subverts the expected response. On one level, Vine is replying to the question by saying that he is not free on Wednesday, but the audience understands that this is really a premise through which to create a pun on both the name of Sheffield Wednesday Football Club, and the word 'manage'. Indeed, all of these puns involve such trickery, introducing a scenario (a man wearing a football over his head; a question about availability; a football team who dance on to the pitch; a match that ends in a martial arts display) and then flipping the interpretation of that scenario with a surprising conclusion (the puns 'getting my head kicked in'; 'manage Wednesday'; 'Charleston Athletic'; and 'Ninjury time'). Vine's art is to skilfully balance the information given in both the set-up and punchline in a way that manages expectation and surprise in the minds of his audience. Of course, the audience also knows that the joke is not likely to resolve itself in the natural or 'expected' outcome; both parties know that the jokes manipulate thought processes in this way, even if they are not particularly cognizant of it.

Much of Mark Thomas' comedy works by incongruously subverting our normal patterns of logic, often by use of what Zijderveld calls 'hyper-logic', which 'beats normal, average logic by hyper-logical, hyper-cunning intelligence'.[35] His CD release *The Night War Broke Out* records a show performed in Edinburgh on the night that Britain and America started their war on Iraq in 2003, amid fierce resistance from the British populace. Thomas mocks US President George Bush's assertion that the two countries were conducting a war on 'terror', calling this idea:

> a mistake, 'cause Terror is a concept [small laugh]… How can you wage a war on a concept, an abstract – fine I – I dunno – you, you want war on abstract concepts, fucking great, you kill a lot less people [small laugh]… Good. Let's have a war on clutter next [laugh], fucking bring 'em on! [laugh continues]…[36]

Thomas' argument is essentially logical: you cannot wage a physical war on a concept because a concept exists only in the abstract. He uses hyper-logic to outdo Bush's 'standard logic', arguing that to declare war on concepts – as opposed to countries or peoples – is more sensible as it avoids needless human suffering.

Thomas gets a big laugh by equating 'war on terror' with a war on 'clutter'. The shift from 'standard logic' to 'hyper-logic' subverts expectations, bringing the 'role and behaviour logic' of standard messages about the need to counter the threat of terrorism into the 'role and behaviour logic' of domestic nuisance.[37] To compare so dark and threatening a force as terrorism with the soft irritation constituted by clutter is silly, but Thomas has supported it by appeal to logic; this hyper-logical argument is rather bewitching and, potentially, persuasive.

If all jokes really do hinge on the use of incongruity, then a manipulation of expectations and of associations is the basic currency of all stand-up comedy; the audience puts itself into the comedian's hands with a willingness to be 'tricked' in exchange for the reward of laughter. The relationship between comedian and audience is a relationship based upon consensual manipulation.

'I'm not that kind of comedian'

Many comedians will assert that their material is simply not the kind of material that has a lasting impact. Isy Suttie believes that stand-up 'definitely' has the power to be a particularly effective way of influencing attitudes in the long term, but dismisses her own abilities in this area, saying, 'comics like Robert Newman and John Oliver are masters of this, but sadly I am not!'[38] Critchley seems to theorize this attitude:

> Most humour, in particular the comedy of recognition – and most humour *is* comedy of recognition – simply seeks to reinforce consensus and in no way seeks to criticise the established order or change the situation in which we find ourselves.[39]

To some extent, Critchley may be right. In the following segment, Eddie Izzard shares his experience of showers with his audience:

The same people who make toasters, make showers [laugh] For they have a turney-button too that lies [laugh] (.) For we know turn-turn-turn-turn for hot [small laugh] (.) turn-turn-turn-turn for cold [couple of people laugh] (.) but the only position we're interested in is the position between there [couple of laughs]... *(puts his hand out as if holding an imaginary dial then watches his hand closely as it makes a barely-discernible movement)* and there [big laugh]... One nano-milimetre [big laugh]... between fantastically hot [big laugh]... and fuckin' freezing [big laugh, applause, cheers and whistles][40]

Izzard then compares shower-users to safe-breakers, miming listening to the dial with comical 'concentrating' facial expressions, and using a stethoscope. The audience continues laughing regularly. Izzard continues:

You have two positions in the shower (.) One position is this *(safe-breaker mime)* (.) and other *(voice gradually escalates to a panicked shout)* is this!

Izzard jumps back as he speaks to press himself against an imaginary wall, facing the spot where he mimed the dial to be. The audience delivers a big laugh and applause. Izzard extends the routine, shouting that everyone must 'stop using taps!' Altogether, Izzard sticks solely to the topic of showers for over a minute and a half, achieving regular and enthusiastic laughter from his audience throughout.

Critchley's interpretation of this routine may be that Izzard is simply recognizing an inconvenience in the lives of his audience. The audience laugh at the recognition, thus celebrating the consensus that they share on this issue. They enjoy the fact that they agree, and they celebrate the ridiculousness of the situation. By collective recognition – even celebration – of the fact that showers do not work properly, Izzard and his audience are merely reinforcing the social truth that showers are inefficient and uncomfortable to use.

This interpretation may not withstand much serious scrutiny. This is a very successful routine; the laughter is enthusiastic and has the unfettered, easy quality which signifies an audience who are comfortable in their temporary loss of self-control. These are not just observations, but finely crafted, crowd-pleasing jokes. Schopenhauer's model may be helpful here to explain the way in which the observations, or 'recognitions', within this routine become successful jokes; the routine is an expression of a conflict between an individual who cannot accept the world as it is, and a world that will not adapt to make itself sensible in the eyes of the individual.

When Izzard recognizes the common failure of showers to function in a helpful way, his audience enjoys the public sharing of experience, and is perhaps thereby released from the negative feelings of irritation and discomfort that usually surround the experience of the shower. Yet this piece of material does occupy the gap between the way things are and the way they ought to be. Izzard's material is not a celebration of the convenience of the modern shower; it is a sharing of the problems with it. The audience see that this design fault is so common that in a room containing hundreds of people, all of them recognize the same problems. Even if the piece does dispel some negativity surrounding this experience – and I would argue it is really just as likely to confirm the appropriateness of negativity as to drive it away – it is certainly 'criticising the established order', and suggesting that a change should occur to improve the situation.

Isy Suttie performs a comic song about the population of a wealthy, insular, *Daily Mail*-reading village succumbing to hysteria and accusing a newcomer of being a paedophile. When asked whether this piece aims to highlight the issues of prejudice and irresponsible hysteria-mongering involved, Suttie replies that her motives were neither so 'deep' nor so specific:

> Sadly it doesn't run that deep, it's just to take the mickey out of the tendency in some people to be narrow minded! It could have just as easily been a murderer, or anyone who was different. I think it's more that I try and chime with what's already inside people and bring it out.[41]

The significance of 'taking the mickey' should not be underestimated. Observational comedy – the 'comedy of recognition' – works exactly as Suttie states. It empathizes with its audience, 'chiming' with their experience and 'bringing out' shared feelings. Thus, common attitudes and observations are exposed, shared and, in this sense, enjoyed. However, the observation is more than just an observation. Suttie does not simply state, 'there appears to be a trend among well-to-do *Daily Mail* readers to accuse innocent people of paedophilia'. This would not be funny. It would be similarly disappointing if Izzard simply stated: 'The temperature of showers is notoriously hard to control.' The mockery and challenge of their statements – the highlighting of the discrepancy between the world as it is and the world as it should be – make these routines funny, and it is these same elements which give the routines the status of real, challenging social commentary.[42]

It is probable that only a small minority of comedians ever think of their work as social commentary. This is perhaps a healthy tendency; the imperative to be funny is a demanding one, and has to be the comedian's priority. As Dan Atkinson states:

> I'm always really shy of talking about comedy as anything more than an entertainment form because I think it's really important to remember that you're there to entertain people, and that's the job. And the other stuff is secondary, but that's not to say it's not important.[43]

What this viewpoint fails to take into account is the fact that the imperative to be funny cannot be divorced from the imperative to deliver social commentary; the two things go hand in hand. Thus, all stand-up sets offer challenge and comment, whether or not the authors themselves intend or recognize it.

Challenging positively

When jokes challenge and attack, they are not solely destructive. The above segments from Eddie Izzard and Isy Suttie debunk the credibility of the current functioning of showers and thought processes of *Daily Mail* readers, but by doing so they necessarily create a vacuum for new ideas to fill.[44] Sometimes challenge can be positive in itself, belittling a negative convention by asserting a more positive idea. In a routine about making personal weaknesses into strengths, Josie Long confides in her audience:

> I guess physically my biggest weakness, er, physically, um, is my stomach *(Long runs her hands around her midriff)* And I've got this thing called polycystic ovarian syndrome, and it means that you carry weight around your middle and it's really difficult to shift, especially if you want to eat up to two chocolate bars a day, which some people do [laugh]. Naming no names [couple of people laugh]… And I thought, well, how can I turn the physical weakness into a strength? You know, turn the physical weakness into a strength, so what I do, is I (.) dress to flatter it! [laugh]… Erm and also, um, and also I've drawn a sea scene [cheers, laughter and applause][45]

Long pulls up her t-shirt as she speaks to reveal a picture painted directly onto the skin of her abdomen, triggering a very positive response from her audience. The picture depicts a square, blue sea with peaks for waves at the top, two fish at the bottom and a boat sailing up the side. There is a mermaid swimming in the patch of sea and the word 'MARVELLOUS' is written in large letters in an arch above it.

The laugh that comes in response to Long's assertion that she 'dresses to flatter' her stomach is, perhaps, in recognition of the incongruity of the statement with Long's image. Dressed casually in a t-shirt and jeans, she comes across as too cool to be scanning fashion magazines in the hope of finding tips for flattering the stomach. This joke also seems to highlight the futility of such beauty advice: even if she wanted to, Long could not change her tummy by 'dressing to flatter' it. The sea scene is a much better solution. It makes Long's stomach into something that is desirable for reasons that seem more legitimate: it is funny and aesthetically appealing, showcasing her talents as comedian and artist. Long continues, speaking over the laughter and excitement created by her sea scene:

I don't know if you can see... I've written the word 'marvellous'
[laugh]... on it (.) there (.) 'marvellous' [laugh]... I just thought...
what's not to love? [laugh]... If it says 'marvellous' on it, like, there's
cynicism and there's cyni – if it says 'marvellous' on it... what's not to
like?... *(Long looks down at her stomach and then cheekily back up at the
audience)* Check this out...

Long taps her stomach, causing ripples to run through her sea scene.
Again, the audience deliver a big laugh and some clapping. Although
Long goes on to admit that she has started doing sit-ups 'in quite a
major way' since devising this joke, the ethos of the routine remains
a celebration of Long's body and new-found body-confidence. She
continues with some comments on the sea scene and more wobbling of
her tummy, before concluding:

Tell you what though, bizarrely, I am now totally comfortable with this
(gestures to her exposed stomach) which is something I never thought
I would be [couple of laughs] If anything I am enjoying myself too
much [laugh].

Long continues by explaining how much she has come to love
performing this joke, now heartily enjoying the opportunity to
expose – and wobble – her belly. The routine emphasizes Long's
delight through her joyful facial expressions, her excited tone of
voice, and her general enthusiasm for sharing what she has done.
Long does attack conventional ideas of beauty and bodily taboos but,
significantly, she does so positively: the focus of the routine is not attack
upon the convention, but the presentation of a delightful alternative
viewpoint.

Freud recognized that joking could perform this positive function.
Over twenty years after the publication of *Jokes and their Relation to
the Unconscious*, in which he laid down the theory discussed above,
Freud identified a special, 'fine and elevating' kind of joking which he
called 'humour':

Obviously, what is fine about it is the triumph of narcissism, the ego's victorious assertion of its own invulnerability. It refuses to be hurt by the arrows of reality or be compelled to suffer. It insists that it is impervious to wounds dealt by the outside world, in fact, that these are merely occasions for affording it pleasure. [...] Humour is not resigned; it is rebellious. It signifies the triumph not only of the ego, but also of the pleasure principle.[46]

In humour, we respond to pain and misfortune with defiance, laughing at troubles rather than suffering from them. This is what is at play in Long's routine about her stomach. She rebels against the world's attempt to impose anguish on her by turning what she believed to be her biggest physical weakness into something in which she can take pleasure. Thus Long triumphs over the draconian norms which dictate what constitutes beauty, and turns a physical characteristic that she was once uncomfortable with into something that she can take delight in showing off.

Kenneth Lash notes that jokes can be an effective way of presenting alternative points of view. First, the comic makes us aware of our 'norms' or 'archetypes', subverting concepts and structures about which we have already decided upon fixed ideas in order to remind us that we take those ideas for granted.[47] A joke may then add to our understanding of the world by allowing us to see that concept in its totality, taking into account other points of view:

Where the failure of the object to fit its archetype is *intentional*, as in the case of wit turning a value upside-down, the incongruity is presented for the purpose of edification through the agency of the imagination. A new norm, to supplant or to modify the original, is suggested; a new point of view is invited. [...] For any given situation, there exists a myriad of possible norms. [...] One of them may seem more true than others, but it does not follow that the others are completely false. [...] Does not each one convey, as it were, an insight into that sector of life which, though it be not yours, nevertheless *is*?[48]

Lash suggests that joking can help us to understand the world better by understanding it more completely. When Josie Long exposes her stomach and sea scene, she reminds her audience that their norms surrounding beauty and bodily taboos are constructed, and that the authority of those norms, however complete and dominant, is essentially tenuous. She further presents an alternative point of view, inviting a positive reaction to her stomach in its norm-defying state and suggesting an alternative approach to beauty as a substitute norm.

If Lash saw this function of joking as a way of understanding our world better, the theatre practice of Bertolt Brecht provides a way of translating this understanding into the possibility of real social and political challenge. Brecht's *Verfremdungseffekt* (commonly translated as the 'Alienation effect', or A-effect) was not only intended to promote awareness among audiences, but also to drive them to act for social change. The A-effect works in just the way that Lash describes; when an object or idea which we generally take for granted is presented as an oddity, its authority as a norm is broken down and other possibilities will, of necessity, get a hearing[49]:

> The A-effect consists in turning the object of which one is to be made aware, to which one's attention is to be drawn, from something ordinary, familiar, immediately accessible, into something peculiar, striking and unexpected. [...] One might have thought that... but one oughtn't to have thought it. There was not one possibility but two; both are introduced, then the second one is alienated, then the first as well.[50]

In Brecht's theory, the intention of presenting multiple possibilities is not merely to encourage a greater awareness, but to translate that awareness into politically useful consciousness; 'to allow the spectator to criticize constructively from a social point of view'.[51]

It is therefore possible for comedy to challenge positively. Yet this positive challenge is no less an attack than its more overtly aggressive counterparts. Long's presentation of her abdomen offers an alternative view in which a feature that she once considered her 'biggest weakness' is not a taboo to be hidden but a joy to be shared. Her routine may be charming and gentle, but is no less an attack upon the norm.

Even seemingly benign joking deals in challenge, and even joking that contains overt challenge must package those challenges in some form of disguise; otherwise we have observations and criticisms, but not jokes. The successful joke must also find the agreement of its audience and, because it does so via a disguise, it is necessarily manipulative. It is true that many of the challenges that comedians make are fairly harmless, such as Eddie Izzard's persecution of the domestic shower, or even positive, as is the case with Josie Long's celebration of her tummy. It is also important to recognize that comedians do not, on the whole, act maliciously: they think of what they do not as 'manipulation' but rather in terms of 'craft'. Yet comedians cannot escape the manipulative nature of their form, and we should therefore question what uses that manipulation may be put to.

This book examines three main aspects of the manipulation employed by comedians. The first is the functional set of manipulations involved in getting an audience to laugh: the management of expectation, atmosphere and perception that form the backbone of successful stand-up performances. The second is the manipulation that might be at play when individuals who outwardly oppose anti-Islamic attitudes or discrimination laugh at Dunham's *Achmed the Dead Terrorist*; that which causes us to permit ideas which we would normally consider taboo to be discussed, or to be treated in a manner which we would generally consider uncomfortable. The third is manipulation in its most dangerous and exciting sense; the possibility that the comedian's influence over individuals could last beyond the immediate contact at the gig, and even take part in a wider social negotiation, having an impact that endures.

Safe Space: From Manipulation
to Influence

As we have seen, the successful joke constitutes a manipulation in itself. A further manipulation comes with the temporary suspension of responsibility which is permitted under the terms of comic licence. Part of the vital role of joking as a form of social negotiation is to provide an abstract safe space in which jokers can operate outside of the restrictions which govern most regular interaction. As Steve Linstead states:

> Humour is often a framework for 'non-real' or 'play' activity, an aside from normal discourse. The fact that it need not be taken into account in subsequent 'serious' interaction does allow messages and formulations to be 'risked' within its framework which would not otherwise be acceptable or possible.[1]

When something is 'only a joke', we allow the speaker licence to subvert our usual standards of honesty and decency. Joking forms a marginal safe space where this potentially dangerous experiment may be held in safety; the subversive ideas posited in joking do not have to affect 'serious' interaction.

Stewart Lee observes that, from ancient societies to the present day, it has been the comedian's duty to posit himself against whatever norms he is confronted with: 'Doing the opposite of whatever appears to be acceptable.'[2] However, a protected space in which this process can occur is necessary on a practical level, if only for the comedian's sake:

> In the Soux Indians they have a guy who's called the Heyoka, and he's like the clown of the Soux nation. He's ideally gay or bisexual, he washes in dirt, walks around backwards, stands on his head, sleeps

outside, y'know. Basically he lives every moment in subversion; in opposition to conventional social norms. I wouldn't like to do that.[3]

Richard Herring notes that failure to adequately separate joking behaviour from everyday behaviour would risk turning social commentary into madness. Herring quips that he sees a 'big similarity' between his own material and the rantings of drunkards and the mentally ill:

> You worry about the insanity of the act kind of *(laughs)* spilling into your real life and you actually becoming insane, y'know, because obviously, on stage you're allowed to […] break the rules and you're allowed to […] be crazy. […] My job is to say the unsayable. […] But a kind of mad person in the street *(laughs)* it is the kind of thing that they do as well. […] When I'm not in the performance situation I wouldn't want to be behaving like the character on stage does.[4]

Herring acknowledges that the safe space can malfunction: if the boundaries between offstage and onstage become blurred then the comedian could risk being merely unacceptable. It is the status of the comedy gig as a protected world apart which makes interaction that would be censored outside of the performance situation credible enough to be worthy of attention.

John Morreall notes that: 'In finding something funny, we are for the moment not concerned about truth or about consequences'.[5] He formulates this in to two key terms. 'Practical disengagement' involves a lack of concern with the consequences of the joke, as 'humour lovers overlook the practical needs of themselves and others'.[6] 'Cognitive disengagement' is a lack of concern with truth:

> As long as something is funny, we are for the moment not concerned with whether it is real or fictional, true or false […] someone listening to a funny anecdote who tries to correct the teller – 'No, he didn't spill the spaghetti on the keyboard and the monitor, just on the keyboard' – will probably be told by the other listeners to shut up.[7]

Practical and cognitive disengagement are important concepts, because they form the basic rule-change by which joking is able to operate as a safe space; between them they constitute a subversion of truth and decency that is manipulative in itself. However, the manipulation does not stop there; the tendency towards practical and cognitive disengagement allows joking to generate more subtle manipulations.

The ambiguous relationship with truth

Critchley suggests that 'the comedian sees the world under what some philosophers call an *epochē*, a certain bracketing or suspension of belief'.[8] For much comedy, it is vital that the audience alter their view of the world so that alternative logics and truths may dominate over everyday common sense. For example, Eddie Izzard presents a world which operates in accordance with many strange rules. In *Definite Article*, fruit has consciousness: pears actively seek to ripen at the most inconvenient moment, and oranges are staffed by a crew of submariners:

> Inside an orange, it's like the film *Das Boot* in there [laugh] … With Jürgen Prochnow going:
> *(Caricatured German accent) 'Don't let zem get in to ze orange!'* [laugh]… '*Most important. All the Juice will get out and will not be good*' [laugh]… '*Zey are breaking in with finger-depth-chargers … Let ze peel come off only in small chunks!*' [laugh][9]

Izzard mimes the person holding the orange, tearing off small pieces of peel, then continues with a less consistent Prochnow impression: ' "Zey are breaking in! Push all the pips into bits they wouldn't expect!" [big laugh].'

Like many of Izzard's surreal routines, the idea of the orange putting up a military defence has its origins in observational comedy. The audience's laughter is fuelled partly by their recognition of a genuine, typical experience: oranges can be difficult to peel. The joy of the routine is that Izzard offers an explanation for this difficulty which is at once absurdly logical and totally implausible. The idea that the orange is fighting back correlates with the initial observation, but is obviously not accurate. The audience gladly accepts, and enjoys, Izzard's topsy-turvy world, consenting to a manipulation of belief in which they temporarily allow the possibility that their fruit is fighting back: if they did not, they could not enjoy the routine's funniness.

The importance of cognitive disengagement may be demonstrated by examining a case in which an audience is forced to re-engage with their common-sense perception of a comedian's material. On stage in Cardiff, Stewart Lee gives an analysis of a joke as told by two different comedians:

> There used to be this Irish comic on the circuit called Michael Redmond, right, and he was great. […] He had big bushy hair, and a kind of long droopy moustache, and deep-set blood-hound eyes and he always used to wear a long brown mac, and carry a little plastic bag. And what he used to do, right, was he'd walk out on stage and he'd stand still in silence for about a minute and a half, looking weird, and then he would say… *(Lee looks dully out over the heads of the audience)* 'A lot of people say to me… get out o' my garden.' [laugh] Now I think that is the greatest opening line ever.[10]

Lee explains that although Redmond always got a good laugh for this joke, it got a 'much better laugh' when used by Joe Pasquale in a Royal Variety Show performance some years later. Lee is certain that Pasquale has plagiarized Redmond's joke, and telephones Pasquale to ask how he thought the joke up. Pasquale replies:

> 'Well', he said, 'I thought if someone looked out of their window (.) and they saw me (.) in their garden (.) they would say, (.) "Get out of my garden"' [small laugh]

Lee then highlights the absurdity of this point, continuing:

> Now, that's not quite right, is it, because (.) if you looked out of your window (.) [one person begins to chuckle] and you saw Joe Pasquale

(.) [a few more people laugh] in the garden (.) you'd just go *(adopts a befuddled expression)* 'Is that?' [laugh]... 'Joe Pasquale?' [bigger laugh]... 'In the Garden?' [laugh]... 'What can he possibly want?' [laugh]... You might even be frightened, right, [small laugh] 'cause that, that joke only works if a kind of anonymous weirdo's saying it. As soon as you introduce a celebrity into it it's kind of structurally compromised.

Lee admits that when Pasquale told this joke in his Royal Variety performance it got a big laugh. It is therefore a funny joke, even when told by Joe Pasquale. Nevertheless, Lee expertly demolishes the joke as told by Pasquale by destroying the 'epochē', in which it makes sense – that is, the world in which Pasquale has a habit of trespassing into the gardens of strangers, and in which homeowners' response to finding celebrities on their property is simply to ask them to leave. Lee identifies that, in reality, people do not react to celebrities as they do to 'anonymous weirdos'. Lee then goes on to make a more general attack on Pasquale, during which the effectiveness of this initial assault becomes clear. As the audience laugh easily at Lee's attacks on Pasquale, they demonstrate that Lee has created consensus for the idea that Pasquale is a plagiarist and liar.

Lee implies that Michael Redmond is the superior comedian as he is the original author of the joke, and the one for whom the joke makes sense. Certainly, Redmond's scruffy appearance and anonymity adds depth and integrity to the joke that Pasquale cannot achieve, and should make the joke as told by Redmond funnier than the joke as told by Pasquale. Yet Redmond too has built his joke on an unlikely sounding premise. His audience surely do not truly believe that he is in the habit of trespassing into stranger's gardens. Lee allows the dubious premise of Redmond's joke to remain intact while also using the destruction of this premise in Pasquale's joke to compromise its credibility. That Lee can engineer so successful an attack on Pasquale purely by dismantling his premise shows the vital importance of the audience's willingness to suspend its disbelief.

The relationship between truth and lies in stand-up is often complex. In this case, it is impossible to be certain how far either Lee or his audience are cognizant of the double-standard Lee has jokingly imposed. It could be a case of straightforward cognitive disengagement: they know that a decision to temporarily accept the dubious premise as fair and truthful will allow them to enjoy the joke, and that a pedantic obsession with accuracy is therefore inappropriate. It could also be related to what Oliver Double calls a 'shared misunderstanding', where · some or all of the participants genuinely believe in a faulty idea and are able to use it as a shared point of reference.[11] All we know for certain is that Lee's audience do not care; their healthy laughter in the routine that follows demonstrates that they have accepted Lee's interpretation and logic without becoming distracted by its validity.

There is, however, a limit to the falsity that audiences can easily accept. Double states that 'truth is a vital concept in most modern stand-up comedy because of the idea that it is "authentic"'.[12] Tony Allen sees authenticity as part of the 'nebulous agreement' which governs interaction between comedian and audience.[13] Dan Atkinson feels that audiences like to believe that what a comedian tells them is true.[14] This is demonstrated in Rhod Gilbert's 2007 show *Who's Eaten Gilbert's Grape?*[15] Gilbert spends a substantial amount of time establishing a close rapport with the audience, before concluding the show with a heart-warming story from his own life which is intended to demonstrate that the world is a positive and hope-fulfilling place. He is sitting in a depressing, dingy hotel room feeling lonely, depressed and old, without much hope of things improving. He orders a burger from room service, and it is delivered by a woman called Bridget. Seeing that he's watching the film *What's Eating Gilbert Grape,* she stays to watch it with him. They arrange to meet again, eventually fall in love, and have just had their first child. As Gilbert has spent much of the show talking to individual members of the audience, they have a sense of community, both with Gilbert and with each other; thus they are emotionally invested in the story and engage with it affectionately.

Their connection to the piece, and to Gilbert, is then shattered when he tells them, quite bluntly, that none of the story is true. As Gilbert offers little further explanation, the audience is left uncertain as to what to believe. Most might have spotted the truth, and will take this throw-away comment at face value and disbelieve the story. However, the length of the show compared to this brief throwaway comment might suggest to others that they are supposed to read the comment as a joke and continue to believe that Bridget and the baby really exist. One way or another, Rhod Gilbert has lied about something important. The next year Gilbert toured with a new show, *Rhod Gilbert and the Award-Winning Mince Pie*, in which he admits that audacious falsehoods (including the baby story) have long been a feature of his material.[16] As he goes on to explain, his long-running claim to originate from the Welsh village of Llanbobl was also a lie: it is just a place that Gilbert made up.

At the Canterbury performance of *Who's Eaten Gilbert's Grape*, the audience remained cooperative even after Gilbert's admission that the story they had invested in was untrue; it was recognized as a joke, and permitted. There was, however, still a tangible sense of betrayal when Gilbert stated that he had lied; indeed, this betrayal is the point of the joke. Gilbert is quoted as saying:

> Fairly early on, I realised that I could have a bit of fun with this whole idea of, 'I've had enough of telling lies, it's the truth', and then everything you say thereafter is a lie. It's funny when you admit to an audience that you're lying on one thing and you tell them 'but the next bit's true,['] then they naturally tend to take you at your word.[17]

Cognitive disengagement is therefore not a universal trait. Audiences do sometimes invest in the truth behind a performance. Total accuracy, however, is difficult in comedy. It is common practice for comedians to adapt true stories in to their funniest form. Usually this involves misrepresentation if not outright falsehood; some amount of equivocation or embellishment. Even the smaller editorial changes involve deceit, as it becomes impossible for the audience to identify the exact point at which truth merges into fiction.

Interviewed in 2008, Joe Wilkinson was working with the creative decision to tell stories that were as true as possible.[18] This inevitably lead to the tricky question of what constitutes 'truth'. Few of any comedian's stories can make it to the stage without editing or embellishment, and between the outright fabrication and the unaltered truth there exists a grey area. Wilkinson's commitment to accuracy extended to rejecting embellishments that would get more laughs through outright lies. However, it was still often necessary to indulge in some level of falsity. He explains by reference to a story he tells on stage in which he overhears a transaction between a salesgirl and a man who wants to buy a crucifix. The salesgirl informs the customer, 'we've got two kinds of crucifixes – plain ones and ones with the little men on':

> I wasn't in the shop, I overheard the man telling someone [about it], do you know what I mean? So, yeah, that is a lie, because I wasn't standing [behind him in the shop] [...] he came out of the shop, told the story to his wife, I was listening. But then, if I told the story how it actually was [...] it's too convoluted. If you wanna get that story across you have to cut out all that bit [...] you can still be truthful, but it is – in a way – it's a whopper. [...] The stories are true, the details are lies [...] because it just helps the stories along.[19]

For Wilkinson, the embellishment of details does not detract from the overall honesty of the story. To say that he witnessed the salesgirl describe a crucifix as having 'a little man on' is a lie in itself, but it is a lie which Wilkinson believes will allow the fundamental truth – the sense of what really happened – to be communicated more clearly. However, Wilkinson is also clear that he does not think comedians have an obligation to be truthful. Being 'as truthful as I possibly can' was what he, personally, was doing 'at the moment'.[20]

Mark Thomas' *Dambusters* is an example of a show that has clear priorities beyond making the audience laugh.[21] The show's tour charted the progress of the Illisu Dam Campaign, which sought to prevent the building of a dam which would have caused environmental damage and displaced thousands of local inhabitants, with particularly ruinous effects for the Kurdish population.[22] *Dambusters* also reported on the widespread persecution of Kurds by the Turkish government, legal system and armed forces. Thomas ends his performance with a long list of real and despicable human rights violations as related to him by the victims, telling his audience stories of physical and emotional violence which happened to real people whom he has met. The effect is deeply harrowing, and far from funny. When asked why he chose to end a comedy show in this way, Thomas is still visibly angered and upset by the memory of the stories he heard:

> The reason to include it was it would be a disservice not to. Because it was true. Because I want people to know. [...] You know, they've had nearly two hours of fairly decent comedy – I think I was pleased with it, do you know what I mean? – I've earned the right [...] they will have that.[23]

That the show be 'decent comedy' was still essential. For Thomas and his colleagues, though, the impetus for the show was inextricably linked with achieving the aims of the campaign:

> We would never talk about the tour. We would talk about the campaign. For us, this was war. This was total war. And we were gonna win. And, you know, we spent three years doing this, and it was gonna be truthful and it was gonna be accurate. I thought, 'I want people to be moved. I want people to feel emotionally moved. I want them to feel motivated. I want them to try and get near, to understand what was going on.' That actually, you know, fucking, the *stuff* that went on was quite vile [...] its *shocking*. [...] And actually, when that happens it would be a fucking insult not to report it. How callous would that be? What should I do? Turn round and go, 'let's put the gag first'? They've had the gags. I wanted to leave them with something that would mean when they left that theatre, they wanted to do something.[24]

The ending of *Dambusters* is conspicuously lacking in jokes. As Thomas states, the decision to abandon 'the gags' was part of an intentional strategy: the sudden lack of joking emphasizes the accuracy of the report and creates a strong emotional response. Yet truth and believability are also vitally important in many of the routines in which Thomas does aim to create laughter. His style, typically, will be highly informative, delivering new information to audiences and updating them on real campaign work, so it is important that the audience are able to trust in the accuracy of what he tells them. Thomas is, however, aware of the ambiguity inherent in the issue of truth:

> Truth. I mean, when you start saying truth it's […] I mean where do we start on that one? […] If you're performing and your objective is to make people laugh, that's your objective. How you get there y'know […] it depends what kind of comic you are, and what kind of performer you are.[25]

As Double notes, Thomas provides an example of the necessary subjection of truth to bias in stand-up comedy:

> In stand-up comedy subjectivity is the whole point. The audience wants to hear the comedian's views, opinions and prejudices, and there is no need to temper these with fairness or balance. This is something that Mark Thomas recognises, admitting that he gives a less fully rounded picture of his opponents than his friends and fellow campaigners.[26]

In telling his stories from a biased point of view, Thomas is delivering the truth as he sees it. His decision to edit the representation of his friends and, more particularly, opponents is similar to Wilkinson's instinct to edit the facts to ensure the clearest possible communication of the vital points.[27]

Stand-up is subject to a clash of interpretations by audiences. On the one hand, audiences accept that much of what a comedian says may be implausible or highly subjective, and that honesty is rarely a priority. On the other, audiences also have a tendency to believe in the accuracy of information presented, and enjoy believing that what they are hearing is the truth. As we shall see, this contradictory approach can open up possibilities for the comedian to move from consensual manipulation to subtle influence.

Suspending values and moving moral boundaries

Henri Bergson famously observed that, 'the comic demands something like a momentary anaesthesia of the heart'.[28] Laughter is usually accompanied by an 'absence of feeling':

> Indifference is its natural environment, for laughter has no greater foe than emotion. I do not mean that we could not laugh at a person who inspires us with pity, for instance, or even with affection, but in such a case we must, for the moment, put our affection out of court and impose silence upon our pity.[29]

Bergson's idea is reflected by many theorists. Morreall's idea of practical disengagement similarly implies the temporary suspension of emotions such as pity.[30] As Lash further states:

> On the part of the observer, any emotion other than one expressive of pleasure will obviate laughter. If viewed sympathetically, the clown's pratfalls can be painful; his terribly strenuous efforts to arouse laughter, piteous. A minor misfortune is not funny until its effects are dissipated, until time has detached us from our angry emotional reactions to the incident. To perceive the comic element at any given moment, emotional neutrality *towards the comic object* is demanded.[31]

Morreall points out the moral implications of this lack of emotional response, stating, 'to laugh about something is not to take it seriously, and for you not to take seriously what I take seriously is for you not to take *me* seriously'[32]:

> As a social species, we depend on each other for emotional support. [...] Displays of solidarity and compassion may be as important as reducing physical pain, for suffering is often at least as much psychological as physiological. Compassion by itself helps reduce our suffering, and *not* showing compassion can itself harm us.[33]

In joking, we permit the participants licence to subvert the important ethical edict that human beings should show sympathy to one another.

The following segment from Jason Byrne constituted the climax of the 'law' episode of BBC Radio 2's *The Jason Byrne Show*:

This is an old story in Ireland, you might know this story which was, which was great – this was the best suing thing ever. There was this couple have moved in to a house and, and the, the wife of the house wen – went into the garage and was cleaning out the garage. So while the husband was at work she, she got the stuff – she got like spirits and paints and stuff – and poured them down the toilet, okay? *(Byrne chuckles as he speaks)* While he was at work. But she didn't flush it, she just poured it down. And she went back down to the garage. He came home from work and did what every man does, got the newspaper, put it under his arm and went upstairs to the toilet, right? And he sat on the toilet *(Byrne chuckles as he speaks)* but the thing that he was doing, is he lit a fag [laugh] right?... On my life, this happened! He lit a fag, right, he threw it into the toilet when he was finished [laughter] (.) and blew up his arse [big laugh] right?... When! [laugh]… When the fire brigade came they just found a man on the ground with his arse blown up, right? [laugh]... And they got him up on to the stretcher, and this is why he sued *(Byrne's voice creases with laughter)* 'cause when they were carrying him down the stairs, the Fireman said, 'What happened to you?' and when he told them, they started to laugh so much [laugh]… On my life, this happened! They dropped him off the [laugh] stretcher… *(Byrne begins to laugh)* He fell down the stairs and broke his leg! [laugh]… This other [laugh continues]… This other lovely story, and this is only about three years ago, there was a bus crash, right, and what happened was, the bus had crashed and keeled over onto its side. Now, when the bus *(Byrne corpses)* [laugh]… when the bus crashed, there was twenty people on it. And on my life, by the time the police arrived, there was twenty-six people on it [laugh].[34]

This is an excellent piece of delivery. Byrne tells the audience that the stories are to be enjoyed by introducing them as 'great […] the best suing thing ever' and 'lovely', then uses his tone and pace to convey excitement about the coming punchlines. He uses his own laughter to catalyse the audience response, corpsing at strategic moments to tell the audience that the joke to come is so funny that he can't contain his own laughter long enough to get the words out.[35] It also reinforces the authority of comic licence, telling the audience that it is acceptable to interpret the stories as jokes and to laugh at them. This is crucial because the subject matter is, if viewed sympathetically, sad and disturbing. The first story involves a man who has been seriously injured, and whose injuries are further exacerbated by the callous behaviour of the medical professionals who are supposed to care for and help him. We could interpret the audience's response as a symbolic 'punishment' for the man's crude and silly behaviour,[36] but such an interpretation could not hold true for the bus crash, which involves an accident befalling twenty innocent people. Although the point of the joke is the savvy behaviour of people who were not injured, emphasis is placed on the seriousness of the crash ('the bus […] keeled over onto its side') and suggests that those on board were genuinely in danger. To laugh at the joke involves momentary disengagement from the plight of those twenty genuine casualties. Byrne's repeated assertions that the stories happened to real people ('on my life!') suggest that the audience are supposed to read these stories as real: far from reducing the power of his tales, Byrne's emphasis on reality is intended to make them funnier.

It is clear that audiences can suspend their sympathy and their concern with the likely practical outcome of scenarios which are presented to them as a joke. Even if Byrne's potentially tragic tales are presented as truths, they are presented in a joking format which gives the audience permission to laugh at their content even though this would be considered highly reprehensible behaviour if the information had been presented in ordinary interaction. It is not only the audience's emotion which is being suspended, however, but also their attitudes. When Morreall identifies that human beings depend upon each other for support, he is not talking about an instinctive emotional response but rather a social attitude that grows out of mutual need. We may assume that Byrne's audience would be repulsed if they witnessed a person laughing at the site of a bus crash or serious individual casualty, or at a second-hand retelling that was presented more seriously: society gives them the attitude that it is important to demonstrate sympathy and wrong to show lack of concern.[37] Yet the attitudes that would cause that repulsion are clearly not active as they laugh at Byrne's comic telling.

Ronald de Sousa refutes the idea that attitudes can be temporarily adjusted in order to enjoy a joke, arguing that, 'suspension of disbelief in the situation can and must be achieved for the purposes of the joke; suspension of attitudes cannot be'.[38] He gives the example of a rape joke which plays upon the assumed promiscuity of its victim, arguing that the hearer cannot find the joke funny unless they agree with the sexist assumptions upon which the joke is based. Certainly, de Sousa is correct in identifying that jokes can and do fail on the grounds that their audience finds them offensive. In Douglas' terms, the joke has trespassed upon attitudes, values and beliefs that are deemed sacred, and thus has been rejected.[39] Failure to reject the joke is not, however, the same as rationally agreeing with it.

De Sousa uses a very simple example to demonstrate the lack of flexibility in audience attitude. He sets up a 'thought experiment' within his writing, whereby he uses the word 'fuck' while making a point about attitudes to promiscuity, and then goes on to say:

> If you snickered at my language, it's because you consider it *naughty*. That is an *attitude*. If you didn't, I'm unlikely to get a chuckle out of you by asking you, just for the present purposes, hypothetically to think my language naughty.[40]

De Sousa recognizes the potential for 'apparent' contradiction here, citing instances of failure to comply with his theory as the exceptions which 'prove the rule'.[41] He claims that when a person who does not have the attitude that an expletive is funny laughs at that expletive, the source of the laughter is the incongruity of considering the joke to be funny. Rather than a 'counter-example', it is 'an instance of the following principle: *It can be funny to suppose that something that is not at all funny might be funny, but only if you actually think it isn't actually funny*' (italics in original).[42]

De Sousa is correct in identifying that such a blatant attempt as his thought experiment is not likely to make his audience suspend their attitudes. Indeed, de Sousa's suggestion of directly asking an audience to pretend that they find a word naughty is manipulative in itself; he has used a ridiculous suggestion to imply that there is no other method by which the audience may be persuaded to suspend their attitudes, thus making the very idea appear ridiculous. If we allow that there may be other ways of persuading an audience to suspend their everyday attitudes in order to appreciate a joke, the idea will appear more realistic.

To take de Sousa's example, the 'naughtiness' of the word 'fuck' is not fixed in an individual's perception, but is open to negotiation on the basis of context and usage. Mark Thomas relates an anecdote in which he attends a formal dinner at the *New Statesman*, where he admits to feeling out of his depth. Unfortunately for him, just as he is planning to leave, a speech is demanded of him: 'Didn't go well [laugh, one person claps]… It didn't, I'll just be honest with yer – head down, fourteen fucks, three wanks and a cunt in five minutes [big laugh, some clapping].'[43]

One of the reference points necessary to understand this joke is the fact that Thomas' regular performance style involves a notably liberal use of expletives. This joke is delivered nearly ten minutes in to the second half of the show. By this point the audience have heard Thomas use the words 'wank' and 'cunt'; instances of the word 'fuck' have been especially numerous. The words are sometimes used as an integral part of a punchline, but are not considered funny in themselves. Thomas' audience certainly do not snicker at his use of language, so we may assume that they do not take the attitude that the expletives themselves are particularly 'naughty'.

Yet Thomas' joke depends upon the audience interpreting 'fourteen fucks, three wanks and a cunt' as inappropriate. The joke derives its funniness partly from Thomas' admission of failure and partly through the incongruous way in which he lists the expletives, but both of these factors rely upon the audience's understanding that Thomas' choice of words was 'naughty' in the given situation. We could interpret the joke as de Sousa suggests and assume that Thomas' stand-up audience laughs at the very fact that the unfunny expletives are presented as funny. However, this interpretation fails to account for the most obvious source of incongruity; that the audience recognizes that the expletives which do not offend in the context of the gig are inappropriate in the context of the formal dinner. They laugh not because it is ludicrous to consider these expletives funny, but because they know that the expletives are genuinely incongruous in that situation. Perhaps they laugh in part because they know that they would also be shocked and embarrassed if they had been present at that dinner speech, despite their liberal attitude to swearing in the context of a Mark Thomas gig. Their attitude to expletives is not fixed, but is open to negotiation.

A more important rebuttal of de Sousa's argument is provided by those instances in which audiences laugh at jokes which present genuinely nasty assumptions. These instances where comedians get laughs for topics which are usually deeply taboo demonstrate that audiences can be worryingly malleable. In 1992, when there was massive media interest in the topic of ritual abuse of children, following accusations against several families in the Orkneys, Jack Dee delivered the following gag at the Duke of York's theatre in London:

> How are you gonna get people in this country to stop smacking their
> children? It would be nice to stop fucking them first of all wouldn't it?
> *(Dee chuckles slightly)* [Big laugh, then appalled ooh-ing][44]

Dee responds to the confused response, achieving laughs both for observing a 'wave of disapproval' to his left and 'a party from the Faculty for Witchcraft and Buggeration' to his right.

This is clearly a difficult joke. The Orkneys story is still fresh, and the audience know that Dee's gag references the recent abuse of real children. Hence, laughing at the joke involves suspending the important moral attitude that making light of such crimes, and turning the suffering of the victim into something to be laughed at and therefore enjoyed, is wrong. Applying the approach which de Sousa took to his rape joke, we would also need to assume that the unpleasant assumptions upon which this joke comments would need to be shared by the audience;

they could not laugh at the idea of children as sex objects or at Dee's flippancy unless they genuinely believed that it was acceptable to treat children, or the topic of abuse, in this way, and did not truly condemn such practices.

Clearly, though, neither Dee nor his audience really share these assumptions or attitudes. The fact that the audience's collective response is to attempt to correct the laugh with a belated (albeit fairly tame) display of disapproval demonstrates that this joke is deemed to have overstepped the mark. Yet the immediate response of this audience is not disapproval but laughter. For the first few micro-moments after Dee makes his shocking statement, the audience is hoodwinked into suspending its disapproval and delivering a big laugh. The correction could be seen as more representative of the attitudes and values by which the audience lives, and by which their society runs, than the knee-jerk reaction of laughter. In the moment that the audience laughs, therefore, they are not demonstrating agreement with the ideas presented, but rather have been manipulated into temporarily moving their moral boundaries by the fact that they are hearing a joke.

What harm can it do?

That joking should allow the temporary suspension of our usual standards regarding truth and morality is important to its role as social negotiation. Joking is a safe space which allows 'messages and formulations to be "risked" within its framework which would not otherwise be acceptable or possible.'[45] If we did not grant jokes some freedom from our own strictures, they could not test them. However, these are tendencies that can be abused. Stewart Lee demonstrates this point in relation to a joke which he heard on a Roy Chubby Brown album:

> There was this one bit where he goes, 'Ah, the political correctness has gone mad, hasn't it? These days you can't say Catholic, you can't say Protestant, you can't say Muslim' – and I'm thinking, 'well you *can* say

those things', right? – and all the audience go 'ooh, yeah'. And he goes, 'you can't say Protestant, you can't say Jew, you can't say Muslim... which is a shame 'cause I like to go in the corner shop on a Sunday morning and buy the paper and go, "'ere's a quid, keep the change you Paki bastard"'. […] And he gets a really big laugh.[46]

Lee feels that this joke abuses the audience's natural tendency to forgive inaccuracy and flout social standards of decency:

> Because first of all, what he's saying isn't true. It's necessary for him to create a false premise – that we live in a society where you can't say 'Muslim', you can't say 'Jew' and you can't say 'Christian' – 'cause that looks heavy-handed and the audience go 'hmm, yeah' – but if he actually said, 'you can't say nigger, you can't say Paki, you can't say –' *(laughs)* people would go, even […] Chubby's audience would go, 'Well... *(Lee makes a conciliatory gesture)*'. So then the punchline doesn't relate to the set-up, because the set-up is about an imaginary Britain, in which you can't use the proper nouns of religions. The punchline is […] it seems to be a response to something else, right? The punchline is a response to a set-up which he hasn't got the guts to make. […] It doesn't make any sense, and it annoys me that the audience think that it's striking some kind of blow for freedom. Because you shouldn't be able to say, […] 'here keep the change you Paki bastard', but you should be able to say 'Jew', 'Muslim' and 'Christian'... and you can! *(laughs)*. […] But that audience definitely feel, from the recording, like Chubby's telling it like it is and thank God for him.

Roy Chubby Brown is allowed to make the inaccurate claim that it is considered unacceptable to name religions in order that he may link that concept to the use of a racist term which is genuinely considered non-politically correct. He thus makes the disallowing of the term 'Paki' appear 'heavy-handed'. Brown uses the tendency towards cognitive disengagement to manipulate the audience into validating an idea which they could not otherwise have approved of: because Brown has merged the term 'Paki' into the same category as 'Christian' and 'Muslim', the taboo against the term 'Paki' appears unnecessarily restrictive.

The tendency towards practical disengagement is similarly abused. As Lee notes, this audience would be unlikely to feel that they could permit a term like 'Paki' if it was presented to them as part of a category of racist terms, but when it is presented at the punchline to a joke the term is interpreted in the safe space where normal rules governing decency are relaxed. Therefore, the term is ambiguous: it is normally disallowed, but may be permitted if presented as a joke about that very restriction. Yet the lowering of the taboo does not stop at accepting the word within the terms of the joke. Lee believes that the gag has gone further for this audience, with the punchline allowing them to assume that the set-up referred to genuine restrictions on offensive language and therefore to agree that 'Chubby's telling it like it is [...] thank God'.

According to Billig, when a statement causes offence, the claim that the speaker was 'only joking' acts as, 'both a claim to be doing something permissible (i.e. joking) and a denial of doing something criticisable'.[47] Howitt and Owusu-Bempah identify that this defence may be so effective that it reverses the interpretation of the event: the blame for the breakdown in social decency is assigned not to the speaker who caused offence, but to the offended party who is deemed to have behaved inappropriately by objecting.[48] Yet it is clearly possible for a joke to be considered inappropriate or offensive. As Douglas acknowledges, the problem with such unsuccessful attempts at joking is sometimes the sanctity or instability of the norm that is challenged:

> There are jokes which can be perceived clearly enough by all present but which are rejected at once. [...] Social requirements may judge a joke to be in bad taste, risky, too near the bone, improper or irrelevant. Such controls are exerted either on behalf of the hierarchy as such, or on behalf of values which are judged too precious and too precarious to be exposed to challenge.[49]

Morreall emphasizes that context and situation are important in determining whether a joke is acceptable. For example, there are occasions when the practical disengagement necessary to enjoy jokes should not be applied: even jokers 'should not laugh at someone's problem when compassion is called for', or, 'promote lack of concern with something about which people should be concerned'.[50] Yet because joking is so complex, and its interpretation affected by so wide a range of contextual factors, it is impossible to discern a hard-and-fast set of rules which may dictate what is, and what is not, acceptable joking behaviour. It is in this ambiguity that the danger lies.

This is exemplified in the debate surrounding racist humour. Kevin Bloody Wilson has often been accused of using racist material. Performing his 2009 *Dilligaf Café* show in Peterborough, he is quick to answer such accusations.[51] His set begins with a film montage of clips, pictures and captions which celebrates Wilson's continued popularity over the past twenty-five years, flourishing despite the efforts of the mainstream media to censor him. A slide bearing the legend 'Friends and Fans around the World' appears, introducing a section of the film in which we see Wilson photographed with 'friends and fans' from various racial groups: a balance which feels distinctly strategic. Early in the set, Wilson indignantly bemoans the fact that he has been accused of racism. He lists ethnic and religious minority groups and advises that anyone who is a member of such groups, and 'a bit thin-skinned about it', should leave immediately. Wilson points towards the door as he speaks, and his demand is met with laughter, cheering and applause from his intimidatingly supportive audience. He explains that the show's title – *Dilligaf* – is based on the military acronym meaning 'Do I Look Like I Give A Fuck'. He then sings a song, also entitled *Dilligaf*, which sums up the show's ethos by meeting critical statements about its subject matter with the acronym.[52] The song does more than establish that Wilson is unconcerned by political correctness (PC). It posits both Wilson – and, by extension, the atmosphere of his gig – as actively anti-PC.

Wilson demands that those who are not willing to play along leave his gig, and dismisses complaints about the offensive nature of his material with the word 'dilligaf'. Many of Wilson's audience already know the *Dilligaf* song, and are able to shout out 'dilligaf' along with him, sharing in that dismissive response. These introductory gestures are an assertion of how the show is to be interpreted. Wilson and his audience are there to joke; people who cannot engage with that joking on its own terms are spoilsports and are not welcome. This reinforces Howitt and Owusu-Bempah's point that:

> Jokers are not held responsible for the joke's content. [...] 'It was only a joke' is held to be an appropriate apology or excuse when a listener protests in some way that the limits of this licence have been breached. Failure to accept this 'apology' results in the butt of the joke being seen as unreasonable.[53]

Anyone who chooses to take Wilson's joking seriously is blamed for failure to accept the terms of comic licence, and it is they who are considered to be at fault.

Despite the clear signification that Wilson's act is all in jest, much of his material presents genuinely aggressive content. Wilson is a white Australian, but identifies himself with 'British' culture (and he implies that this is equivalent to 'lad' culture) by highlighting cultural similarities between Britain and Australia. He also notes that he spends a lot of time in Britain, and enjoys doing so. By contrast, he says that he cannot understand why Muslims 'come here', as they do not like 'our' culture, do not 'let us shag their women' and 'don't even drink'.

It is clear that the term 'Muslim' is used here to imply difference and 'otherness' of nationality, ethnicity and culture as well as religious belief. Wilson's statement does not acknowledge that there are many Muslims who are British by birth, citizenship and culture. There is some incongruity present in the juxtaposition of Muslim and 'lad' cultures, and a cosy statement of shared culture in the implication that British culture boils down to 'shagging their women' and, particularly, drinking. Above all, though, this is a sheer statement of superiority, designed to give its audience the pleasure of identifying what they share and contrasting this unity to the 'otherness' of the outsider:

> Laughter produces, simultaneously, a strong fellow-feeling among participants and joint aggressiveness against outsiders. Heartily laughing together at the same thing forms an immediate bond [...] and simultaneously draws a line. If you cannot laugh with the others, you feel an outsider'[54]

Wilson's joke implies that promiscuity and, particularly, consumption of alcohol are defining features of British culture. While this is arguably true of the culture that Wilson is addressing – or at least of the way in which his audience would like that culture to be interpreted, at that moment in time – cognitive disengagement is needed. Many non-Muslim British people would be excluded from 'British culture' by such a definition. While terrorism has given a high profile to a minority of Muslims who object to Western culture, it is inaccurate to apply this attitude as widely as Wilson's statement implies. A dissenter may also point out that many Muslims are born and raised in Britain, so do not actively choose to 'come here'. Such factual niceties are not wanted: they ruin the joke. Similarly, it would be deemed inappropriate to deprive the audience of their practical disengagement by highlighting the offence that this statement could cause to those whom it is designed to exclude and oppose.

Wilson follows this gag with some jokes about blowing Muslims up, both in revenge and as a measure to prevent terrorist attack. He also sings a song about a taxi driver named Mohammad Achma-lick-my-arse. As Wilson has already placed all of the responsibility for offensiveness onto the 'thin skin' of those who are offended, it is clear that the participation of both Wilson and his audience in these exchanges is intended to be excused by comic licence. Indeed, Wilson's suggestion that those who are likely to be offended should simply leave the gig is intended to emphasize that his material is harmless: if those who are offended simply remove themselves, the performance cannot affect them.

Michael Phillips argues that participation in an event like Wilson's gig will necessarily constitute racist behaviour. Even those who would never participate in prejudice against Muslims outside of the safe space provided by comic licence are committing a racist act because it is their actions, rather than their intentions, which define racism:

> Consider the German soldier who volunteers to march Jewish victims to the gas ovens *out of simple patriotism*, or the Klansman who ties nooses at lynchings for *business reasons*. Each may (in principle) act

with heart and mind uncorrupted by racist beliefs or feelings (though obviously this is unlikely). Does this mean that they have not acted in a racist manner? Suppose that all the German soldiers at Dachau acted out of patriotism and all the Klansmen at the lynching were there for business reasons. Would this mean that none of those who participated in such events were guilty of racist acts?[55]

Phillips believes that defining racist behaviour by result rather than by intention is the more socially helpful interpretation:

> The point of the moral category 'racist', to begin with, is to allow us to identify and to condemn certain pervasive forms of mistreatment (both for the sake of the victim and for the sake of justice). Accordingly, we ought to adopt that use of 'racist' that best serves this end.[56]

Kevin Bloody Wilson's implied claim that participation in these racist acts has no effect outside of the gig is spurious. As a form in which to transmit ideas, jokes have the advantage of being eminently repeatable, and thus able to spread ideas to a much wider audience: an effect that is intensified by Wilson's use of catchy and memorable comic songs. Not only does the joke package the idea in an entertaining form which rewards both teller and hearer with the benefits of humour, it also allows sentiments and stereotypes to be reintroduced in a variety of packages so that it does not become onerous. Howitt and Owusu-Bempah state:

> It would be conversationally problematic to introduce the ideas underlying racist jokes so repeatedly in normal conversation. […] It is not simply that jokes give the teller a degree of license to express such views but, provided that the teller has a repertoire of such jokes, it allows prolonged repetition of basic themes which would tax conversation otherwise.[57]

As the joke is transmitted, each new person who laughs validates the sentiment expressed.[58] The joke may be shared under the guise that it is 'only a joke', but according to Howitt and Owusu-Bempah, it is far more significant:

> Jokes, in general, do not begin and end with individuals, they are transmitted socially, changed and embellished. [...] Jokes are communicative acts which play a significant role in social exchanges – a medium through which society disseminates and generationally transmits its dominant attitudes towards outgroups. Racist jokes, therefore, act as propaganda in support of a racist ideology.[59]

According to Howitt and Owusu-Bempah, jokes do not only transmit existing stereotypes, but also teach new ones. Philips claims that a joke will be incomprehensible to a person who does not have a pre-existing knowledge of the stereotype upon which it plays.[60] Howitt and Owusu-Bempah demonstrate that the opposite is true: the hearer can spot the exchange as a joke and discern that the reference point needed to interpret it is a stereotype.[61] The hearer then calculates what the stereotype is and recognizes that they were expected to have a pre-existing knowledge of it. If surrounded by an audience who are laughing, the hearer can discern that the stereotype is acknowledged by their peers. The joke thus succeeds in transmitting racist attitudes, keeping stereotypes alive by teaching them to the uninitiated and to new generations.

In his influential analysis of *The Nature of Prejudice*, Gordon W. Allport deconstructs the process by which prejudice may come to result in the most extreme of discriminatory acts such as lynchings, pogroms and massacres. He states that 'any negative attitude tends to express itself in action. Few people keep their antipathies entirely to themselves.'[62] Allport identifies a five-point ladder of discriminatory behaviours. The first point is *antilocution*, simply talking about prejudices. The scale then escalates through *avoidance* of the 'disliked group', *discrimination* such as exclusion from certain rights and opportunities or segregation, then on to acts of violence: *physical attack* and, finally, *extermination*. The earlier stages are harmful in themselves because they are discriminatory

behaviours; they also create the possibility of action progressing to its
more dangerous stages:

> While many people would never move from antilocution to avoidance;
> or from avoidance to active discrimination, or higher on the scale, still
> it is true that activity on one level makes transition to a more intense
> level easier.[63]

Wilson's audience may be unlikely to indulge in actual violence.
However, Wilson's gig is certainly guilty of antilocution, and the demand
that anyone who is likely to be offended leave the theatre, coupled
with the apparent absence of any representatives of the persecuted
minorities at his gig, could suggest that this event has already made
the transition to avoidance and discrimination. There is no explicit
policy excluding minority groups, but their exclusion from this event is
nonetheless a fact. In this context, activity is unlikely to progress on to
actual violence. However, it is only the presence of activity in these less
extreme stages, Allport claims, which has made actual violence possible
in those contexts in which it has historically occurred.

The fact that Wilson feels the need to rid himself of accusations of
racism, and has the enthusiastic support of his audience for doing so,
suggests that Wilson and at least a sizeable proportion of his audience
do not consider themselves racist and do not want to be considered
racist by others. If, therefore, they are drawn in to genuine racism, we
must assume that this is the result of manipulation which allows the
audience, and perhaps the performer, to believe – or at least claim to
believe – that their actions are not racist. Kevin Bloody Wilson's material
manipulates the audience into committing racist acts and perpetuating
racist attitudes through the allowance of comic licence.

Comedians and audiences understand that stand-up can be an
interaction in which the audience learns from the world view presented.
Within the first ten minutes of his performance of *From Caliban to the
Taliban* in Aberdeen, Robert Newman declares that his task for the
evening is to tell the story of American (and, as it transpires, general
Western) history from a less honourable perspective than that which

he says is being disseminated by the propagandist Hollywood machine. He says:

> Now of course I know, yes, these Hollywood films and documentaries made by the Academy of Arts will reach millions – my little show, 300 of yeh, [small laugh] right up on the north-west bit of Europe [laugh] on a Thursday night, but I'm hopeful [laugh] [...] because I believe that there's a special property about us being all in the same actual physical space together which means that I can utterly brainwash you [laugh][64]

Although it is framed as a joke, this is a statement of intent from Newman. While 'brainwash' is an exaggeration, he believes that he can use his relationship with the audience to educate and persuade them. He states that he is actively seeking to achieve this. The implication is that he believes that the relationship that exists between stand-up comedian and audience has more persuasive power than that which exists through other mediums, in this case, film-making. The audience's laugh suggests that they recognize the idea that live interaction can be especially influential.

In stand-up comedy, there is a dangerous merging of two contradictory interpretative forces. On the one hand, comedy is about laughs rather than accuracy, and it is acceptable (within limits) to abandon ethics and ideology where necessary. On the other, joking provides us with social criticism, and successful stand-up allows an individual a platform from which to have his messages heard and understood. Furthermore, audiences have incentives to comply with the ideas presented by a comedian; many theorists view laughter as an effective reward for audience cooperation. Schopenhauer describes laughter as 'a pleasant condition' to which 'we give ourselves up gladly'.[65] Freud states that laughter can be used as a 'bribe', offering its 'yield of pleasure' as a reward for 'taking sides without any very close investigation'.[66] There are also punishments for those who fail to go along with the comedian's ideas. Philips suggests that laughter can unite a group in a 'community of feeling', and further notes that the community created is so strong in its acceptance of the joke's premise that it becomes very difficult for an individual to object. Doing so would frame the individual as an 'outsider', leaving them open to isolation or mistreatment, while joining the 'community of feeling' by laughing at the joke legitimizes the premise as an attitude shared.[67] The danger is that stand-up allows the comedian's utterances to have persuasive power at the same time as removing the restraints which would ensure the quality of those comments.

Part Two

The Tools of Manipulation

A Manipulative Environment

Successful stand-up comedy manipulates audience response. When we consider whether a stand-up act went well, we are assessing whether or not the comedian took charge. Most obviously, we judge whether the comedian was able to get the audience laughing; sometimes he will have been looking for more varied responses, and we credit his ability to create shock, pathos or uncertainty. The acid test is always whether the mass reaction was under the comedian's control. This is not to say that audiences are duped. Rather, they are willing collaborators in their own manipulation. As was noted in Part 1, a good gig allows its audience the satisfaction of reacting in unison, and of doing so easily, without any explicit negotiation or feeling of effort. Audiences look to the comedian to lead their responses, and will be disappointed if the comedian does not succeed.

In a well-organized gig, everything works together to make the audience laugh. This part of the book addresses some of the key methods used to manipulate audience response. We begin with some of the most subtle and pervasive of stand-up's manipulative tools: the venue in which the performance is delivered, and the register in which the comedian chooses to communicate.

How the venue manipulates[1]

Audiences rarely notice how the space in which a comedy gig takes place has been arranged to maximize their responsiveness. Before they arrive at the venue, much work may already have been done to encourage them to laugh. There are a handful of spaces in the United

Kingdom which are specially designed as comedy clubs, for example The Stand's venues in Edinburgh, Glasgow and Newcastle, and the Comedy Store's postings in London and Manchester. However, the majority of comedy nights take place in spaces that were not primarily designed for performance, such as pubs and bars. It is with the selection of a suitable venue that the manipulative process begins.

Kent-based comedian and promoter Dave Bailey outlines some of the factors he considers when selecting a venue:

> I discounted many venues before even trying. I knew a high street pub would be impossible, as there are just too many distractions. [...] A high street pub would be too noisy, and with big screen TVs, pool tables, fruit machines – the comic would be fighting a losing battle.[2]

Interviewed before a performance at the Horsebridge Arts and Community Centre, Matthew Crosby explains that the layout of a room can be important. For example, it is best to avoid having doors by the stage, or at least to take them out of operation for the duration of the performance; obviously, physically pointing the audience's gaze away from any traffic in and out of the room makes it easier for the comedian to hold the crowd's attention. In the Horsebridge, however, this is not possible, as the only entrance door is at the side of the stage, and the location of the lighting rig and shape of the room makes any relocation of the stage impractical:

> If you've got a performer on stage and the door opens and someone walks in, it's very, very hard for an audience – you can see the eyes drifting! [...] One time [...] and it was quite exciting, we had a fireman burst in and go, 'Oh. I must be in the wrong place', which was brilliant [...] and a gift for the night because we were all making jokes about it. [...] But most of the time [...] if someone walks in, you just see the eyes of the whole room drifting [...] I mean as a compère it doesn't matter, I'll just drop what I'm doing and talk to those people [...] but if you're actually trying to craft something bigger than, you know, banter or crowd work then it can be really, really tricky.[3]

Ideally, then, the promoter is seeking a room where the audience's attention can be directed towards the performance, and where any competition for the audience's attention is minimized. Rarely will the promoter have the luxury of a space that is perfect. As Crosby's experience demonstrates, the onus is often on the comedian to compensate for some of the problems the room may present. The opportunity to comment on these can even be a 'gift'. On the whole, though, a well-run night will be proactive in identifying and neutralizing those elements that might compete for the audience's attention. Oliver Double recalls making the most of a 'motley collection' of improvised comedy venues while working with the Red Grape Cabaret:

> Sometimes this would mean taking obvious steps, like turning off televisions, jukeboxes or one-armed bandits while the show was on. Other times, it would mean rearranging the space, finding the best place for the stage to be set up, adjusting the lighting and rearranging the seating. Usually, this turned an undoable gig into an acceptable one, an acceptable gig into a joy.[4]

Exploiting the space to increase the efficacy of the performance is an integral part of the show's delivery. At the same club at the Horsebridge, Crosby took similar steps to manipulate audience behaviour. For example:

> We did this thing of moving the tables to the front. Now, a few people don't like this [...] especially because these are big tables [...] so it means that the first person is still quite far away from the act [...] but at the same time we had a problem with people not wanting to sit in the front. So we move the tables to the front, people automatically want tables 'cause they wanna put their drinks down, so you make the front seating much more appealing.[5]

In rearranging audience seating, Double and Crosby were each addressing the other great concern of the stand-up venue: to create a space in which energy flows freely between performer and audience, and throughout the room. Few theorists have turned their attention to stand-up spaces, so the majority of work that has captured professional knowledge in this area relates to traditional theatre architecture. In this field, practitioners and theoreticians tend to agree that there is such a thing as a good and a bad space for performance, that everybody can tell one from the other, and that it is primarily instinct through which we recognize and create such spaces. Influential theatre director Peter Brook states:

> There are no strict rules to tell us whether a space is good or bad. In fact, all this relates to a kind of rigorous and precise science which we can only develop by continuous experiment and empiricism based on fact.[6]

The key to a good space is its ability to promote a high level of quality interaction between performer and audience. As Iain Mackintosh explains:

> The chief purpose of theatre architecture is to provide a channel for energy. Although this energy flows chiefly from performer to audience the performer is rendered impotent unless he or she receives in return a charge from the audience.[7]

Mackintosh argues that the arrangement of some spaces is conducive to this process while others destroy the possibility of such communion between performer and audience.

In stand-up, the aim is for this flow of energy to combust into the specific response of laughter. As Double states:

> Funny lines, gestures and mimes flow from the comedian to the audience, and laughter, applause and heckles flow back. The audience is energised and bonded into a group by the comedy and the performer is energised by the audience's responses. Comics must be able to generate this energy in the audience, or there will be nothing to fuel their performance.[8]

To produce laughter, an audience needs not only energy but also confidence. To laugh is pleasant, but can also be risky; to be caught laughing heartily when other audience members are silent could be embarrassing. It is therefore important that the energy that causes laughter flows freely and easily between people. As Bergson states:

> You would hardly appreciate the comic if you felt yourself isolated from others. Laughter appears to stand in need of an echo. [...] Our laughter is always the laughter of a group. [...] How often it has been said that the fuller the theatre, the more uncontrolled the laughter of the audience![9]

When asked what makes a good space for stand-up, the majority of comedians interviewed suggested features which pack the audience in tightly, instinctively adhering to Bergson's observation that a 'fuller' space brings the opportunity for more 'uncontrolled' laugher. Energy can be lost in empty space but a tightly packed room concentrates the crowd's response, making it more likely to combust into laughter. Related to these factors is the need for acoustics to amplify the laughter, rather than letting it dissipate, so that the laughs that have already come can better fuel those being created. As Dan Atkinson explains:

> Low ceilings, hard surfaces, rowed seating – if you're having tables, very, very small tables – very dark, lights only facing the stage. Low stage, so that people feel close to the comic and they know that it's not a theatre performance and that there's going to be interaction. And, basically, what all that does – what you're aiming for – is that you have the audience as one homogenised group. [...] You want them all to forget that they are in a group or single, you want them all to be believing they're one lump, enjoying it all together. Which is quite a nice thing, when that does happen.[10]

When asked about the tendency to reduce empty space in a room, Atkinson replies:

> Yeah, it's crucial. That's a technicality about the laughs. Because if you've got high ceilings or a half-full room the laughs get lost a bit, dissipate. It's like doing comedy in a tent's usually shit because the fabric just lets the laugh out. So you want nowhere for the laugh to go and for it to just sort of bounce around the room.

A tightly packed space is unlikely to be as comfortable as a sparsely populated one. A successful night's stand-up with a large audience may be associated in the audience's mind with many uncomfortable annoyances: having to stand owing to lack of seats, having to perch on a table or bench, not being able to see the performer easily, having to push through a crowd to get to the bar. Yet both Mackintosh and Brook welcome these implications. As Brook states, 'Nothing is so unimportant as comfort; comfort in fact often devitalizes the experience.'[11] A comfortable audience is simply a less efficient conductor of energy. Mackintosh concurs: 'A less densely packed house seated in ever greater comfort becomes ever more passive, ever more comatose.'[12] Practical experience in stand-up comedy supports this idea. Matthew Crosby explains that the performance space at the Horsebridge is 'really relaxing', and 'that can often be to the detriment of a room'.[13] He gives the following example:

> I've been to gigs where the front row's sofas [...] and they're using the exact same logic that I used with the tables up the front, they go, 'well obviously people are gonna want to sit on a sofa rather than a hard chair.' But if you're on a sofa [...] you're not upright, ready to laugh. [...] You could become very passive and treat it like you're just watching telly.[14]

Another important factor in managing audience energy is promoting a feeling of excitement about the show. Dan Atkinson feels that a good comedy club will purposefully enhance the perceived status and authority of the comedy gig itself:

> The conditions need to be right [...] the more polished it is, the better. People feel they're being treated to an experience. So if you have, y'know, lights down at the beginning, search lights, intro music, announcements and stuff, it makes it really exciting. And before you've even seen anything you're well-disposed because you've been primed to believe that what you're about to see is good.[15]

Matthew Crosby adds that audiences like to feel that they have come to a popular gig; encouraging the appearance of commercial success increases the audience's confidence in the show.[16] Occasionally, the space can be manipulated to enhance this impression. Crosby recalls performing with sketch troupe Pappy's Fun Club at the Tobacco Factory in Bristol:

> They had 250 seats, and we were going 'oh, this is fantastic, it's a sell-out show,' and they said, 'well, we could have another 150, and we'd move the stage back and we bring in chairs at the side.' But it felt great, you know […] 'cause, like, every seat was full.[17]

It should be noted that promoters can be fairly oblivious to the dynamic of their venues. Many comedians can relate horror stories of badly run comedy nights in which they felt they were set up for a fall by management who failed to optimize the environment and expected the performer to struggle against unnecessarily difficult circumstances. Such experiences are often related with a still-tangible sense of anger and frustration. Yet the very fact that performers feel so let down by bad practice demonstrates that the use of the space to enhance audience responsiveness is an integral part of the craft; it is noticeable when the effort is not made.

Even the show's publicity can be used as a manipulative tool, being carefully pitched to ensure that the 'right kind' of audience attends. Comedians commonly draw a distinction between 'comedy-savvy' audiences and less specialized or sophisticated ones. A comedy-savvy audience is one which is highly literate with comic forms and devices. They know the comedy scene reasonably well and can distinguish and articulate differences in comedic style. Therefore, they are less likely to engage in futile attempts to consume all comedy in the same way. As Matthew Crosby elaborates:

> There is such a thing as taste, and there is such a thing as opinion, and people seem to forget that in comedy. […] An example that's sort of been used by many different people, that's comparing it to music, is you would never go to a night called 'Music Night' […] they would want to go, 'well what kind of music are you playing?' […] Whereas,

if someone goes, 'oh there's a comedy night happening,' you would go without sort of going, 'well what kind of comedy is it going to be?'[18]

The savvy audience are more likely to choose to view a style that suits them, and to engage with that style on its own terms. Understandably, many comedians express a preference for this type of audience, feeling that such proficiency on the audience's part allows the comedian freedom to indulge in the more complex comedic forms and material that they – themselves highly proficient with comic devices – find more interesting.[19] Dan Atkinson relates his experience with his own comedy club:

> I ran a gig for five years [...] and there were a couple set up in opposition. Where I ran my gig it was all about the experience of the audience. It was all about making everything as funny and as fun as possible. So the brochures would be, sort of, hand-drawn, thirty-two page comedy magazines. [...] And we ended up getting a really, really high class of audience; people who were comedy-savvy, who knew what was lazy from a comedian and would genuinely love when a comedian did something comedically interesting. On the flip side of that, there was a bar next door that put on comedy in their bar and they just put posters up and then people went and they got the meat heads. So it does make a huge difference how you sell it.[20]

Stewart Lee delivers a peculiar kind of comedy in that his aim is often to create a feeling of uncertainty among the audience as to how they should respond.[21] It takes a particularly savvy audience to appreciate such an unusual approach, and Lee has a novel way of attracting them:

> I [...] always try and put some bad quote on a poster – like 'monotonous, boring and repetitive' or something – if I can find something like that, to just try and thin the audience out a bit. I don't have to deal with the problem.[22]

This strategy is designed to make Lee's job as a performer easier. By highlighting criticisms levied at the unconventional aspects of his act, he makes his show appealing to people who enjoy unusual comedic approaches. At the same time, he sends a message to that portion of potential punters who would respond negatively; if they are not up for a challenge, they should not come.

This raises an interesting possibility for audience manipulation: by pitching the publicity in a particular way, a performance could implicitly invite certain individuals while excluding others. The choice of venue and the price of a ticket may also carry an implicit message about who the show is for.[23] Hence the type of audience attracted to a particular performance may be manipulated. However, while this is a strong possibility for comedians like Stewart Lee, who has the experience and credibility to mount a solo show and hence some control over the location of the performance and the messages sent to prospective audience members via its publicity, comedians performing on the circuit rarely have such luxuries. While Atkinson is aware of the possibility of selecting 'good' audiences to perform for, he cites this as 'a minor possibility because you've got to earn a living'.[24] The most profitable gigs are the ones generally cited as the artistic nadir; the stag and hen dos and the notorious 'corporates'. While a good gig ensures that everything works together to support the comedy, the gig provided as a sideshow at a big party confronts the comedian with an audience who have other priorities. As Josie Long outlines:

> A lot of the big clubs, the way they do it is they set up deals with offices for parties or corporate things and they set up, kind of, deals with stags and hens, and with group bookings so [...] the atmosphere necessarily changes because of that. Because it's their party so they think it's their big day, so they're a bit like, you know, 'Woo! Talk about Karen! Talk about Karen!' They're not there thinking, 'I love this comedian, I'm glad I'm going to see this comedian.'[25]

For the majority of comedians, then, there is little leeway to either select or directly manipulate the nature of the audience to which they perform. Isy Suttie sums up the situation: 'Clubs which give out home-made cakes are the nicest to play, but sadly they pay the least!'[26]

The venue is a delicate and complex manipulative tool. In some respects it is an unreliable one; the art of managing something as ethereal as the flow of energy, or of attracting a specialized audience, cannot be reduced to hard-and-fast rules. Rather, creating a conducive space for comedy performance involves sensitive adaptation to myriad factors in changeable circumstances. Yet those spaces that comedians speak of most fondly adhere to some common standards of good practice: they pack audiences in tightly, minimize the empty space in the room, eliminate competition for audience attention and proactively set positive expectations for the night. The fact that audiences are generally ignorant of the way that both they and the space have been arranged to enhance their responsiveness only makes the manipulation more complete.

The playground and the drinking-place

In *Homo Ludens,* the seminal analysis of play, Johan Huizinga observed that, 'all play moves and has its being within a play-ground marked off beforehand either materially or ideally, deliberately or as a matter of course'.[27] Playgrounds are, 'forbidden spots, isolated, hedged round, hallowed, within which special rules obtain. All are temporary worlds within the ordinary world, dedicated to the performance of an act apart'.[28] Playgrounds cover a wide range of social environments which operate in accordance with their own, particular etiquette; Huizinga's examples range from the temple to the card-table, and include the stage and the screen.[29] Just as the act of joking is often theorized as something which transports joker and audience to a theoretical safe-space, so the comedy venue itself is a material playground; a physical safe-space which operates in accordance with the marginal rules of comic licence.

Mintz observes that generally a comedian will '[establish] his or her comic persona', in the early stages of the gig, in order to 'establish that the mood of comic licence is operative'.[30] However, the precise nature of this licence will be finely nuanced. For example, we expect and permit different types of subversion from Frankie Boyle, who is 'infamous for his willingness to comically stamp around on sensitive issues',[31] than we do from Josie Long, who markets her shows under such titles as *Trying is Good* or *Kindness and Exuberance* ("cause […] pretty much that's the perfect distillation of how I think you should live your life').[32] One feature of the gig's playground, then, is that the extent and nature of its subversion is largely set by the comedian, negotiated both through their persona and, where possible, by the careful control of venue and publicity described above.

A further feature that almost all stand-up comedy venues have in common is a licence to sell alcohol. Most comedians and promoters agree that running a successful gig without alcohol would be very difficult, if not impossible. Dave Bailey generally 'discounts' immediately any potential comedy venues that are not licensed:

> No alcohol for the audience would make things very hard for the comics […] it's very difficult to get any kind of atmosphere going. English reserve takes over and what you get is people politely listening but not relaxed enough to really laugh.[33]

Alcohol is usually not only offered to the audience, but its consumption actively encouraged. In an example fairly typical among stand-up performances, the first half of *Eric's Tales of the Sea* concludes with Eric (a former submariner who prefers not to disclose his surname in connection with the show) explicitly advising the audience to go to the bar during the interval, as it is an established 'rule of comedy' that the more they drink the funnier the second half will be.[34]

There is a direct and obvious manipulation of audience mood and receptiveness involved in the use of licensed venues and the encouragement of alcohol consumption. As Dave Bailey notes, alcohol is not a neutral element that happens to be present at many comedy nights, but rather a drug which lowers inhibitions and thus encourages responsiveness. The fact that whole audiences are persuaded to imbibe chemical stimulants as a matter of convention is really a striking manipulative coup for stand-up, especially as it has become so embedded a part of the culture as to go largely unnoticed by audiences.

On a more theoretical level, it could be argued that the presence of alcohol itself imports a subversive, democratic culture. Anthropologist Kate Fox has noted that 'the drinking-place is a special environment, a separate social world with its own customs and values'. She argues that drinking-places tend to be 'socially integrative, egalitarian environments' in which the usual rules governing social hierarchy do not apply.[35] This describes an atmosphere which is conducive to challenge, and thus to joking.[36] This is not to say that drinking-places are naturally and universally socially inclusive, nor that behaviour within them is entirely unregulated. Indeed, the opposite may be true: subcultures attached to specific types of drinking-places often have a powerful impact on the behaviour conducted within them.[37] In fact, the culture of the drinking-place allies with the particular kind of control needed within stand-up venues. Both environments offer freedom from convention but also have their own behavioural code. By using licensed venues and thus adopting the culture of the drinking-place, comedy nights are importing a particular etiquette and audience attitude that subverts mainstream norms, allowing a more subversive culture to come in to play.

The creation of a subversive playground has clear possibilities for manipulation. When the audience come to the gig they know that they are entering a space where marginal rules apply, and they broadly authorize the comedian to set these new parameters. Huizinga has noted that a 'play-community generally tends to become permanent even after the game is over…the feeling of being "apart together" in an exceptional situation, of sharing something important, of mutually withdrawing from the rest of the world and rejecting the usual norms, retains its magic'.[38] Lockyer and Myers identify that this feeling of community – 'sharing the comic experience' – is one of the things that draws audiences to comedy.[39] Perhaps, then, the use of the playground also has implications for influence. The audience know that when they leave the playground of the gig they re-enter the world in which the mainstream rules apply; yet those rules have been questioned and their validity reinforced by the 'play-community'. This notion is explored further in Chapter 8.

The illusion of spontaneous conversation

Most comedians' material is reusable, and its development is a long-term process. Jokes are planned in advance and routines repeated in front of several different audiences, being edited according to audience response with the aim of making them more reliable. This is no secret. Yet the majority of comedy enhances the feeling of 'unexpected and unpredictable potential' by adopting the trappings of spontaneous, conversational interaction. Drawing on empirical data assessing what motivates audiences to attend live stand-up comedy, Lockyer and Meyers find that, 'many respondents described the appeal of live stand-up comedy in terms of its unexpected and unpredictable potential', which included 'the ways in which the stand-up comedian responds to the dynamics of the specific audience'.[40] Just as the stand-up venue is subtly arranged to encourage laughter, so the register in which the comedian delivers their material contributes to the creation of a manipulative environment.

Most stand-up performances maintain the appearance of being spontaneous. Joe Wilkinson states that there are still some audience members who are taken in by the illusion of spontaneity. Even audiences who are comedy-savvy enough to be aware that comedians both plan and repeat material will opt to believe in its spontaneity, suspending disbelief for the duration of the show in order to enhance their enjoyment of the material:

> The audience has to suspend their belief as well [...] but some people just literally do [believe it's spontaneous], I've had people say to me 'do you do different stuff every night?' and you're like 'Jesus Christ! Yeah, I write all that stuff in a day!' Do you know what I mean? [...] But

people do, they want to believe it, even if they want to believe it [just] for that time.[41]

Wilkinson confesses that he still buys into this process himself when watching other performers, choosing to believe in the spontaneity of material which he knows is part of a well-rehearsed repertoire.

Eddie Izzard's writing process is well documented. New material tends to be loosely planned offstage, but it is through experimentation in front of live audiences that the material is honed to completion.[42] Once formed, this material can be repeated in roughly the same shape on subsequent nights. Thus Izzard develops a show which is planned and repeatable. He experiments with new material by embedding it in the old, so that any given show is likely to feature a small amount of real improvisation.[43] His delivery style allows him to convey complex, pre-planned ideas and well-formed material in a babbling, hesitant manner which maintains the illusion of spontaneity. It is usually impossible to be certain to what extent any given moment is improvised, planned or repeated from other performances.

In the following segment taken from his show *Glorious*, Izzard re-tells the Judeo-Christian creation story:

> So then God created the world and the first day he created light and air, and fish and jam and soup [laugh]; potatoes and haircuts and arguments and [small laugh] small things and rabbits and people with noses and… er… jam – more jam, perhaps [laugh] – and, er, and soot and flies and… tobogganing and [small laugh]…showers, and toasters, and grandmothers [small laugh] and… er… Belgium (.) and [big laugh][44]

There is a long pause here to allow the audience's loud and hearty laugh to spread out. Izzard then produces a list of the things created on the second day. This list mirrors the structure of the first; snappy and rhythmically pleasing, but also littered with hesitations and 'ers' which suggest that Izzard is searching his brain for appropriate examples.

Izzard's list purposefully juxtaposes items with no obvious connection to one another, moving from potatoes to haircuts, and abandoning objects altogether as he moves on to the more abstract concept of 'arguments'. This creates incongruous links, and the apparent randomness of their selection enhances the feeling of spontaneity. In fact, randomness is the very criteria by which items are selected. The audience may easily discern that Izzard is purposefully, and falsely, creating the impression that he is ad-libbing. Yet it is unlikely that Izzard's audience are paying attention to such a dull fact. Instead, they are buying in to Izzard's game, pretending along with him that the material is fresh and unscripted. Hence they laugh when Izzard – apparently by accident – includes 'jam' twice. The speed with which Izzard spots his 'blunder', and the ease and fluency with which he acknowledges it, may suggest that it is not a mistake at all. His delivery style seeks to underline the uniqueness of the encounter. The audience are allowed to feel that this conversation is an event which cannot be repeated: a live, special encounter which they share with each other and with Izzard.

Izzard does not seek to deceive his audience, and openly admits that his material is not spontaneously improvised. He states:

> What I do does have a sense of spontaneity because I start out going 'right, now... fish... er... fish' [...] but I always know roughly where I'm going to end up. The unfortunate thing is if people think it's totally improvised, then when they realize it isn't, they'll think I'm letting them down [...] I prefer everyone to know exactly what I'm doing, because that means I'm good at what I can do rather than what people *think* I can do.[45]

Yet, as Ben Thompson observes, the appeal of Izzard's style is, none-theless, largely derived from its apparent spontaneity:

> One of the things that makes Eddie Izzard such an exciting comedian to watch is the sense that his set is evolving as you watch it. [...] However honest he is about what he does, people still seem to have

something invested in the idea that he's plucking it all out of the air as he goes along.[46]

At the same time, audiences are capable of accepting the fact that most comedians perform pre-prepared material, and that this material probably has been, and will be, performed to other audiences. During a performance of *The Impotent Fury of the Underprivileged* in 2008, Daniel Kitson makes no secret of this.[47] At the start of the show, Kitson says that he has argued with the management of the venue because he refused to put an interval into his one-hour-and-forty-five-minute-long show. Kitson asserts that his show has been designed in that format, and later explicitly refers to the fact that he has 'written and rehearsed' the show. This openly acknowledges the pre-prepared and repeatable nature of his material, and even demands respect for the craftsmanship and commitment involved in his creative process. Kitson's audience accepts this point, remaining cooperative even after the illusion of spontaneity has been dispelled.

Eddie Izzard likewise acknowledges the writing process on stage. Continuing his creation story, he describes how, by the seventh day, God began to rush his creations to meet his deadline, producing such faulty items as Rwanda, the 'Leaning' Tower of Pisa and Mrs Thatcher's heart. The next week 'the People' begin to bring the rushed inventions back. Izzard uses a whining tone to signify the disgruntled People and his 'James Mason' voice to signify God (God in italics):

'Rwanda doesn't work very well.' [small laugh] 'Infrastructure's fucked.' [laugh]
    'Terribly sorry. I'll, er, put some more jam here.' [laugh] *'And, er, a mountain of cabbages,'* [small laugh] *'and… a radiator'* [bigger laugh]…
    'Thank you. That's just what we wanted' [laugh][48]

Izzard then mimes the dejected People hauling a load on a rope and explains: 'This is them dragging Rwanda back [laugh]. To lay it out on the map.' Izzard's mime of the country being laid on to the map receives very little response; it is possible to pick out a small handful of individual laughers, but the audience as a whole has failed to follow. Smiling, Izzard acknowledges the (apparent) failure of his joke by direct reference to the writing process. Miming the jotting of a note onto a pad, Izzard says: 'No one got that. [laugh] Never do that bit again! [laugh]'

The device of making editorial notes on the mimed notepad explicitly references the fact that Izzard intends to perform his material for a different audience. Part of the comic power of this device may be its cheekiness; by acknowledging that the material may be repeated, Izzard breaks the rules and punctures the illusion which the audience and he have collaborated to maintain. Yet the device also adds to that illusion. By making notes for future performances to different audiences, Izzard highlights the uniqueness of his current encounter. The next audience will, apparently, not receive that piece of material: this material is for the current audience only, and they have power over it. The audience are thus reminded of their important role as collaborator, and favourably contrasted to future audiences who will play no part in developing that particular joke. By acknowledging its failure, Izzard makes the map joke appear to be a kind of secret shared between himself and his current audience.

Stewart Lee comments, on stage, upon the fakery involved in Izzard's 'improvisational' style. Lee delivers a list of three items which, although clearly intended as a joke, gets a poor response. During a routine which analyses the reasons for the joke's failure, Lee says that a friend advised him to make the items in his list more random:

> And I thought yeah, I will, but I won't write them down. You know? I'll come out every night and I'll just make them up, I'll exist in the moment, I'll trust it to chance, I'll improvise like Eddie Izzard (.) pretends to do [laughter, some clapping, a few 'oohs']… No! And when you've tried to do it you realise why he doesn't. It's hard – it's hard to do. It's much easier to just go 'er' in every sentence and give the illusion of spontaneity [bigger laugh][49]

The way that Lee's audience respond demonstrates the presence of contradictory interpretations that run alongside each other when an audience enjoys Izzard's material. On the one hand, the laughter of Lee's audience signifies that they recognize the truth: they know that Izzard's work is not as improvised as it appears to be. The 'oohs' imply that such an observation would be considered an insult: they accuse Lee of treating Izzard harshly by acknowledging that the appearance of spontaneity is mere pretence. This suggests that everyone knows that the material is not spontaneous, but that it is considered bad form to say so.

Constructing spontaneity

All stand-up performances involve both spontaneity and planning. It is the balance of one against the other which differs widely. Even in the most meticulously planned set, the exact nature of the material's delivery will usually be adapted to fit the specific situation and the particular participation of any given audience. Referring to a performance of the 2008 *Edinburgh and Beyond* tour, Dan Atkinson states:

> You should approach each gig on its own merit and play it accordingly. So there were – what? – 250 people at the Gulbenkian [Theatre], and so you have to play it slightly larger. But if there were ten people and we'd all played it like we did it wouldn't have worked because it feels false. If you're delivering to a huge amount of people, you have to make bigger gestures and if you did that, y'know, in an intimate setting [...] so yeah, I think a comedian is able to adjust the pitch of their performance, even if they're doing the same thing.[50]

It is therefore highly unlikely that any comedian would be able to produce exactly the same series of words and gestures on any two nights, even if he wanted to. Jimmy Carr's material often takes the form of long strings of packaged jokes. On the whole, the rhythm of Carr's delivery follows a concise and repetitive pattern, with a paced set-up, followed by a pause before the punchline, the next joke being introduced just as the laugh is beginning to ebb away. This means that, in a successful performance, the laugh becomes an integral part of a repetitive rhythm so that it is not only clear when the laugh is expected, but there is a tangible void when the laugh fails to appear. The jokes themselves are tightly structured and it is often clear that they have been planned word-for-word. There is apparently little space for Carr to spontaneously tailor his set to the needs of the moment. Yet Carr is necessarily doing just that. While Carr's material can be scripted, the audience's reaction cannot be. When the audience laughs, Carr will pause. The length of that pause will depend on the longevity of the laugh, Carr adapting the rhythm of his delivery in response to the input of the specific audience to whom he is performing. Carr listens not only for the length of the laugh, but also for the qualities within it, reacting differently to a loud, bursting laugh than to a reserved, uncomfortable one. A heckle, or other unexpected occurrence, may cause him to veer off script entirely in order to address the unforeseen interruption.

On the other hand, the impression of spontaneous conversation given by comedians who perform in a more conversational register is almost always a construct, whether or not the comedian is particularly conscious of the methods they are applying. Jo Brand began her career in the 1980s with a concise, deadpan delivery, and later adopted a more chatty style which purposefully lacked the marked fluency of her earlier work. The following transcripts document two separate performances in which Brand delivers the same piece of material. The first is in her early deadpan style, and was recorded for *Friday Night Live* in the mid-1980s.[51] The second is from Brand's 1994 video *A Big Slice of Jo Brand*:

My flatmate actually advised me to buy *Cosmopolitan* magazine because, let's face it, all their articles are about how to get a husband, aren't they? Despite the fact that they may be rather thinly disguised as articles on more general topics for the ever so slightly feminist woman [small laugh]. For example, I read an article in *Cosmo* last week about how to speak knowledgeably on quantum mechanics theory, [laugh] whilst giving someone a blow job, [big laugh] and asking them to marry you all at the same time [big laugh]. I tried it…but the man on the cheese counter at Safeway [laughter and applause]… said he didn't think it was terribly hygienic [laugh] quite so near to the Red Leicester [big laugh].

–Jo Brand, Friday Night Live c.1988⁵²

And a friend of mine said well, you know, if you wan' a partner just read *Cosmopolitan* magazine because all their articles are about how how to get a husband, aren't they? They are! Although they're disguised, y'know, as – as articles on slightly, slightly, slightly, slightly feminist issues [couple of laughs] But they're not really, 're they? [small laugh] Um, for example, you know, I read an article in *Cosmo* recently about how to talk knowledgeably at parties on quantum mechanics theory, [laugh] er, whilst giving someone a blow job [laugh] and asking them to marry you, all at the same time. Now I tried that, but unfortunately [one person laughs] the man on the cheese counter at Sainsbury's, [laugh] er, didn't go for it, strangely [laugh]

–Jo Brand, A Big Slice of Jo Brand, 1994⁵³

Brand's earlier, deadpan style is very successful. In fact, the routine as delivered in this style gets bigger laughs than the 1994 version, and some applause. There may be various reasons why the 1988 version is more successful. For example, the fact that the 1988 routine is part of a short, tight set, whereas the 1994 routine comes at the beginning of a longer, solo show, is likely to have an impact. Yet some of the credit must go to the deadpan style itself. Brand uses a strong rhythm and intonation which cue her audience to laugh at the right moments. The material is beautifully concise, so that the jokes are communicated smoothly and clearly.

However, there is a danger that the marked, unnatural rise and fall of Brand's intonation and the rigid rhythm of the set would become irritating and tediously predictable after a while. In an interview with Oliver Double, Brand herself observed that the deadpan style was essentially limiting:

> It's impossible to keep that up for any longer than about twenty minutes without the audience getting bored shitless, to be honest. Because there's something about that rhythm that's slightly sort of narcoleptic.⁵⁴

The decision to change to the chattier style was a conscious one. Brand actively took measures to achieve the change, putting herself forward to compère in the knowledge that this would force her to converse more directly with her audience and to improvise.[55]

The difference is clear in the above transcriptions. Brand delivers the 1994 version with less fluency than she was able to do almost a decade earlier. She appears less certain of what is coming next. While the tight delivery of the 1980s implies that Brand is in total control of her material and demonstrates the meticulous planning behind its delivery, by 1994 Brand is disguising the prepared nature of her material. Fillers such as 'um' and 'er' have become commonplace in her speech, as have meaningless, accidental repetitions; for example, 'how how to get a husband' and 'as – as articles'.

Brand's whole relationship to her audience has changed. The 1994 persona seems more approachable; Brand smiles when her audience laughs, sharing their enjoyment, her bright red lipstick enhancing the effect. In 1988, Brand retains a sullen expression throughout the performance, allowing her audience to laugh while appearing bored with both the world she caustically observes and the immediate situation. In the 1994 version, Brand calls for her audience's involvement in the material via hedges such as 'you know' and tag questions such as 'right?' or 'isn't it?'[56] The use of the question 'aren't they?' in the 1980s set, with its deadpan delivery, does little to request an audience response. Brand drawls the question out so that it seems to enhance the feeling of boredom with the *Cosmopolitan* culture, rather than energizing her audience to respond in agreement. This use of 'aren't they?' does not request confirmation from the audience, but rather imposes Brand's own confirmation of her statement upon them. In 1994, the same question is delivered in an open, inviting way. Although it is Brand who fills in the audience's response ('they are!') this is in keeping with the deceptively one-sided nature of the conversation, and still serves to enhance the feeling that she is inviting a two-way interaction.

Even comedians who are, genuinely, roughly improvisational in their approach tend to have a planned structure in which to frame their spontaneity, and chunks of repeatable material that may be utilized if they are needed or relevant. Ross Noble is an improvisational comedian for whom any given show is likely to contain a significantly higher-than-average proportion of ad-libbed material.[57] Noble is also among the minority of comedians in his ability to confidently improvise a whole show. However, he has also stated that he uses prepared and repeated material. In a sense, even the use of prepared material is spontaneous in this context; Noble does not plan his use of stock material, but rather mixes ad-lib and pre-formed routines in whatever proportion seems right at the time.[58] For Noble, preparation for a show is focused more upon internal structures within the performer:

> It's less about sort of coming up with a show, and more about just getting up to match fitness, you know. Just mentally – well, physically as well as mentally – just being in that headspace. 'Coz even with, like, improv, it's not necessarily about the speed of invention, it's about the application of it. And pace as well. […] The pace, if you like, that's just as important a skill – a muscle – to exercise as anything else.[59]

Noble's idea is a difficult one to articulate and his meaning is difficult to accurately pin down or develop in any terms that are not his own. The process of 'getting up to match fitness', 'being in that headspace' and 'exercising' the 'skill' or 'muscle' is itself a kind of planning. Perhaps it is even an embryonic method of writing. At root, Noble appears to be talking about a process which marshals the performer's previous experience and hones his skills, preparing him to draw, if not on actual material that has been delivered before, then upon the structures, thinking patterns and rhythms by which it came into existence.

The three main categories of comic theory define 'funniness' not by what a joke says – its content and wording – but by what it does. Those jokes that may be interpreted by the superiority and relief theories work by performing a task – the comedian either illustrates the superiority of one group or concept over another, or expresses an unspoken tension or desire. In incongruity theories, the joke is created by the structure in which ideas are placed, presenting 'some object of perception or thought that clashes with what we would have expected in a particular set of circumstances'.[60]

Although a focus on form and structure over individual content is a natural side effect of processes which seek to find common ground between jokes, there is a significant trend for comic theory to posit structural and formulaic factors as the root of funniness, rather than its means of communication. This implies that there are two parts to the writing of a joke. The idea transmitted in the joke varies widely, and is often the result of a moment's inspiration. However, such ideas are built upon the foundation of cognitive processes that are pre-determined. This is not to imply that jokes lack variety, for there is no formula that can satisfactorily provide a comprehensive range of jokes. What this common basis does mean is that each joke is built on established structures of thought which enable both teller and hearer to recognize a diverse range of comic forms and utterances as jokes; when we create a joke, we find that some of the ground work is already done for us. While it remains an awe-inspiring feat on Noble's part to be able to ad-lib an entire show, it should be noted that there is some preparation achieved in the form of structure and experience. His ad-libbed jokes are not completed until the moment of the performance, but they find a pre-prepared base in his experience and understanding of comic forms. By tuning in to comedic structures of thought, the comedian is able to repackage spontaneous occurrences in to gags.

Looking clever: A 'higher' kind of comedy

The techniques which enhance the appearance of spontaneity become particularly manipulative in those cases in which the comedian receives kudos for his apparent quickness of wit in responding to a supposedly unpredictable situation. As resident compère at the Edinburgh Stand, Bruce Devlin performed very frequently in the same venue. At the beginning of a show, Devlin would typically converse with the audience, picking out individuals and asking them questions about themselves.

The result would be unpredictable and Devlin would, apparently, be forced to improvise spontaneous responses to the answers put forward by his audience. In reality, Devlin was able to impose certain limits. First, Devlin's persona is an aggressive and somewhat arrogant one; his joking responses were already guided by the fact that he is expected to insult the audience. Devlin was also in charge of the questions, and could therefore determine the direction of the conversation. He might ask punters what they do for a living. Answers to such a question may be very varied, but will typically fall into a series of categories which allow Devlin to apply tried-and-tested responses. When an audience member says that he is a student, Devlin might ask him what he studies before pointedly asking, 'and what call centre do you hope to work in?' Anyone who works with children may expect to have their job title reinterpreted as 'paedophile'.

In November 2005, Devlin performed both of these gags during the audience warm-up.[61] They seemed like fresh, ingenious responses, and the audience's laughter was perhaps due in part to their appreciation and respect for Devlin who, although cruel, appeared very quick and clever in his ability to produce spontaneous put-downs. In November 2006, both gags appeared again in the audience warm-up, and the audience reaction was just as keen.[62] These jokes have probably been performed on many other occasions, and each time their success relies upon the audience's perception that Devlin is spontaneously ad-libbing to an unpredictable stimulus. Without this impression, the joke would probably fail. In reality, though, Devlin's initial question pushes punters in a helpful direction, causing them to deliver the feed line for an established gag to which he can provide the punchline.

Devlin cannot be accused of dishonesty. Anyone who visited the Stand regularly could spot the formula and tumble the ruse. Like many other comedians, Devlin adopts the trappings of spontaneity in order to give his material the important feeling of freshness and excitement which characterizes much comedy. As we have seen, many stand-up comedians tend to flavour their delivery with an appearance of spontaneity which is faked to a greater or lesser degree. However, many consider genuine and successful ad-libbing to be the more exciting and artistically commendable part of their work.

Dan Atkinson spends much of his stage time compèring, but aims to avoid the 'bag of tricks' approach:

> There is a bag of responses – there are stock lines that all compères are allowed to use, and I try desperately not to. And I have my own stock responses – more than responses, I have a stack of experience and I've been in these situations many, many times before, so I'll find the same situations cropping up, the same kinds of people cropping up. And I try as hard as I can to not use them. [...] I've learned to be fairly quick and so it's a shame not to use that. And I try to respond to everything on its merits and its own circumstance. So I have got them and I do use them, but my default is to not use them, because I think that's when you're being a real comedian.[63]

Knowing how to successfully utilize stock responses as Devlin does is a skill in itself; as Atkinson notes it takes a 'stack of experience' to develop this repertoire. Yet Atkinson feels that spontaneous reactions force him to develop as a performer in a way that is not possible when he chooses to fall back on stock responses and structures. Audiences also seem to value improvisation, willing the comedian on and giving them more leeway for failure. As Atkinson observes, 'you'll be surprised how indulgent audiences will be if you are being genuinely improvisational. They will allow you to fail a couple of times on the search for something good.'[64]

The writing of a joke is not the whole act of creation. Joking is a social process, existing only in interaction with a hearer; as Zijderveld points out, 'a joke [...] is only meaningful in the interaction between human beings. It is also in this interaction that the joke is born.'[65] Thus the act of performance is an integral part of the joke's creation and involves a great deal of creative skill, even if the gag has been performed many times previously. Yet Atkinson is not alone in citing real spontaneity as both the essential heart of the form and the aim to which it aspires, but for which there can be no prescribed method. As Atkinson elaborates:

> I think it's more exciting. That's why stand-up's crucially such a live art form. The best gigs are the ones that you're going to where you'll see stuff that couldn't happen anywhere else, and you've been part of a special moment. And that's what everyone strives for. But ironically, you can't force it. You have to forget about that for it to happen.[66]

The illusion of spontaneous conversation is one of stand-up's most pervasive manipulative tools. Audiences want to believe that they are participating in a unique and spontaneous encounter. As Zijderveld notes, 'stale' jokes lose their attraction, 'a joke [...] draws its power from being new and rare'.[67] Stand-up generally needs to give the impression of spontaneous conversation in order to allow the material to feel fresh, and to create the chummy atmosphere in which jokes work best. We must remember, however, that this impression is constructed in order to manipulate audience responsiveness. This trick can also be manipulative in the deceitful sense. Audiences and comedians have great respect for genuinely ad-libbed material: when a comedian is able to create the impression that old material is genuinely written on the spot he gains respect for a piece of magic that he never delivered.

When an audience enters a comedy gig, they are entering an environment in which everything works together to make them more responsive. They will not usually be cognizant of the extent to which the arrangement of the space, the publicity and the very register in which the comedian delivers his material has been contrived to enhance the excitement of the event and make them more likely to laugh. Audiences unconsciously consent to this, buying in to their own manipulation, but it is manipulation nonetheless. Into this playground steps the comedian, who creates the rules in this marginal space and has his own tools for managing audience response. It is to these tools that we now turn our attention.

Manipulating Responses

The extent of control

When compèring the *Edinburgh and Beyond 2008* tour, Dan Atkinson demonstrates the control that a comedian exerts over his audience with great assurance.[1] Atkinson's demeanour is friendly, and expertly manages the contradiction of talking to and controlling a crowd while maintaining a persona that appears slightly shy and awkward. Atkinson chats several times to audience member Sam, who is sitting in the front row. Sam becomes known by the audience; a kind of supporting character. Once Sam's celebrity is established, Atkinson pulls the following stunt: he makes a joke about paedophilia – one which is purposely 'crass' and 'not particularly funny' – and then hops off the stage, holding up his hand as if to elicit a high five, crying 'Paedos Sam!'[2] Sam automatically raises his hand to high-five Atkinson, at which point Atkinson lowers his own hand, failing to meet Sam's high five, and, turning away, retreats back onto the stage chiding, 'Now, that's not ok, Sam!' The audience deliver a big laugh. Atkinson has tricked Sam into an inappropriate response, displaying approval for an unacceptable topic.

Asked offstage about this joke, Atkinson describes it in the following terms:

> Yes it's cruel. Basically, the point behind it is an abuse of status. And it works every single time. [...] It's partly to do with picking the right person, someone who's open to the gig and enjoying it and happy to chat. [...] So you chose someone suggestible, and then there's an ambiguity as to whether they're high-fiving the joke or the notion of paedophiles. And you sort of dress it up so it seems like, maybe to

them they'd be high-fiving the joke, and then you pull out. And the
comedy comes through abuse of power.[3]

This demonstrates a couple of crucial points about the nature of the
control that comedians exert over their audiences. First, the control is
not limited to ensuring that audiences recognize a joke and laugh at
it, albeit that this element of control is absolutely vital. The audience's
determination to deliver the 'correct response' extends to an audience
member attempting to participate in an excruciating social *faux pas*.[4]
Secondly, the incident demonstrates that audiences are aware of the
fact that they are complying with the performer's attempts to control
their responses: the joke references this very aspect of the performer–
audience relationship.

Reflecting on the incident offstage, Atkinson describes Sam as 'an
excellent audience member'; one whose consistent cooperation with
the comedian showed that he would be the perfect victim for such a
practical joke: 'He was very good [...] he played it straight. He didn't
try to take his own laughs but he still answered the questions. It was just
what you want.'[5] It is Sam's competence at delivering correct responses
which gets him into trouble. He has been a good supporting character
within the show because he plays along, recognizing the response that
the comedian requires and delivering it. The joke is that Atkinson uses
this against him; the incongruity that the correct response of cooperating
with the comedian should also be a fundamentally taboo response in
the wider social context. That the audience recognize their own drive
to cooperate, and thus their own submission to the comedian's control,
is a prerequisite for their understanding and appreciation of this joke.
The fact that Atkinson's joke 'works every time' suggests that this is a
universal, reliable trait among comedy audiences.

Nick Helm bursts onto the stage of the Horsebridge Arts and
Community Centre as the audience applaud, crying, 'Keep it going!'.[6]
The audience comply, continuing their applause until Helm is ready
to start speaking. Helm's tall, heavy-built frame roams the stage as he
belts out one-liners in a growling, west-country accent. His material

includes such gems as, 'I won a swimsuit contest... I ate fifty-seven swimsuits!'; 'My mate was in the army, he ate all the pudding rations... He got shot for desertion!' The timing and pace are all wrong, and the aggressive way in which Helm screams through his lines squashes any charm and playfulness that the jokes might have had. Helm does not allow his audience space to respond, but rather celebrates his comic dominance immediately after each punchline, kicking and punching the air or thrusting his pelvis forward, crying out phrases such as, 'You're welcome!' and 'Oh (.) my (.) God!'. By any conventional measure, Helm's delivery is very poor.

Therein lies Helm's genius. The Horsebridge audience are laughing from the outset, but seem initially uncertain of how to take Helm's belligerent style. Helm does not step out of his aggressive persona, nor give his audience any direct sign that his act is meant ironically, but rather keeps barking out jokes, relying on the audience's knowledge of stand-up to provide them with the appropriate interpretation. Gradually, the audience start to feel at ease, and join in with the game. After several of his poorly executed one-liners, Helm addresses the uncertainty in the room growling: 'This is happening. Get on board!' The audience deliver a big laugh, and proceed to respond confidently and in unison to the material that follows. Helm has got his audience under control.

The set evolves into a gentler mood as Helm delivers some comic poetry and finally finishes with a sing-along, providing accompaniment on the guitar. He briefly tells the audience the words to a sweet and lyrical song that they are required to sing. The tune and words both seem very simple, but Helm has told the audience their lines too quickly for them to really catch on. The first couple of attempts to sing as a group are a shambles, and Helm demonstrates frustration at the audience's incompetence – which he knows he has manufactured.

There is then a detour, as Helm identifies an audience member who has not been joining in and attempts to bully him into doing so, trying to haul him up on stage and eventually moving the microphone down into the audience, placing it directly in front of the man and standing over him until he sings. By the time Helm gets back to the stage, the words to the song and the accompanying chords have been repeated interminably. So when Helm, apparently despairing, tells his audience to give it one more go, the audience are able to deliver the song in perfect and harmonious unison. Helm looks up, his facial expression demonstrating impressed surprise, and keeps the music going so that the chorus is sung again. Thus the initial, messy confusion ends in a harmonious group rendition.

It is impossible to tell how much of the routine was pre-planned and how much of Helm's act was worked out in the moment. Whatever the balance of premeditation and spontaneity, the result was a performance which led the audience through seismic changes in pace and atmosphere orchestrated by Helm's expert control of their responses. As we have seen, extracting laughter by successful joking always involves some level of manipulation. What Atkinson and Helm demonstrate is that the manipulation of response extends beyond the procurement of laughter, with comedians being able to control a greater range of audience behaviour. When a comedian performs, he is not just relying on good jokes: some other manipulative effort is being made, and a large part of this effort consists of the way that the material is structured, packaged and presented.

The other reasons for laughing

Defining the word 'joke' is no easy task. At the outset of their book about jokes, Carr and Greeves provide the following definition:

> A joke, for the purposes of this book, is defined primarily as something you say deliberately to evoke amusement. It's a thing of words, a unit of communication. Not simple slapstick, not just storytelling, not mere wordplay – although it undoubtedly can contain all of these. It's a formulaic verbal construction designed to elicit a response – laughter. Beyond that, it gets a bit more complicated.[7]

That Carr and Greeves impose the broad qualification 'for the purposes of this book' is a clue to just how slippery the concept of joking is. It seems safe enough to claim that evoking amusement is a universal purpose of jokes, but even this fails to adequately explain some joking situations. The motivation of jokers is often not so simple: for example, a joke can be told in order to hurt or exclude, or to frustrate an opponent's argument, and can be recognized as a joking statement even when there is no third party present to laugh at it. If we perceive a joke as cruel or lack the ability to interpret it, or if we understand the joke but do not find it funny, we will still generally refer to the utterance as a joke. That we can recognize a cruelly intentioned or unsuccessful example as a joke implies that we recognize joking by characteristics other than intention and success. Laughter is a measure of a joke's success, but not a defining feature. Even in stand-up, unified laughter is not always the sole aim. In Mark Thomas' *Dambusters*, for example, informing audiences and motivating them to act was at least as important an aim as the promotion of laughter.[8] Often, Stewart Lee actively avoids unified laughter, feeling that 'there is something unpleasant about lots of people all laughing at the same thing *(laughs)* in the same way. It seems a bit like a – a rally, you know.'[9]

Determining how successful a joke has been is similarly tricky. John Limon claims that:

> A joke is funny if and only if you laugh at it. [...] A joke at which the audience smiles or nods its approbation is a failed joke; a joke at which the audience laughs is a good joke in proportion to its laughter.[10]

The idea that only jokes which procure laughter are funny is, perhaps, fair enough in situations where all audience members respond in unison, but it is of little help in defining the funniness of jokes which receive a mixed response. The idea that jokes are good 'in proportion to [their] laughter' has a similarly limited application. Compare routines by Josie Long and Michael McIntyre. The laughter that McIntyre gets is likely to build to a louder volume and more hysterical pitch than that present in Long's routines. McIntyre's performance is geared towards working his audience in to a frenzy; Long prefers a less slick approach, disrupting such linear accumulations of energy and thus inviting what she feels is a deeper and more authentic level of exchange with the audience.[11] She references this preference within her own performance.[12] Both are legitimate approaches. Commercially and in terms of volume of laughter, McIntyre is undoubtedly the more successful comedian. Yet among certain factions of the comedy world, Long is the comedian who commands greater respect. Fans admire her interesting comedic approach, and the act's DIY aesthetic and resultant artistic integrity, as well as her funniness and ability to reflect the shared human experience. Laughter and ticket or DVD sales are, therefore, not universally considered the most important markers of success, and nor is laughter the only thing ever demanded of comedians. As Dan Atkinson states:

> The best comedian is not necessarily the one who gets the most laughs, in my view. […] I think the best comedian is the one who has some sort of a synergy of, yes, making people laugh – that's the first thing, you have got to be funny, if you're not being funny or making people laugh then you're failing – but it's how you're making people laugh, and also giving them something to think about as well.[13]

As we have seen, joking is fundamentally about the subversion of boundaries, and for this reason it tends to have trouble sticking within its own limits. Designing a definition of the word 'joke' that can satisfactorily represent all of its forms is as difficult as designing a comic theory that fully explains all of the ways of being funny. Yet there are few instances, certainly within stand-up, where the human competence to recognize joking fails: audiences can usually tell a joking utterance from one that is intended to be taken seriously.

The following discussion focuses on the construction of jokes, in terms of text and performance. For the purposes of this chapter, a joke is defined by content rather than response, and by the joker's intention to make a joke, rather than their intention for that joke to result in laughter. As incongruity is the only element in comic theory that is generally considered to be universal, the current definition states that a joke must contain incongruity. It must also be instinctively understood by the audience to be a joke: the comedian must signal that the utterance takes place in the safe space where cognitive and practical disengagement are permitted. This enables us to examine the fact that the relationship between joking and laughter is not necessarily a straightforward matter of cause and effect.

In his study of the techniques that characterize successful speeches by political speakers, Max Atkinson demonstrates that much of positive audience response stems from the audience's cooperation with the speaker.[14] Like comedians, political orators will seek 'displays of approval' from their audiences; just as a comedian cannot claim to have given a successful performance if he does not draw laughter, a politician relies on the applause and supportive utterances of his audience.[15] Cooperation between audience and speaker is vital; the speaker must give clear signals as to when a response is wanted and when it should begin, and must pause to allow the display to occur. Meanwhile, the audience must give the desired response, starting at the right moment and continuing for the right length of time, not interfering with the continuation of the speech.[16]

The audiences of stand-up performance and political speaking share the same incentives to cooperate. In either case, the audience may have a personal loyalty to the speaker. As Max Atkinson states, this is the case when leading politicians speak to their own party: it is similarly true when a famous comedian faces an audience who have paid for a ticket specifically to see him. The audience know, instinctively, that their response is necessary for the success of the event, and are committed to making the required effort to ensure that the event is indeed a success. Above all, the audience will not want to risk giving an incorrect response. As Max Atkinson states:

> We tend to feel very uncomfortable when, as members of a collectivity, we fail to co-ordinate our own behaviour with that of everyone else. [...] When we are seen to step out of line, we draw attention to our ignorance of how to behave properly on such occasions, and may find our social competence called into question. It threatens exposure to the

horrors of public ridicule and humiliation. [...] At public gatherings, there is thus considerable pressure on all those present to conform and 'go along with the crowd'.[17]

Atkinson argues that audiences do not applaud only because they hear an idea that they like, but rather when the linguistic packaging of the utterance tells them that it is time to do so. The same process is at work in stand-up comedy. According to Max Atkinson, 'three out of every four displays of approval occur in response to about half a dozen verbal devices'.[18] These techniques constitute ways of structuring utterances which signal clearly to the hearer that a display of approval is wanted, and when it should begin.[19]

These 'packaging' techniques, which get the laugh more through the way that statements are delivered than the actual incongruity of the material presented, are common in stand-up. They are ingeniously manipulative, partly because they can be very hard to spot. Well into the second half of the show filmed for his 2004 DVD *Monster*, Dylan Moran embarks on a long critique of romantic relationships and gender differences.[20] Moran manages his audience's response expertly, and seemingly effortlessly. While the performance of this highly successful routine relies on a complex range of skills, it is possible that part of the reason for the apparent ease with which Moran cues his audience to laugh is the fact that they are working to a pattern. Max Atkinson demonstrates that audiences are skilled at identifying patterns and discerning how and when to react to them.[21] One such pattern for Dylan Moran is the list of three items. In the following example, Moran compares male and female attitudes to falling in love:

> Because it's actually men... you'll find (.) who are the far more romantic. [couple of laughs] Men are the people you will hear say: *(Moran pauses to light a cigarette)...* 'I've found somebody'... [few laughs] 'She's amazing... If I don't, if I don't get to be with this person, I'm fucked.' [laugh]... 'I can't carry on.' [laugh starts, Moran cuts it off] 'I – no I mean it – I, she's totally transformed my life. I have a job, I have a flat, it mea, means nothing. If – I can't stand it, I have to be with her. Because if I don't, I'm gonna end up in some bedsit, I'll be

alcoholic, I'll have itchy trousers. I can't' [laugh]… 'I can't walk the streets anymore'… That… is how women… feel about shoes. [big laugh and applause][22]

This segment demonstrates two main uses of the list of three. The first, 'I'll end up in some bedsit, I'll be alcoholic, I'll have itchy trousers', is based on the commonly used joke structure of 'establish, reinforce, surprise'.[23] The first item is 'bedsit', and introduces the idea of lonely and inadequate living conditions. The second item, 'alcoholic', reinforces the image. The third item, 'itchy trousers', is a surprising twist on the theme; the joke lies in the surprise. The 'list of three' pattern is also described by Atkinson as a commonly used 'claptrap'; audiences well understand that the completion of a three-part list is a prompt to applaud.[24]

This pattern is so well established that its form can be used even when there are not three items in terms of content. Thus Moran's second three-part list is actually a breakdown of one concept expressed in a single sentence; by pausing twice Moran turns 'that/ is how women/ feel about shoes' into a three-part list. The fact that a list of three is being used signals to the audience that a response may soon be necessary; thus although the joke is funny in terms of content, the response it receives is also partly due to the fact that it is delivered in such a way as to elicit response.

Most strikingly, Moran's use of three-part lists becomes so successful that it plays a greater role than content in dictating the point at which a joke is deemed to have been completed. Here Moran is discussing the comparative abilities of men and women to argue against each other:

And the arguments do seem to be unfairly racked in, in, in, in women's favour because of the, the, I think the arguments are made in different places; all male arguments are very early-seventies, Soviet-made, uni-directional, [small laugh] trundling behemoths [small laugh] (.) That say the same thing again and again and again. [small laugh][25]

On paper, 'unidirectional' is an inadequate punchline; it is certainly no more incongruous than the idea of an argument being 'early seventies' or 'soviet-made'. Yet it receives a laugh, albeit a small one. In a sense, the audience is applying the pattern inappropriately; having learnt that the completion of a three-part list is usually a good joke, they laugh in response to the list even though no joke has been made.

Moran is only able to extract laughs through packaging because his show is full of funny jokes; therefore it could be argued that the tendency to laugh in response to a verbal device is, in real terms, unimportant. However, this view underestimates the importance of what a laugh does. The effect of a laugh extends beyond the moment in which the laugh takes place, creating and reinforcing feelings of consensus and unity both between the members of the group who laugh together, and from the audience towards the joker.[26] Furthermore, it confirms the status of the comedian as a successful and funny performer, each laugh increasing the audience's vital faith that the comedian can make them laugh again, and telling them that laughter is indeed the correct way to respond.[27] By structuring material to keep the laughs coming regularly, the comedian manipulates the atmosphere and attitude of his audience to his own advantage. By utilizing the audience's instinct to respond to verbal devices, giving them clear cues regarding when and how to respond, the comedian can make the most of the unity that laughter implies, and the pressure to conform that accompanies it.[28]

It is unlikely that many comedians consciously apply these techniques. These verbal devices are used instinctively even in everyday conversation[29]; comedians, similarly, utilize them naturally, by instinct. Whether the thought process behind these devices is as detailed as knowingly using a list of three items or contrastive pair to create a prompt for responses, or is merely the result of a comedian having a vague, instinctive knowledge that it will 'sound better that way', analysis of stand-up demonstrates that they are widely used to manipulate audience response.

Patterning and the 'unfinished' gag

Comedians are aware that their audiences can learn patterns and respond to them. Richard Herring explains that he often jokes about the joke pattern itself, building the expectation that the punchline is coming before changing the direction of the joke altogether.[30] He notes that even surprising patterns are essentially utilizing the audience's competence with patterning:

I think it is about surprise, but I think that means that – certain audiences, you know, are more sophisticated [...] and certain comedians are more sophisticated with the way they hide stuff. [...] I [might] see a comedian who tricks me with a basic [...] pull back and reveal joke, [because] you can set it up so beautifully that you don't see the twist coming, you know. Whereas a lot of comedians who will just do [...] these jokes [...] – 'I was sitting in my nappy doing a poo, and my Mum came in and said "what are you doing?"' and, you know, 'I was twenty-eight years old at the time', it's that basic kind of joke – which a comedian will see that coming a mile off, but occasionally you'll get a comedian who can really hide those. [...] You've gotta keep moving and you've gotta keep changing and you've gotta, kind of, surprise yourself. [...] [But] Peter Kay's continued success shows that some people just like to be spoon-fed [...] they obviously know what's coming and they love it [...] that's fine.[31]

Stewart Lee often comments directly on the patterning tendency during his performances. In his show *90s Comedian*, he identifies that one-half of the audience are more in tune with the jokes than their counterparts on the other side of the stage. Lee teases the section on his left for being slow to adapt to the ethos of the show, and points out that this is going to be a problem, implying that the material in the second half of the show will be difficult and harrowing.[32] Lee intersperses jokes about the 'mixed ability' level of the audience with other material which focuses on the show's key themes of terrorism and religion for a few minutes, and then he comes to the following:

I don't know if you know but the Catholic Church are very worried about you all reading *The Da Vinci Code* and in fact in January last year the Vatican actually issued an official statement reminding Dan Brown readers that the books are largely fictional and full of historically unverifiable information.[33]

The line is delivered with a subtle, wry smile, but the tone and pace are calm; vocally, Lee gives no signal that this is anything other than a simple statement of fact. The statement is accompanied by a repeated downward bounce of Lee's left hand, which accompanies each new syllable and draws attention to the utterance as an important point containing specific detail which requires close attention. This is one of Lee's joke patterns: the joke is not made explicit but demands that the audience make some of the imaginative effort to complete and interpret the joke themselves. Thus, although Lee does not explicitly make the link between this comment and the Bible, the attitudes and information he has conveyed before this point give the audience sufficient hints that they should identify the Vatican's statement as hypocritical: we are able to assume that Lee would take the view that the Vatican has based its existence on a text that is, itself, 'largely fictional and full of historically unverifiable information'. Koestler's theory of bisociation provides a useful model through which to interpret this process. According to Koestler, jokes are 'the perceiving of a situation or idea [...] in two self-consistent but habitually incompatible frames of reference'. Diagrammatically, he expresses this idea with a line representing a concept (M1) crossing an incompatible concept (M2), creating a joke (L) at the point where those lines cross.[34] Lee's joke works on a subversion of this incongruity theory: M1 is given, but the audience must discern M2 from hints that litter the surrounding context, and then follow the concepts through for themselves to point L.

Having delivered the line, Lee pauses for a long time, taking a pace forward then back, keeping his eyes on the floor and waiting confidently until some of the audience catch on. Franklyn Ajaye identifies such pauses as a useful technique for allowing an audience to catch up with a 'cerebral' or subtle joke; it gives them time to make the links and leaps of thought that the joke leaves them to create for themselves.[35] In this case, some of the audience not only laugh, but commit to keeping the laugh going while Lee goes on to draw a sharp intake of breath and make a gesture which seems physically to weigh up the extent to which each side of the audience is now following along. On this occasion, however, the laugh fails to envelop the whole audience. Lee goes on to turn to the left-hand section of the audience – the side that he has said are lagging behind – and says:

> Six minutes time, I tell you (.) you'll be fine, right? But you're right not to laugh at that. It's not a proper joke, right? It's just (.) based on a shared set of assumptions, doesn't work.[36]

A little under six minutes later, Lee is talking about the fact that the funeral of Pope John Paul II was arranged for the same day as the wedding of Prince Charles and Camilla Parker Bowles, causing the wedding to be moved to avoid a conflict. Lee jokes that they should not have cancelled the wedding because 'that's what split screen television technology was invented for', before going on to make another 'cerebral', or perhaps incomplete, joke:

> Although it is hard, isn't it, to imagine which one of those events would have been the most distressing to watch… [laugh] you know? [laugh continues]… the public veneration of a wrinkled old corpse….

This, admittedly, is an easier joke for the audience to 'get' than is the *Da Vinci Code* joke. Lee utilizes a common joke structure, making a statement which would be appropriate to one of two concepts that he has introduced ('the public veneration of a wrinkled old corpse' as a description of the Pope's funeral – a statement which is itself incongruous in its irreverence) and then matching it instead with the other concept ('the public veneration […]' as a description of the royal wedding). Unlike the *Da Vinci Code* joke, which provides minimal information from which 'M2' may be discerned, this latter joke directs the audience straight to it. Both, however, make use of the audience's awareness of Lee's pattern. Like the *Da Vinci Code* joke, this latter joke makes an observation, hints at a shared reaction to it and then leaves the audience to identify the funny angle associated with it. This is Lee's pattern in terms of content, and is accompanied by a verbal and physical pattern which cues the audience to pay attention and identify it. In this latter gag, Lee slows his pace as he comes to the end of the utterance, and then leaves a long pause. Having made a sharp downward movement with his left hand during the final section of the utterance, he now repeats that movement twice with more emphasis, mirroring the movements that accompanied the *Da Vinci Code* joke. Once the line has been said, he opens his mouth and closes it again, giving an emphatic nod, as if he had been about to carry on speaking but had stopped upon realizing that the audience, finally, are able to keep up. The laughter now sweeps around the whole of the room.

Although Lee stops speaking, his movements suggest the carrying-on of the utterance, clearly signalling that the audience should be filling in the remainder of the words in their own minds. Now familiar with the formula, knowing that such a simple statement of facts is supposed to lead them to search for the presence of incongruity, the majority of the audience deliver the laugh. Lee goes on to recognize the pattern that he has established, saying that they now have a section of the room ahead of the punchlines, and emphasizing that the audience should indeed be making the effort to complete the jokes in their own minds:

> And if you, if anyone had anticipated that joke and was holding back from laughing out of kind of politeness to me [laugh]… thinking, 'oh he won't like it if we guess his jokes' right, [laugh]… I don't care, I would welcome it. I think it's good, right, 'coz if you think about it (.) I have to write about an hour and a half of jokes every [year] – that's quite hard, right? [couple of chuckles] but what's just happened suggests (.) that with the correct (.) encouragement of audiences, [small laugh] I wouldn't have to write any jokes. [laugh] I could just come out with a list of topics [laugh], read them out [couple of chuckles], and you (.) could think of something amusing about them [laugh starts] in your own heads [laugh] then if you didn't like the show (.) that would be your fault [laugh].

While this joke is built on the premise that Lee is reacting to an unexpected behaviour from his audience, the whole incident has been created by Lee's own expert craftsmanship. Over the course of just under ten minutes, Lee is building his audience's capacity to work to a specific pattern. He rewards their cooperative tendencies while punishing the uncooperative, in a bid to create the unity that will be essential to get the show through the challenging and controversial material that follows. These jokes reflect upon this process, identify those who are and are not 'up to speed' – meaning those who do or do not recognize the pattern and respond accordingly – and praise those who are 'ahead of the punchlines', indicating that Lee is well aware of the process in which he is involved.[37]

Offstage, Lee acknowledges that he actively trains his audience to work with the unusual pattern of his joking.[38] This much is manipulative, as it involves using his skill to lead the audience to adopt certain cognitive patterns. However, the purpose of Lee's oblique style goes beyond manipulation to influence:

> Part of the pleasure of any piece of art (and I think stand-up is art), is having the fun of figuring out for yourself. [...] I build that in quite self-consciously, giving the audience the pleasure of figuring it out for themselves. People often say as a criticism of me that it's so slow and it's really obvious where it's going. But it isn't obvious where its going, always, it's like what I do is I give them just enough information for them to figure it out for themselves, and they laugh before I've actually finished the thing off. Y'know, and I like that, 'cause it means they're, sort of, engaged. [...] I often don't finish [jokes]. You sort of do half a joke, and just leave it [...] and also that has the effect that there's normally about ten per cent of the audience going, 'What was that? What's everyone laughing at? He hasn't finished!' And then I feel they've got to raise their game. [...] Because basically, I think everything's so passively consumed in the world today, and spelt-out for people, that you're trying to remind an audience that they are having an actual live experience, that they will have to listen.[39]

For Lee, then, re-educating a modern, hyper-mediated audience to connect with live performance presents both a challenge and an opportunity:

As well as everything being spoon-fed today there's, like, amplification and noise, fast editing. [...] So you kind of feel [...] the way to get people's attention is to kind of do the opposite of that, because you can't compete with that level of volume and speed and information. The only thing you can do is, like, go right back to basics.

For Lee, the 'unfinished' joke is a mechanism for engaging an audience more deeply; forcing them to do some of the work so that they cannot consume the material passively. This enhanced level of engagement necessarily means that audience members who are able to follow the odd patterning of Lee's material will connect with it, and cognitively process it, in a more profound way than other modes of performance, with their 'noise' and 'fast editing' can ever encourage.

Comic Licence and Manufacturing Consensus

The structure of an act, and the establishment of comic licence

In his essay, 'Stand-up Comedy as Social and Cultural Mediation', Mintz suggests that all jokes, even those which appear benign, serve as social challenge; they 'contain a critique of the gap between what is and what we believe should be'.[1] Both the comedy event and the person of the comedian must therefore operate under comic licence, allowing a 'dysfunctional' persona to revel in 'dysfunctional' views of the world which can easily be discounted and rejected, so that the gap may be identified and attacked within a safe structure. Equally, however, the comedian's marginal observations may be 'publically [*sic*] affirmed under the guise of "mere comedy," or "just kidding,"' in which instance the comedian becomes the 'comic spokesperson', revealing that gap and championing the attack upon it.[2] This view is reflected in Linstead's idea of joking as a 'bracket' in which ideas may be experimented without the danger of infecting everyday interaction.[3] The point is that, for the joking to work, all of the participants in the stand-up event must recognize that what is said occurs under the auspices of comic licence.

Mintz identifies two key processes that comedians undertake at the start of their acts in order to establish an atmosphere in which social practices may be questioned, and the boundaries of consensus tested. First:

The comedian must establish *for the audience* that the group is homogenous, a community, if the laughter is to come easily. 'Working the room,' as comedians term it, loosens the audience and allows for laughter as an expression of shared values rather than as a personal predilection.[4]

The comedian will then establish his own comic persona, a process that 'allows the audience to accept that comedian's marginal status and to establish that the mood of comic license is operative'.[5]

Here Mintz is deconstructing the complex process of 'warming up' the audience. This is not only a matter of relaxing the audience and ensuring that they are capable of producing laughter easily; the warm-up also allows the comedian to establish that comic licence is in operation, and that all following statements are to be read within the safe bracket of the joke. Furthermore, the comedian asserts that the disparate collection of individuals in attendance is in fact a unified group with a shared consensus, thus allowing the group to feel secure in the knowledge that their laughter is acceptable to their peers, and any potentially risky value-judgements involved in the joking are shared with others. The comedian is established as the focus of this group, and their immunity as a 'dysfunctional' accepted.

Although Mintz discusses these functions in relation to the earliest moments of a stand-up set, stating that they occur before, and essentially as a separate entity to, the 'comedy routine itself,' this is really only part of the process.[6] The 'warm-up' may in fact involve an ongoing effort which extends throughout the set, allowing the comedian to extend into more controversial, complex or difficult material as the audience become more attuned to the ethos of the gig and the persona of the comedian. Indeed, it is this ongoing attention to the need to firmly establish and maintain comic licence that allows Stewart Lee to pull off an impressive feat of crowd control: obtaining applause for the terrorist activity of the IRA.[7]

This moment occurs during a routine about the 2005 London Bombings, performed in Cardiff in 2006, in which Lee compares Al Qaeda to the IRA:

> But, Cardiff, who are these inhuman bombers that strike, they strike at the very heart of our society with no respect for human life, without

even the courtesy of a perfunctory warning? It makes you nostalgic, doesn't it, for the good old days of the IRA. [laugh] 'Coz they gave warnings, didn't they? They were gentleman bombers. [laugh] The finest terrorists (.) [small laugh] this country's ever had (.) [small laugh] we'll not see their like again. [laugh] Let's, let's have a little clap for the IRA, come on, give them a little clap. [Audience applauds] Give them a clap, right. 'Coz the IRA, they were decent, British terrorists. They didn't wanna be British, [laugh] but they were. [big laugh] And as such they couldn't help but embody some fundamentally decent, British values. [laugh] We'll miss 'em now they're gone. [small laugh][8]

Perhaps Lee's audience will permit some mitigating factors here. It is likely that many of Lee's audience are too young to remember the time when the threat of IRA bombing was a dominant public concern. This routine is performed in Wales, while the main threat of IRA bombings, and indeed of Al Qaeda attacks, was focused on England. Thus it could be argued that the notion of the IRA will be more distant and less emotive to this audience than it might be to an audience of older Londoners. Yet it cannot be argued that Lee is on safe ground here. Some of his audience are old enough to remember the IRA bombings of the 1980s. The resurgence of terrorist activity by Al Qaeda, and the death and injury that accompanied it, made terrorism a current and emotive topic when this routine was performed in March 2006. That Lee successfully persuades his audience to issue applause for the terrorist activity of the IRA is a striking demonstration of the comedian's ability to manipulate the boundaries of consensus.

Remembering this routine over four years later, Lee recalls the rationale behind this piece:

The extent to which Islamic terrorism – well, Islam's – been so demonised and yet, when I was a kid in Birmingham and the IRA were blowing up nightclubs and killing teenagers [...] the notion, forty years later, that you would have Irish theme pubs just seems impossible, you know. And everyone loves Ireland now. So I thought that it would be an interesting thing to do to, sort of, use the language in a manipulative way [...] to say that the Irish terrorists were better;

that they had *(laughs)* like, achievable aims and they always phoned
in warnings and stuff like that. But also there's an element of truth in
it whereby that style of terrorism, whereby it was a bargaining tool,
seems just so old-fashioned now, compared to things where the aims
seem much less [clear] – or more simple in a way, which is just, sort
of, punishment. [...] But, I mean, it was really, really good fun using
that. [...] Because people applaud it, I think, before they realise what
they're applauding, because you couch it in a language that sounds
reasonable. [...] But yeah, the thing there was definitely to, sort of,
wrong-foot the audience, and I try and do that a lot to get them to [...]
applaud or laugh at things that I then criticise them for laughing or
applauding at.[9]

As Lee states, the use of 'a language that sounds reasonable' is one way
in which this set manages to convince the audience to applaud. Lee
presents his subversive idea in such a way as to make it seem logical.
Close analysis of this set reveals that structure – the positioning of this
moment within the show as a whole and the build-up to it – is also
vitally important in allowing Lee to perform this contentious piece of
material not only safely (in that he does not lose the cooperation of his
audience), but with an explicit, if perhaps reluctant, display of approval
in the form of applause. Lee has arranged his material in such a way as
to deliver the controversial idea that the IRA were 'decent', 'gentleman
bombers' within a logical order and time frame which allows the
audience gradually to warm up to the point where, around eighteen
minutes into the show, he can request and be granted applause for IRA
terrorism.

Having begun his show with a brief set of jokes about its unusual
length and structure, and the behaviour expected of the audience,
Lee begins the show proper with an immediate, but so far inoffensive
reference to the 7 July bombings:

Now on, um, Thursday the seventh of July, 7/7, I woke up, in London,
er, at about midday. And already I can sense people going yeah, 'course
you did Stew, you slept through that (.) major (.) news event, because
you are a lazy... stand-up comedian [small laugh][10]

Although Lee's joke poses no serious ethical dilemma – it chastises his own failings, and says nothing about terrorism or its effects – this introduction already begins to minimize the emotive impact that a reference to that day, and those events, may have. While the device of beginning the story with a significant date is rather dramatic, the way that Lee phrases his date – 'Thursday the seventh of July', which suggests a date in the calendar, rather than '7/7', which more specifically denotes the July bombings – functions to begin a process of detachment which distances the audience from traditional reactions to the events which happened on that day. Lee further minimizes the impact of the event by saying that he slept through it, despite being in the very city in which it occurred. Rather than describing the bombing from the perspective of its immediate victims and witnesses, as is the common and more emotive approach employed in the mainstream media's handling of the story, Lee gives us an account formed from the point of view of one who was not immediately connected to events. The result is that the terrorist activity and the damage and pain that it inflicted are placed into wider perspective and deprived of the iconic power that made '7/7' a widely emotive topic.

This first joke completed, the topic of terrorism immediately gives way to less dangerous material, as Lee goes on to explain that his oversleeping was due to his having arrived home late the night before following a gig in Lincoln, with the routine easily evolving on to a set of jokes which mock the lack of sophistication of the Lincoln audience, and Lee's own foolishness in dealing with them. He then loops briefly back to the topic of the July bombings, describing how he, not having heard the news that London had been bombed, incongruously misinterprets his emails and text messages:

> And the first thing I did on 7/7 when I woke up, was I checked all my emails, right, and the first one in was from an American comic called Jackie Kashian, that I'd worked with in Perth in June, and it was just one line it just said… 'are you alright?' [couple of laughs]… So I emailed back (.) 'yes, fine, thanks how are you?' [laugh]… And the next one was from a New Zealand comic called Ben Hurley who I'd worked with in Auckland in May, same thing, one line, 'are you

alright?' [small laugh]... so I emailed back 'yes fine thanks how are you?' [small laugh]

Lee explains that he got approximately fifteen further emails and twenty text messages from friends around the world, all asking 'are you alright?', and gets a good laugh as he goes on to explain: 'Now, as you may or may not know, I did have quite a difficult year.' Lee deviates onto the various medical and legal problems that had beset him, and returns only very briefly to the story of his own personal and insular experience on the day of the London bombings. Again, the joke is at the expense of his own ignorance, rather than the events of the day:

> So it had been (.) a difficult year, and [laugh]... while I was touched [laugh]... that all of my friends had chosen to enquire after my welfare, it did seem strange [couple of laughs]... that they had all chosen [couple of laughs]... the same morning to do that [laugh]

From here, Lee launches into a routine about an endoscopy that he had earlier that year, leading smoothly into a routine that discusses Joe Pasquale's theft of a joke from lesser-known comic Michael Redmond. Again, this material puts Lee on safer ground. The topics are not as emotive, nor are Lee's approaches as taboo, as Lee's later discussion of terrorism. Lee talks about his endoscopy in such a way as to expose his own embarrassment. The routine also relates ignorant and insensitive comments made by Lee's doctor and nurse on the fact that his medical notes describe him as a 'famous comedian'. There is no moral dilemma caused by Lee's mockery of either himself or the people who, in the context of the endoscopy, hold a high status. It is mockery of those with low status and genuine anguish, as is the case when a tragedy with many victims like the July bombings is discussed, that causes moral difficulty.[11] Similarly, when Lee comes to attack Joe Pasquale, he frames Pasquale as the high-status 'mainstream' performer, attributing to Redmond an obscure and more vulnerable status. Altogether, this detour on to safer subjects allows Lee to talk for over ten minutes without any reference to terrorism or the July bombings.

Returning to the story of the seventh of July, Lee now arrives at the routine which will culminate in asking the audience to applaud the IRA. He is now just over fifteen minutes into his show, and has laid the ground for more controversial material. We rejoin the story at the point at which Lee has realized that something must have happened; he switches on the television news, paving the way for the first bit of really dangerous material on the subject of the July bombings. Lee reads out quotations from victims who had survived the terrorist attacks in a way that makes them appear ridiculous: an impassive near-monotone, which serves to place the statements out of context and suggests that they should be taken literally:

> By now it was about three hours after the London Al Qaeda bombings, and on TV news there was all these kind of insensitive news journalists, running around, trying to get statements out of bomb survivors that weren't really in a fit state to give statements. And I, I started writing them down, right. This was, um, a guy (.) that had survived the King's Cross Bomb, and he said to camera, he said, 'the rescue workers have been amazing, really amazing. I mean, I take my hat off to them… I'm not wearing a hat' [laugh]… 'obviously' [laugh]… 'but if I was' [laugh]… 'I would take it off' [laugh]

The audience's laughter has a quality of uncertainty, and their reaction to the joke paves the way for Lee to explicitly address his audience's discomfort surrounding the treatment of this topic as entertainment:

> Laughs over here, a smattering of applause, and then (.) doubt spreading towards the back corner [laugh]… Now, don't judge me for this, ok, don't be uncomfortable, I am a human being like you, I'm a member of society, I watched that news report, I thought I hope these people are ok, and things don't pan out too badly, er, for the world situation. But on the other hand I am also a comedian so I was thinking, 'mind you, it's quite funny I should write it down' [laugh][12]

By beginning this routine with a reference to the 'insensitive news journalists' and 'survivors that weren't really in a fit state to give statements', Lee excuses the survivors and places the blame for the ridiculous statements that they made on to the journalists. While in reality the bomb survivors remain the butt of the joke, by accusing the journalists of exploiting the survivors Lee gives the audience a way out of the moral dilemma; the journalists are at the root of the ridiculousness of these statements, and it is they, not the audience, who are the opportunists guilty of exploiting the pain of the survivors. The audience may therefore redirect blame for any trespass of decency towards the journalists, and away from themselves and Lee. In talking about his own dual reaction to the bombings – as a compassionate member of society and as a comedian – Lee emphasizes both the licence and protection afforded by his status as comedian, and that it is possible to operate in this mode while also remaining a responsible and compassionate individual.

Lee has given his audience an easily discernable set of rules; by highlighting both his status as comedian and the marginal nature of the stand-up event, Lee tells his audience that here, within this performance, it is acceptable to laugh at serious and emotive subjects. Following this gag, Lee delivers one more statement from a bomb survivor. The audience laugh, reaffirming the acceptability of the topic. From there, Lee immediately goes on to the section transcribed earlier, asking, 'But, Cardiff, who are these inhuman bombers [...]?', and going on to gain applause for the IRA's approach to terrorism.

It is important to recognize that Lee's audience are not delivering an unqualifiedly positive response. There is an uncomfortable quality to the laughter given in response to the bomb survivor statements. When Lee asks for applause for the IRA, the DVD footage offers close-ups of various audience members, revealing that some are not clapping. Those who do applaud appear uncomfortable, both during the applause and afterwards. Interestingly, the applause is very short. Max Atkinson demonstrates that audiences instinctively and regularly keep this kind of display of approval to a length of between seven and nine seconds, and that applause may usually be expected to 'begin to get underway either just before or immediately after the speaker reaches such a completion point'.[13] This applause lasts for a mere three seconds, and the audience hesitates, leaving a pause between the completion of Lee's request and the beginning of the applause, which begins in a gradual and uncertain canon rather than bursting out in impressive unison. Several of the audience members who can be seen during this routine have their hands held up to their faces, covering their mouths. One woman, having applauded the IRA, fiddles with the fingernails of her right hand and briefly glances at the fingers, seemingly unsure about whether she should be going along with the joke and allowing herself to become complicit in the statements Lee is making, or pointedly withdraw her participation from the event. While the DVD naturally represents an editorial choice regarding which audience reactions will be highlighted, this choice is telling in itself: Lee explains that the audience close-ups in his DVDs are chosen to 'preserve for the viewer that feeling of not being sure how you're supposed to respond'.[14]

According to Lee, this is success:

> [It's] counter-intuitive in a way, because the most obvious thing to do in stand-up is to try and get everyone on side, but I like to create a feeling of confusion in the room where people don't really know if they're supposed to be laughing or not. […] I would ideally try to create a number of varied and contradictory [responses] by using language that's manipulative in such a way as some people might respond to it differently to other people. But I also like the audience to be aware that they're being manipulated, I think; y'know, that's half the fun of it […] part of the joke.[15]

In Chapter 7, we will come to a further discussion of why Lee takes this unusual approach to stand-up comedy, and the influence he exerts by doing so. For our present purposes it is important only to note the level of Lee's manipulative skill and his awareness of it. He seeks purposefully to create feelings of uncertainty and discomfort. The audience will be aware that they have been manipulated; that they know that they have been tricked is part of the joke; the enjoyment of Lee's skill in orchestrating the manipulation is 'half the fun of it'.

By contrast, when Lee states that the IRA 'didn't want to be British but they were', thus turning the bombers from heroes to victims of mockery, the laugh is louder and more comfortable; perhaps embodying a feeling of relief that the IRA are once again placed in the position of 'other', being criticized rather than praised. This example represents a common technique employed within Lee's work. By including safer gags among more controversial ones, Lee ensures that laughs come regularly, asserting that comic licence is still in operation.

There are many factors which make the IRA routine work. Lee's audience have come specifically to see him, and are therefore likely to be well prepared for the controversial flavour and ambiguity of attitude which characterizes much of Lee's most distinctive material. Part of the joke is the outrageousness of what the audience is being asked to participate in, and Lee's blatantly manipulative abuse of power. However, it is the structure of Lee's material, the gradual build through various stages which expose and refute the taboo of discussing the bombings in such frank terms, which allows Lee's audience to come to terms with the topic, and provides them with a moral escape route. Through the expert structure of this routine, Lee builds a network of mitigating factors which absolve the audience of responsibility for their compliance. Most importantly, he emphasizes to them that the whole activity takes place under the rule of comic licence, and therefore need not have any consequences in the 'real' world. That they are still left in some doubt about the acceptability of their actions is part of Lee's joke and a testament to his expert management; that they comply at all is a product of the set's ingenious structure.

Manufacturing consensus: The (selective) use of logic

Zijderveld sees jokes as powerful entities which expose our dominant ideologies; in fact, evidence of what a society jokes about is a better indicator of its preoccupations than the evidence of a more straightforward opinion poll.[16] Like Douglas and Lash, Zijderveld sees the element of 'challenge' as vital to joking: for Zijderveld joking is about deviating from the 'norm' in order to expose the perceived notion of normality and allow us to question why it should be so.[17] Zijderveld therefore identifies four categories of joking, which represent four areas of human experience in which the joker may deviate from the norm: 'socio cultural and political life at large'; 'the meaning of language'; 'traditional emotions'; and 'traditional logic'.[18]

Zijderveld identifies two ways of deviating from traditional logic:

> [T]he joke can deviate from normal logic in that it transports logical thinking into the realm of the absurd, or it can deviate from our standard logic in that it beats normal, average logic by hyper-logical, hyper-cunning intelligence.[19]

Taken together, Zijderveld's idea about the function of logic in humour and his suggestion about the very real social impact joking may have create important opportunities for the comedian as manipulator. 'Hyper-logic' implies that the joker has created an idea that, although ridiculous, is based upon a logical, often rigorously factual, premise. Human beings harbour a set of characteristics which may make them susceptible to the use of biased logic and hyper-logic. First, as Allport identifies, effort is 'objectionable'; people are innately lazy when it comes to testing received opinions and ideas, and it stands to reason that we might be especially reluctant to test ideas when rewarded with laughter for not doing so.[20] Lippmann further states that human beings necessarily have a rather detached and contrived relationship with reality; unable to know of every event and occurrence in the world around us, or to comprehend the complexity even of our own limited experience, we necessarily interpret our environment by simplifying it, thus creating a pseudo-environment based on the limited information we are able to obtain and process. Self-interest also plays its part in constructing the pseudo-environment:

> For the real environment is altogether too big, too complex, and too fleeting for direct acquaintance. We are not equipped to deal

with so much subtlety, so much variety, so many permutations and combinations [...] we have to reconstruct it on a simpler model before we can manage with it. To traverse the world men must have maps of the world. Their persistent difficulty is to secure maps on which their own need, or someone else's need, has not sketched in the coast of Bohemia.[21]

This combination of theories points to some significant possibilities for stand-up comedy. If an audience thinks in the way suggested above then they have both the incentive to adopt the comedian's logic as a premise, and the experience and well-practised skills to traverse the world using the given 'map'.

Analysis of stand-up demonstrates that this is a staple method for manufacturing consensus. Consensus is particularly vital in Mark Thomas' work. While it is true that Thomas attracts a rather specific audience who are likely to be predisposed to agree with him, his material does challenge the consensus of even this specialized audience. Much of Thomas' material is potentially controversial, with past shows having encouraged audience members to participate in political protests including direct action and acts of civil disobedience. For example, Thomas has encouraged his audience to harass the police by creating excess paperwork, and to prank call a military airbase, RAF Fairford. He has also praised the efforts of campaigners who have broken the law with various acts including trespass and vandalism.[22] As Thomas encourages his audience to see the purpose and virtue of potentially dubious actions that have physically taken place in the real world, he discusses and encourages activities that the mainstream of the British populace would not contemplate carrying out for themselves.

Just as Stewart Lee gradually builds consensus for the controversial use of terrorism as a topic for amusement over the first fifteen minutes of his show, Thomas will generally make an early effort to assert the moral virtue of his standpoint and justify his position. His 2007 show *Serious Organised Criminal* attacks part of the Serious Organised Crime and Police Act (SOCPA) which made it illegal to hold demonstrations in a designated area surrounding Parliament Square without first applying for, and receiving, police permission.[23] The show discusses Thomas' campaign to have this law repealed, which hinged on the tactic of submitting as many applications to demonstrate as possible. This would create administrative difficulties, waste police time and make the law costly to maintain, while at the same time exposing the foolishness of having such a law in the first place. It is vital that the audience agree that the law is not only unjust, but also defeatable; if Thomas cannot muster consensus on these points his audience will neither enjoy, nor be persuaded to act upon, the material that he will present. He thus sets to work almost immediately to dismantle the authority and validity of the law.

Thomas begins his story by introducing SOCPA:

> I should explain, tonight's show is about the Serious Organised Crime and Police Act. It's the bit of the law that David Blunkett brought in to get Brian Haw the peace campaigner.[24]

By introducing SOCPA in these terms, Thomas subtly reduces the law to an attack upon one individual, which implies a rather cowardly and disproportionate approach by former Home Secretary Blunkett and the government to persecute one person. That the law should have been brought in to attack a peace protestor, whose right to protest we may assume Thomas' audience would broadly uphold, appears suitably despicable, and from this starting point Thomas easily establishes the idea that to quash Haw's rights by limiting everybody else's rights is tyrannical. Thomas further explains that a judge has decreed that the law cannot be applied retrospectively, and thus does not apply to Brian Haw, 'so the very man they brought the law in to get, it doesn't work for'.[25]

Thomas goes on to continue to reduce the authority of the law, showing it to be ridiculous in detail and application as well as in concept. Finally, he comes to one of the more outrageous examples of SOCPA's unreasonably oppressive application:

> It then gets weirder. My mate Sian (.) is having a picnic on parliament square (.) and the police come up to her and go 'you've gotto move,

move right now', she goes 'no, no it's a picnic', 'no, no, no unlawful
demonstration.' She went 'no, for the love of god, doily, cucumber
sandwich' [laugh]... 'picnic'. The cops go, 'ah, cake' and point at her
cake. It's a Victoria sponge with one word iced upon it, and that word
is 'peace'. And the police deem her cake to be a political cake [laugh]...
and she therefore needs permission from the police six days prior to
breaking the Tupperware seal [and] exposing said cake to the public
arena [laugh]... And I thought any law (.) that means we can be
arrested (.) for a cake... we can play with [laugh]

In delivering this segment, Thomas emphasizes the words 'picnic' and
'cake', popping their satisfyingly short and punchy syllables out so that
the bouncing hardness of the sounds is juxtaposed with each word's
homely, innocent connotations. Thomas also places stronger emphasis
on each of the words 'deem her cake to be a political cake', again
creating an incongruous juxtaposition between a soft and innocuous
object and the criminal purpose which the police are claiming it serves.
He delivers the lines with an increasing sense of frustration, until by
the time he says 'arrested for a cake' he is virtually shouting; he then
draws back with a cheeky expression and wry smile as he says, teasingly,
'we can play with'. Turning the ridiculousness of the law back against
the law itself appears noble and just; Thomas can therefore proceed to
tell stories in which he and his colleagues create a nuisance, safe in the
manufactured consensus that he has created for such activity.

Mark Thomas elicits consensus by appeal to logic, and, in the above
cases at least, that logic is intended as a serious argument. When
Thomas asserts that SOCPA is an unsuccessful attack on one man and
allows innocent people to be arrested for a cake, a critical audience may
perhaps identify that he is over-simplifying the situation. Nonetheless,
despite the manipulative selectiveness with which Thomas has chosen
to tell the truth, he has taken undeniably sound logic as his premise; he
asserts as a fact that the most high-profile demonstration in the SOCPA
designated area is unaffected by the law, and at root Sian's story does
boil down to police intervention over a Victoria sponge. Both these
facts lead to the logical conclusion that the law is ridiculous.

Thomas' 2009 tour *It's the Stupid Economy* placed particular emphasis on the participation of the audience in his political activism.[26] The audience was invited to submit policy ideas which were then debated in the performance. Audiences cheered for the policy they wanted to keep through a series of knockout rounds, until one winning policy remained. This policy was incorporated into the *People's Manifesto*, upon which Thomas immediately started campaigning and which was eventually published as a book.[27] The *Manifesto* was even represented by an official candidate in the 2010 General Election.[28] When audiences suggested and cheered for policies, it was in the knowledge that these were intended to result in real action, having real, practical effect.

At the Maidstone performance, the vast majority of the policies read out on stage, and certainly of those supported by the audience, similarly embody the kind of leftist and liberal values that characterize Thomas' work both as stand-up and activist.[29] Although this audience is broadly united in political and social opinion, there are some topics which remain contentious even in this context of heightened unity and consensus. The policy suggestion 'Make assisted suicide legal, not difficult' receives a mixed response. This is perhaps partly due to the way in which Thomas delivers the suggestion – by pausing after the word 'legal' he makes 'not difficult' sound like a joke and attracts a sprinkling of giggles – but is also an indication that the audience has some moral difficulty with the statement. Thomas successfully mongers support by identifying assisted suicide with compassion and personal freedom: 'Let people choose to die with dignity? I think so.' He then puts the piece of paper on which the proposed policy is written defiantly on top of the pile of suggestions that have made it through to the next round. The audience give a solid display of approval, delivering strong, full applause. The policy does not gain sufficient support to win, but is taken seriously and supported throughout the rest of the show. That the audience response goes from uncertainty to definite support suggests that Thomas has won the audience's consensus on an issue about which they were initially uncertain. He has done so by creating a 'map of the world' upon which the audience's approach to the issue of euthanasia is solely about dignity. With such a map in operation, the audience have little choice but to accept euthanasia as a humane practice, and its denial as a callous means of inflicting humiliation and suffering.

When handling the similarly controversial topic of abortion in 1998, Thomas begins his routine by establishing for his audience that the correct approach is to support his view in favour of the legalization of abortion, which he achieves by highlighting the illogical premise at the heart of the 'pro-lifer's' fundamental argument:

> They have this whole *shit* of, like, 'we are here to save lives'. Now, the year before abortion was legalised two hundred and fifty women died at the hands of backstreet abortionists, so technically speaking you're not actually saving fucking lives.[30]

In a later routine on the same subject, Thomas mongers support for his pro-choice approach both by calling on the expert opinion of his mother, explaining that she was 'a midwife in Glasgow before abortion was legalized, and she's militantly pro-choice', and subtly categorizing women who have abortions as victims, and the pro-life demonstrator as aggressor.[31] He explains that his father was both a lay preacher and the 'rudest [...] man in the world', and celebrates the 'heckle' that he used to launch at pro-life protestors who demonstrated outside a Marie Stopes clinic near their home:

> My Dad would drive past, lean out the window and go 'you fucking zealots! [laugh and few claps] What the fuck are you doing fucking intimidating vulnerable women like that? Call yourself a Christian? Read your bible: John 3!' [laughter and applause][32]

Thomas employs a combination of appeal to basic values and logic, highlighting the emotional distress that the protestors caused to vulnerable women by publicly chastising their decision to terminate pregnancy. It is easy to gain consensus for the idea that causing further distress to the vulnerable is morally wrong, and thus Thomas gains consensus for his approach to the topic.

Furthermore, the use of a joke (in the form of his father's ingenious heckle) to make the point means that the premise receives immediate validation from the audience. By giving them a cue to laugh, Thomas provides an opportunity for the audience to express its support for the pro-choice premise. This reaction exerts pressure on the group: it tells each member of the audience that the crowd agrees with Thomas. Having established this ground rule, the following, more controversial, joke achieves laughter with little difficulty. Thomas relates an encounter with a pro-life supporter which took place at a *New Statesman* dinner:

> I'm sitting thinkin', 'fucking hell, if you're one of these people who thinks all life-giving fluid is sacred I'm off to the fucking toilet for a wank' [laugh]… 'I've just committed genocide, love' [laugh]… 'There you go, there's a massacre on your napkin,' [laugh] 'now shut the fuck up' [laugh and a few claps]'[33]

Thomas then mimics his Edinburgh audience, saying, tuttingly and in a Scottish accent, 'there was no need for that'. This is a device Thomas has established and used several times previously in the show, imagining that some of the audience will dislike his more vulgar moments and characterizing them as stern puritans. This allows him to voice the disagreement and disapproval that he imagines his audience might feel, and dismiss these reactions with ridicule.[34] In this case, his comment addresses the vulgarity of the preceding jokes but, interestingly, not the controversial premise. Thomas has done all the work necessary to persuade the audience that, for this routine at least, they need to take the pro-choice side of the argument; it is the vulgarity, not the politics, of his statement that receives comment. The audience is trapped by a persuasive cycle: their laughter reinforces the validity of Thomas' stance, but it is Thomas who is creating scenarios in which cooperative responses such as laughter, which validate his points, are the natural – indeed the only 'correct' – response.[35]

Comedians themselves show awareness that controversial material can be made palatable. Joe Wilkinson expresses a view which is commonly held among comedians:

> I don't think there is anything that you shouldn't [talk about], any subject that is taboo, really, because it depends how you do it [...] Every subject is there to be, sort of, pulled apart but it depends. [...] In very skilled hands it's funny and it's insightful and it's not just shock, in the wrong hands certain topics should never be talked about.[36]

Wilkinson gives the example of the high-profile case of the disappearance of three-year-old Madeleine McCann, and the abduction of nine-year-old Shannon Matthews, which received much less media attention although it happened soon afterwards. The discrepancy was bemoaned as indicative of attitudes towards class and appearance. Shannon came from a poorer family than Madeline who, as a golden-haired preschooler of ruling-class stock, seemed to capture the public's imagination more readily. While the topic of Madeleine's disappearance was one that preoccupied the public and formed an obvious point of reference for stand-up comedians, Wilkinson felt that to joke about this story was not worth the trespass of moral boundaries involved, explaining: 'Comedy isn't the most important thing in the world [...] it's not important enough to get a laugh out of a tiny [...] girl going missing.'[37] However, Wilkinson felt that when comedians made jokes about the discrepancy between the levels of media coverage surrounding the disappearance of Madeleine McCann as compared to the similar story surrounding Shannon Matthews, a worthwhile point was being made:

> Some people have made some great points on stage [...] about the story, not about the girl [...] about the media's perception of this story. [...] So there are things of that story that are worth talking about. [...] So there are things around the issues... so no topic is taboo.'[38]

Although Wilkinson links his comments strongly with personal preferences – noting, importantly, that the decision of what he should talk about generally comes from his personal sense of what he wants to say rather than what he feels he can get away with – in practice, he is referring to the same techniques that are at play in Mark Thomas' various pieces of consensus-building. When Wilkinson talks about having a specific approach, such as tackling the topic of Madeleine McCann from the safe angle of an attack on the media, he is talking about finding a point on which consensus is easily established and building outwards from there. So in the case of the media-focused Madeleine McCann joke, the comedian may use the ostensible premise of an attack on the media to approach a topic which is certainly going to be very sensitive and raw to the audience. For Mark Thomas, the starting premise is incontestable values and ideals such as decency, humanity and freedom, from which he is able to construct a logical pathway to consensus on more thorny issues such as abortion and euthanasia.

It is clear that Thomas' Maidstone audience were not wholeheartedly in favour of euthanasia, and it is unlikely that abortion was really such a clear-cut issue for the Edinburgh audience as their hearty laughter suggests. This is the danger of comedy logic. Issues do not need to be considered in full, nor assertions backed up with incontrovertible evidence; comic licence excuses the speaker from the demands of such rigorous quality control. Yet the effect on the audience's thinking is ongoing, with the joking premise being carried over as the logical foundation on which the rest of the show is laid; it creates a feature on the audience's 'map of the world', which they use to traverse the rest of the gig.[39] Examples such as those discussed above show how this principle may easily be carried further than we might think.

In some cases, this might serve a healthy societal function. It is important to the notion of democracy that a range of views be heard, considered and continuously tested. Thomas' routines about abortion and euthanasia may use joking logic to circumvent preconceived or knee-jerk attitudes, and so force his audience to engage in healthy questioning of their ideas, whatever their attitudes may have been on entering the gig. However, this also points to a potential danger inherent in these techniques consensus-mongering. By permitting comedic logic to function like rational argument, they allow ideas that are presented as merely ludicrous to be validated with reference to the real, rather than the joking, world. Of course audiences must continue to enjoy subversions of common sense and logic; but it behoves all comedy audiences to be aware when and how they are being manipulated, and to what end.

Persona and Status

What is persona for?

In 2007, a full Gulbenkian Theatre waits for Jenny Eclair to take the stage.[1] The audience already know what their comedian looks and sounds like, and can even make an educated guess at the topics they expect Eclair to address, and the attitudes that she will take towards them. In buying their tickets, the audience have invested in the Eclair image: a cool, trashily sexy glamour girl with masses of energetic cynicism, who pays no heed to the sacred boundaries that surround bodily and behavioural taboos.[2] Unsurprisingly, the vast majority of Eclair's audience are, like her, female and over forty years of age; the public do not need to see the show to understand that Eclair's comedy will be tailored towards a specific demographic.

The stage is unusually cluttered for a comedy performance at this venue. There is a *chaise longue* covered with a fluffy pink throw and cushions, a pink table sporting large, sparkly gems, and a large picture frame suspended from the ceiling, framing a projector screen. When Eclair herself appears, she is decorated with similar glitz; a purple shirt covered by a sparkling gold jacket, and glittery gold shoes with a killer heel. Eclair's material, like her appearance, suggests that she is an extreme personality. She is often outrageous, relating tales of behaviour she has indulged in which her audience would not dream of replicating. Yet Eclair is easy to relate to. This show focuses on the reality of getting older, and Eclair discusses in detail the changes in her body, lifestyle and attitude that have come with middle age. Her language is littered with tag questions such as 'don't you?', 'wouldn't you?', 'don't we?', which call upon the audience for confirmation that they share her experience. She has soon established a strong sense of bonhomie.

Eclair tells the audience how her life has settled into gloomy normality with middle age. She relates an incident which she feels demonstrates that her dull ordinariness has reached embarrassing levels. She is sitting at home with her husband when, in great astonishment, he calls her over to the window to see a frog which is sitting in their pond. 'Well!' says Eclair, '*I put down my knitting!*' The audience deliver a loud, bursting laugh.

The joke is successful, and it relies for its success upon the audience's understanding of Eclair's persona. The word 'knitting' focuses the clash between the image of Eclair the party girl and the cosy domesticity she has described, and moves it up a notch. That she can rely upon her persona as a key reference point for a joke demonstrates one of the key functions of the comedian's persona: that of economy. Eclair does not need to explain for the audience that she is not the type of person who knits because the clarity of her persona tells them this. They can thus deduce, quickly and effortlessly, that the word 'knitting' is intended as a joke, and that it is a good one. As Dan Atkinson explains:

> The theory is, to be successful, you need a very clearly defined stage persona. If you look at any well-known, successful comic you can probably sum up what they do in two or three words. And that's very crucial, because you want as few barriers between yourself, the audience and the comedy. So if they know who you are and where you're coming from very early then it's easier – they know what you might think on a subject [...] and if the audience can pre-empt how you might address a subject, it allows it to be funnier. It allows them to buy into it.[3]

Clive Barker theorizes this professional knowledge, and in fact sees the persona as an essentially limiting structure, stating:

> Audiences are remarkably eclectic in what they will take at large and yet discriminating within very narrow boundaries as to what they will accept from individuals. [...] The unifying principle seems to be that

the audience like to know where it is in a relationship and tends not to like being disturbed.[4]

Barker also makes a separation between the performer's 'image', which is 'the residual memory of a performer outside the performance', and the persona, which is the representation that the audience encounter on the night. Image and persona have different functions, because 'the image attracts an audience to a theatre. The performance persona is what sends them home happy.'[5] As Barker further notes: 'The image or persona is a fabrication. It is a part played as consciously as the actor assumes his role.'[6]

In his 2008 documentary *Rob Brydon's Identity Crisis*, Brydon allows his search for a comic persona to be shown with a striking level of candour which reveals the stage personality for the construct that it is.[7] Although he had already established a successful career as a stand-up comedian, Brydon had previously performed in character as Keith Barret. Faced with the task of putting together a show that explores his personal sense of national identity, Brydon is forced to create an onstage personality which represents the 'real' Rob Brydon. Although he is an experienced performer, the seemingly simple task of 'being himself' proves difficult. The first show in which Brydon delivers material about Welsh identity, performed at the Glee Club in Cardiff, receives a negative response from the audience. In retrospect, he lays the blame on the aggressive negativity of his persona. He admits that he had been 'mean' and 'very judgemental'.[8]

To tackle the problem, Brydon decides to adopt a more cheerful, optimistic persona. He demonstrates that this is a conscious manipulation of audience perception, saying:

> So what I'm going to do is smile a bit more and be a bit friendlier, and I'm gonna be wary of making the Welsh character in my jokes the victim or the [...] butt of the joke every time.[9]

Brydon then puts this into practice, changing the standpoint from which his material is delivered. We see him going over material from the Glee Club gig, saying, 'I should, sort of, change "we couldn't have a Welsh rapper" to "we've got Welsh rappers" – to make it more positive.'[10]

Brydon's final gig demonstrates his honed new positive persona. He opens by declaring everything 'lovely'; it is 'lovely to be here', the audience is lovely, the building is lovely, he's feeling lovely.[11] When he mocks the Welsh, he does so from a positive starting point. For example, he introduces a routine about Welsh pilots by claiming that they are 'the best in the world'. He then plays on the traditional stereotype that the Welsh are dim-witted by introducing the character of a Welsh pilot who attempts to fly an aeroplane without knowing how. Although the actions of the Pilot character are extremely dangerous, he is given an endearing optimism and determination. Throwing his arm forward in an enthusiastically blasé gesture, he cries, 'You know what? I'm gonna 'av a go!' The audience responds well, and Brydon clearly feels more comfortable with his new persona. This friendliness has longevity: a review by Steve Bennett written a year later describes Brydon as 'a natural wit with a disarmingly charming manner. He's the hot towel of comedy: warm, cosy and refreshing.'[12]

In moving from the negative to the positive persona, Brydon kept much of the same material, changing mainly its attitude and approach. In reviewing the gig, Brydon observes, 'It shows what you can do if you just change […] the attitude to it – you can say anything, really.' The reverse has also been demonstrated; if the audience will not accept a comedian's attitude, they will not accept his material. While Brydon makes the fair point that audiences do not want to be abused, the fact remains that several comedians do succeed with exactly the kind of attitude that Brydon adopted in the Glee Club gig. The difference may not be that the audience would not tolerate anti-Welsh material – for the edited material is still a thinly disguised jibe at the Welsh – but that they would not tolerate it from Brydon. Barker suggests that we could:

> Consider the material in terms of consistency with the persona and
> as an enabling set of structures through which the entertainer works,
> rather than in terms of literary excellence or comic invention.[13]

This implies that the persona can actually dictate the material to some extent, imposing limits on the comedian as writer.

In his bestseller *The Tipping Point*, journalist Malcolm Gladwell observes the following difficulty in comprehending the complexity of other people's inner make-up, even when we know them well:

> If I asked you to describe the personality of your best friends, you could do so easily, and you wouldn't say things like 'My friend Howard is incredibly generous, but only when I ask him for things,' or 'My friend Alice is wonderfully honest when it comes to her personal life, but at work she can be very slippery.' You would say, instead, that your friend Howard is generous and your friend Alice is honest. All of us, when it comes to personality, naturally think in terms of absolutes: that a person is a certain way or is not a certain way.[14]

Allport further notes that we tend to assume all people who give the appearance of belonging to a particular category will embody all of the characteristics we assign to that category:

> *Overcategorisation* is perhaps the commonest trick of the human mind. Given a thimbleful of facts we rush to make generalizations as a large tub. [...] There is a natural basis for this tendency. Life is so short, and the demands upon us for practical adjustments so great, that we cannot let our ignorance detain us in our daily transactions. We have to decide whether objects are good or bad by classes. We cannot weigh each object in the world by itself. Rough and ready rubrics, however coarse and broad, have to suffice.[15]

The persona is clearly manipulative in that it is a skilful presentation of the performer's personality that controls perception in order to direct the audience's interpretation and facilitate the gag. It would be possible for Eclair to enjoy both parties and knitting, but she knows that the fact that she aligns herself with one of those things leads her audience to overcategorize; because she likes parties, they assume that she will shun knitting. Thus the statement 'I put down my knitting', which would be dull and ordinary in most contexts and from most other people, is turned into an effective joke.

As we have already seen, the relative truth of stand-up material is usually ambiguous. The level of falsity in a persona is similarly difficult to pin down. In some cases, the fictional nature of the persona is overt. When Brydon performed as Keith Barret, it was always clear that Barret was a character and not intended to represent the performer's offstage personality. In the vast majority of cases, however, the correlation between the offstage personality and the onstage persona is complex and slippery.

Mark Watson talks about many aspects of his life that are verifiably true: he has a wife; he went to university; he has worked as a regular panellist on television quiz show *Mock the Week*.[16] There is no reason for the casual observer of his work to imagine that he is not representing himself and his life accurately. There has, however, been a striking element of untruth in Watson's persona: for the first few years of his stand-up career, Watson chose to perform in a Welsh accent, while his natural accent is English. Watson was never entirely deceitful about the fact that his accent was artificial; this information was always in the public domain and was, for example, referenced several times on the *Chortle* website by 2007.[17] Yet the 'Welsh' persona was successful only because he upheld the falsehood onstage.

Watson is not alone in deceiving his audience. No comic persona can accurately and fully represent the person who exists offstage, nor can any character act divorce completely from the real-life performer. Double has suggested that there is a spectrum of types of persona, ranging from the 'naked self' to the character comedian.[18] For different points on the spectrum, the persona will bear different relationships to the offstage personality. Some comedians see the stage persona as a genuine part of themselves exaggerated. Josie Long says that she is consciously trying to develop her persona into 'a small part of myself amplified; like the best part of myself amplified'.[19] Towards the other end of the spectrum are placed comedians like Alexei Sayle. Sayle does not appear as a character act in the way that Rob Brydon appears as Keith Barret, performing under his real name, but still refers to his stage persona in the third person, thus keeping the identities strictly separate.[20]

All personas, wherever they fall on the spectrum, must involve some manipulation of perception and some honest reflection of the perfomer's real attitudes. As we have seen, personas such as Mark Watson's, which appear to be plausible representations of the offstage personality, are often the most deceptive. As Double observes of modern stand-up comedy:

> Truth is a vital concept in most modern stand-up comedy because of the idea that it is 'authentic'. The boundary between offstage and onstage is blurred and, in many cases, the audience believe that the person they see onstage is more or less the same as the person they might meet offstage. This inevitably means that there is an assumption that what the person onstage says about his or her life is more or less true.[21]

At the other end of the spectrum, character comedians present an obvious element of invention, in that the characters in which they perform are discernibly fictional. They may therefore be excused from any charge of 'not being what they appear to be', by virtue of the fact that they are not pretending to be anything other than a comedian performing a piece of fiction. Yet there is a basis of truth behind character acts which is crucial to our enjoyment of the performance. Al Murray performs as the 'Pub Landlord', a ridiculous bigot whose attitudes and arrogance are not shared by Murray himself.[22] It is important, therefore, that audiences read the casual bigotry of the Pub Landlord through the lens of Murray's mocking performance of that bigotry. They need to discern Murray's real attitudes as well as the Pub Landlord's, if they are to understand the act. In any stand-up act that presents a clearly fictional and absurd character, the creator of that character will be a discernible and important presence within the act.[23] If we can identify the creator and share his attitude towards the character, we can laugh comfortably. This dual presence is one of the defining features of a character act.[24]

However, the comedian's manipulation of audience perception can prove unreliable. Al Murray has a relatively high profile as a celebrity in his own right, and any reasonable interpretation must be that he and the Pub Landlord are two separate entities. Yet Murray has been accused of performing in contexts where the ironic intention of his material might be lost on, or ignored by, an audience who appreciate its bigoted qualities. Stewart Lee cites Murray's early performances as the Pub Landlord as being 'amongst the greatest stand-up I have ever seen […] a bulletproof satire of the soft right',[25] but goes on to say that, 'the places the character appeared and the attitudes of the punters who flocked to see him in the noughties have inevitably changed the way the material is received'.[26] Even in this seemingly clear-cut example, there has been ambiguity around the audience's interpretation of the comedian's intention. Murray himself is quoted in a 2007 interview as saying, 'That's what's fun about doing this. People still don't know what I think.'[27]

While Murray has perhaps courted misinterpretation, Jo Brand has been plagued by it. Brand is a married, heterosexual woman, who often references her husband in her act. Before her marriage, boyfriends and trying to find them were staple topics. Nonetheless, rumours that Brand is homosexual have achieved such prominence that Brand says she has had petitions from lesbian groups asking her to tell people that she is heterosexual; the public association of Brand with lesbianism has been so strong that these groups feel that she is 'giving them a bad name'.[28] That such a misinterpretation of Brand could take root, despite both a lack of supporting evidence and the existence of evidence to the contrary, shows how stubbornly we adhere to our own overcategorizations.[29] Matthew Crosby discusses a similar problem in relation to Josie Long:

> She got an email from a website that said they wanted to champion 'pro-cardigan, anti-punchline comedy' – that's what they described it as – and they said 'we think you're an example of that' […] What Josie does isn't anti-punchline, she writes really, really good jokes but […] they're almost so good you don't see them, you don't realise that you're

laughing at set-up – punchline. [...] And the fact that, you know, she would wear a cardigan [...] informs but doesn't dictate what she does. So yeah, I hate people who see [...] glasses, or who see a reference to an obscure movie, or who see, you know, like an interesting indie band T-shirt and think that's the act.[30]

Clearly, comedians can find the process of presenting themselves difficult to control. While Dan Atkinson is aware of the theory that a defined and easily interpretable persona can be very useful, he has found that establishing such a thing is very difficult in practice. It appears that part of the difficulty is in seeing this necessarily personal process from the outside. Atkinson states, 'I don't really know how I come across', and later elaborates as best he can, 'I'm quite amiable onstage, I think, maybe slightly charming or whatever – I don't know – friendly, a friend of the audience in a sense.'[31] Although, at the date of this interview, Atkinson did not feel that his persona had yet taken form, as an audience member it was possible to spot defining characteristics in the persona presented on stage. Atkinson was indeed 'amiable', 'friendly' and 'charming', perhaps also little chaotic. Even if Atkinson struggled to find consistency or simplicity in his own persona, audiences were still looking for, and identifying, what absolutes they could. It is all they can do. Audiences, being human, are programmed to simplify people into easy-to-use categories.

There is a natural basis for the ambiguities between representation and reality experienced by both the audience and the comedian themselves. Erving Goffman interpreted what we might think of as 'personality' as a series of day-to-day performances in which the individual presents their part.[32] We have seen how comedians claim certain characteristics for themselves and implicitly demand that the audience play along; Eclair's knitting gag relies upon exactly this process. Our everyday interactions involve a negotiation of the perception of self which is, in essentials, the same:

When an individual projects a definition of the situation and thereby makes an implicit or explicit claim to be a person of a particular kind, he automatically exerts a moral demand upon the others, obliging them to value and treat him in the manner that persons of his kind have a right to expect. He also implicitly forgoes all claims to be things that he does not appear to be and hence forgoes the treatment that would be appropriate for such individuals.[33]

Our performances are not always intentional deceptions: as Goffman states, 'the performer can be fully taken in by his own act'.[34] Indeed, we are well trained never to think of some of our most important performances as representations, and instead confuse them with indubitable reality:

> And when we observe a young American middle-class girl playing dumb for the benefit of her boy friend, we are ready to point to items of guile and contrivance in her behaviour. But like herself and her boy friend, we accept as an unperformed fact that this performer *is* a young American middle-class girl. But surely here we neglect the greater part of the performance.[35]

We would be quick to identify the 'guile and contrivance' of the girl's 'playing dumb' as manipulative, yet the more complete manipulation is surely the one that goes unnoticed even by its performer: the girl is also taken in by her own performance of behaviour appropriate to her age, nationality, class and gender. Just as Goffman's exemplar is more controlled by her 'young American middle-class girl' role than in control of it, comedians may also find themselves trapped by their own image. We see an example of this when Rob Brydon is forced to change the attitude of his material to fit his image, and when comedians are unable to fully control the perception of their personality, leading to spurious assumptions about who they are.

Often, then, the comedian is not so much manipulator as manipulated. They are not always able to maintain control over the presentation of their own personality, and can have difficulty seeing themselves from the outside. Furthermore, as Goffman demonstrates, the manipulation of one's own image is a process in which we are all engaged during every interaction we undertake. The comedian is, therefore, arguably no more manipulative than anybody else. Yet it is clear that the persona is a manipulative device and, often, it is one that the comedian can use quite consciously to manage their audience's interpretation of their material. When Eclair uses her manufactured image as a shortcut to a laugh, she demonstrates the application of an advanced skill which allows her to control both the audience's perception of her and the way in which that perception is utilized. Interviewed just as he was becoming established, and before regular TV appearances had given him the fame he currently enjoys, Joe Wilkinson demonstrated just how controlled the use of persona can be. He shows not only an acute awareness of how he is perceived, but also a sense of assurance regarding his ability to manage his own representation:

> I'm a bit grumpy, I guess, a bit, like, of an outsider. [...] I'm definitely aware of what I'm doing, and also I change that [...] [as I'm sure] a lot of comedians [do], I change that kind of slightly dependent on the room. [...] I did a gig in Aldershot on Saturday night and they were a slightly older audience and a slightly smaller audience and [...] maybe less comedy savvy, you can just tell. And so I wasn't quite as grumpy about it, do you know what I mean? I was slightly more upbeat. [...] They needed to know that I was enjoying it rather than hating it. [...] Whereas I did, last night, a gig in Greenwich which was really rowdy, and then I do a lot less in that and I'm grumpier, because [...] it's a bigger clash. The less I do in a rowdy room the bigger the show looks. [...] So you have a persona but you have to, sort of, scale it up or down depending on where you are or what the situation is.[36]

Dysfunction and the marginal world

In the year after his deceptive *Who's Eaten Gilbert's Grape*, Rhod Gilbert toured with a new show, *Rhod Gilbert and the Award-Winning Mince Pie*. As outlined in Chapter 2, Gilbert admits that he has had difficulty living in the real world, and has, in the past, built his persona upon a few blatant lies.[37] He has therefore been trying to live in the real world and desist from making things up, because 'apparently, people don't like it'.[38] The show that follows is superficially about Gilbert's attempt to live in the real world, but is structured to deteriorate into implausible tales that take place in his imaginary world. As Gilbert states at the beginning of his show, living in the real world is not the sensible choice: 'I don't know how you all do it. It's madder than anything I could make up [laugh]'.[39]

Foremost among Gilbert's previous deceptions has been the invention of his 'hometown' Llanbobl. Gilbert has previously been in the habit of asking audiences if they had ever heard of Llanbobl, and says that various confused and fraudulent people had claimed that they have, or even that they have been there. One man claimed that his daughter had moved there. Gilbert expresses his befuddlement that a place he made up has actually been attracting new residents. He invites the audience to imagine what would happen if the daughter married a local boy. On one side of the church would be her family, and on the other side, 'people I made up!'[40]

There has been an ongoing dispute with a 'Rugger Bugger'; an audience member whom Gilbert met following a gig and with whom he has since communicated via MySpace. The Rugger Bugger insists that his team thrashed Llanbobl, and his arrogance eventually provokes Gilbert to retaliate. He creates a map upon which Llanbobl is shown, and sends it to the Rugger Bugger, inviting him to visit. A projector screen behind Gilbert then shows footage shot secretly from Gilbert's car, following the anti-hero as he drives around Wales trying to find the fictional town. The Rugger Bugger stops at a pub and goes in to ask for directions. Gilbert hurriedly jumps out of the car and goes to perch a mince pie on Rugger Bugger's windscreen (a reference to the show's title, but one which Rugger Bugger can have no hope of understanding). Rugger Bugger emerges from the pub, with an amused-looking barman, and gets back into his car. He then notices the mince pie and gets out to pick it up, looking bemused. The video ends with a black screen across which is written 'Llanbobl 1 – Reality 0'.[41]

If Gilbert's show is ostensibly about trying to live in the real world, it is really a demonstration of the real world's inferiority. It is delightful to think of Llanbobl, a place which Gilbert invented, full of people he made up and refugees from reality. In defeating the arrogance of Rugger Bugger, Llanbobl scores a symbolic win against the real world. This is mirrored in the rest of Gilbert's show. Gilbert embarks upon a realistic, observational piece about motorway service stations, but the honesty of his initial observations quickly develops into implausibility as he makes improbable claims about his service station experience. He explains that he was offended by a fellow customer who gave the toilets a lower rating than he had on the customer feedback board. Other people saw it happen, and Gilbert is embarrassed by the implication that his standards are lower than those of the other customer. The story is plausible enough, until Gilbert claims to have thrown that other customer into a toilet cubicle and locked him in there in an attempt to terrify him into reconsidering his verdict. The story concludes with Gilbert sitting on a camp chair in the service station, refusing to move until the discourteous staff tell him what award the mince pie they have sold him is supposed to have won. Gilbert's sit-in forms a symbolic protest against the validity of the real world; a ridiculous place that does not work as well as the one he makes up.

If comedians offer us a 'better' world, they also offer us better ways of dealing with the one we already have. Mintz claims that the comedian's weaknesses are a vital tool for persuading the audience to permit the element of social challenge in their material. If the comedian appears to be abnormally cynical, promiscuous, idiotic, and so on, the audience can ascribe any attacks that they do not like to the comedian's dysfunction. They can 'forgive and even bless his "mistakes"', because he is considered 'physically and mentally incapable of proper action'.[42] However, if the comedian stumbles upon a piece of social commentary that expresses the shared but repressed view of his audience, he becomes their 'comic spokesperson'.[43] It is true that many comedians work hard to suggest that their relationship with the real world is deeply dysfunctional. For example, Dylan Moran appears drunk and socially awkward, as well as unhealthily cynical. Lee Evans is incompetent; he is clumsy and foolish, unable to comprehend, or interact normally with, the world that surrounds him. However, neither comedian occupies a low status in their audience's perception. Moran showcases his talents and intelligence, using poetic language and a wide and often complex vocabulary. He often performs in front of projections of his own sketches, each one signed by him so that the audience may be aware that it is he who possesses this talent.[44] Similarly, Evans has showcased his musical abilities. At the end of a show at Wembley arena he performs a song that does not get many laughs, but is rather intended to be impressive. He plays the piano and sings, eventually introducing a large choir and his father, who performs a solo.[45] It is not necessary for comedians to be wholly sad characters. Far from wanting comedians to be dismissible dysfunctionals, audiences will happily accept and admire a comedian's talents.

Indeed, dysfunction is often presented as a way in which to triumph over life's imperfections.[46] Much of Lee Evans' material is based on the premise that he is incapable of coping with the world around him: one routine suggests that he is unable to use an aeroplane without becoming anxious and awkward. Yet if this is his dysfunction, he is also able to enjoy the fact, making others laugh at his anxieties and even earning money and fame for doing so.[47] If Dylan Moran is a cynical drunkard, he is a very successful and likeable one. From his 'dysfunctional' standpoint, he is able to issue advice that might help us to lead better and happier lives. For example, during a routine that disparages self-help books, Moran makes the following, seemingly popular suggestion:

> Or release your potential, that's another one. [Small laugh] Now that's a very, very dangerous idea. [Small laugh] You should stay away (.) [Small laugh] from your potential, [Laugh] I mean that is something you should leave absolutely alone. [Laugh] Don't, d, you'll mess it up... [Laugh] It's potential, leave it... [Big laugh] And anyway it's like your bank balance, you know, you always have a lot less than you think. [Big laugh] So don't look at it, n-no, leave it.[48]

A 'functional' person could not suggest such a course of action, knowing that it is much safer to pay close attention to their bank balance and that they will find life more fulfilling if they examine their 'potential' and try to make use of it. Moran, however, is able to offer us a comforting alternative which promises an easier existence. Thus, his dysfunction seems rather appealing.

Although the dysfunctional characteristics of comedians may be useful in giving them licence to criticize and subvert conventions with the excuse that it is all in jest, such characteristics are eclipsed by those abilities which demand respect and admiration. In the playground of the gig, the comedian occupies a very high status, and is able to create and manage the rules of interaction. This provides opportunities for manipulation as, within his self-created world, the comedian can dictate his own terms.

Democracy and the force of personality

Most comedians take a fairly modest view of their own position and their power to influence. Few comedians see themselves as dictators of opinion, even when a gig is going well. For Mark Thomas, the particular strength of stand-up as a political form is its 'democracy':

> That interaction exists in no other art form in this dynamic [...] there's actually a kind of democratic feel to it, if you like [...] that actually the voice of the audience affects the outcome. Y'know, your laughter affects the outcome, the way you react affects the outcome, what you shout affects the outcome [...] actually comedy is more open than any other art form to put-down and challenge.[49]

Establishing democracy within the gig is important to Thomas. He actively encourages more articulate participation, for example inviting the audience to correct him if he quotes a fact or statistic incorrectly, or asking them whether they went on some of the public demonstrations that he mentions.[50] For him, the audience's right to disagree bolsters, rather than damages, the possibilities for influence:

> It's about play, it's about interplay. It's about expectation and defying expectation, and if you can't make that political and change people's minds, then you're in the wrong fucking game. It's intrinsically there.[51]

Josie Long describes the interplay between comedian and audience as a two-way process, but with the emphasis on a friendly sharing of interests. Long has run various projects alongside her shows which allow the audience to join in with the show's theme. Audiences of Long's *Trying is Good* were encouraged to take postcards away with them and draw or write about any eccentric or 'odd' people they encountered, sending them back to Long when they were completed.[52] The *Trying is Good* DVD, which Long released at the end of the tour, features a gallery of contributions sent in by audience members. When asked why she includes interactive projects in her shows, Long replies:

> My dream of doing stand-up was getting to meet other people who were kind of like me. [...] I wanted to meet people who were doing creative things. [...] I just really like the idea of, like, getting to bring out little creative parts of people, getting to engage with people and make people a bit kind of fired up to doing their own little projects. [...] I also think it gives the show some heart, you know? Like, it's not just you coming on going bang-bang-bang goodbye [...] it's making it live a bit.[53]

For Josie Long, therefore, the whole point of stand-up is to have a genuine interaction, to share personal interests with others and see what interests them: this is not compatible with the idea of a comedian who imparts wisdom from on high, but rather with a reciprocal relationship where the status gap between performer and audience is kept to a minimum.

Joe Wilkinson hopes that the issue is simpler. When asked whether he thinks stand-up is a particularly effective means of persuasion, he responds; 'I'd like to give people more credit than that – do y'know what

I mean? I'd like to, but maybe I'm wrong.' For Wilkinson, stand-up is essentially no more advanced as a method of persuasion than everyday conversation:

> I think that's as simple as someone hearing someone's opinion. I don't think it matters whether it's stand-up or a conversation, really. […] Yeah, of course […] taking on any new piece of information can change your perception [but] […] I don't think […] it will have a profound effect on people. […] If me and you were talking about something in a pub, that's got as much chance of changing your perception as hearing something onstage.[54]

Wilkinson concedes that a comedian may be at a slight advantage because the position they are in appears 'exciting' to the hearer, but, like Thomas and Long, he assumes his audience to be formed of intelligent people capable of bringing their own analysis to the debate.

Stand-up is undeniably democratic to some extent. Few forms of art, or of performance, are held to so immediate and emphatic a measure of audience approval as stand-up, where the audience's appreciation needs to be demonstrated through their laughter and their disapproval can be communicated equally clearly through their silence or, more distinctly, through heckling. Understandably, comedians can feel very vulnerable at times, and often think of their authority as rather precarious.

According to William Cook: 'The implicit understanding that allows the audience to pitch in on equal terms with the person behind the mike – a comedic right to bear arms – is the first article of comedy's unwritten constitution. […] Heckling is what makes stand-up special.'[55] Cook's choice of words says much about the way heckling is understood among comedians and their audiences. He celebrates the unique dynamism that heckling brings to stand-up encounters, but he does so in the language of war: when an audience member chooses to interject they are 'bearing arms'; going into battle. Stand-up folklore contains several tales of dramatic battles between comedian and heckler; vicious encounters which ended in emotional, intellectual or even physical violence orchestrated by at least one of the parties.

These stories serve as darkly delectable reminders of stand-up's dangerous nature. They are, though, acknowledged to be the exception rather than the rule. As Ritchie states, 'a lot of heckling is pointless and destructive but it can really make a gig if done right'.[56] Comedians commonly acknowledge that hecklers are trying to add something to the gig, albeit that these attempts can frequently be drunken, clumsy or inartistic. Cook quotes Robert Newman's view: 'I've always loved heckles. [...] I've always loved playing around with them. [...] I hate comics who take a heckle as an affront to their authority. You've got to work with a heckle, you've got to say yes to it.'[57]

Heckling is an important component of stand-up comedy's dynamism as well as its democracy. Mark Thomas views the right of the audience to intervene as a welcome component of the democratic process, even when hecklers attack the comedian rather than cooperate with him. The audience's right to redress bolsters their power at the expense of the comedian:

> It is often the case that articulate hecklers can express the mood of an audience and beyond that can challenge the comic on a host of issues. [...] There have been cases where the audience can express outrage at an idea and rein in comics.[58]

Dan Atkinson reinforces this point with reference to a comedian who was booed offstage in Liverpool after material that referenced the abducted child Madeleine McCann and murdered child Rhys Jones badly misfired:

> Yet for all the offence caused, it actually displays one of the finest points of stand-up comedy: the right of the audience to interact with the performer and express immediate and forceful disapproval. It is emphatically and instantly democratic.[59]

Yet the comedian's aim is to control a mass reaction, and their craft relies on maintaining the attention of the group. This surely involves claiming a more particular authority; indeed asserting some control over the mass reaction is necessary if the show is to run smoothly.

As we have seen, this control can be a matter of facilitating friendly cooperation by giving clear punchlines as indicators of when and how to respond, but it can also involve careful manipulation of the audience's consensus. In truth, by placing themselves on a stage and in front of the only microphone in the room, comedians adopt a position of leadership, managing not only the audience's behaviour, but also their attitude towards the material presented.

Opportunities for the audience to challenge the comedian are, in practice, limited. In 2000, Tony Allen received funding from the London Arts Board to become an Advocate Heckler at Speakers' Corner, an area of London's Hyde Park where a diverse bunch of self-appointed speakers gather informal crowds.[60] Speakers' Corner aims for real freedom of speech, and the right of the crowd to reply – to heckle – is an important part of this democratic ethos. Part of Allen's rationale for the project was the recognition that some people would be too 'lazy, shy or intimidated' to heckle.[61] Significantly, the funding request form that Allen submitted for the project also cited his own expertise as a heckler, noting that some existing heckling practices were merely irritating and implying that the ability to heckle in a way which supports the democratic ethos is a specialist skill: 'I believe that I am developing a style of heckling which undermines the traditional reductionist banter, but more importantly, is not seen by other speakers as a disruptive activity.'[62] In stand-up, as at Speakers' Corner, to heckle successfully requires great courage and eloquence; it is a skill in itself. This casts doubt on the notion that the mere acceptability of heckling within stand-up is enough to empower the audience.

Even when an audience member is willing and able to introduce and uphold a challenge, the democratic ethos of the interaction can be difficult to maintain. Cook relates the common notion that the punter 'pitch[es] in on equal terms'.[63] This is surely overstating the case, reflecting the romanticized view of stand-up's democracy rather than the typical situation: an individual trying to make an uninvited contribution, battling a comedian who already has licence and the attention of the

crowd, and who is much more experienced, better prepared and in possession of the room's only amplification device. Assuming the gig is going well, it is generally accepted that the comedian will be at a distinct advantage. This means that witty or genuinely challenging heckles, although comparatively rare, are particularly exciting and memorable, but it undermines the potential for true democracy.

Performing at Soho's Wam Bam Club in 2008, Richard Herring encountered a particularly persistent heckler: a young man who repeatedly disrupted the set over a period of around ten minutes, until finally being thrown out by the venue's security when he began aggressively moving towards the stage.[64] Early in the battle, Herring institutes a belittling strategy, advising the heckler in an ostensibly kindly fashion that he ought to try to be funny, and to wait for a pause so that the audience can hear the heckles, which are otherwise drowned out by Herring's microphone. A little later he plays at purposefully leaving gaps for the heckler to fill:

> Remember the rule about not speaking when the microphone's on because we can't hear you. Try and wait for a gap… there was one, you missed it [laugh and some applause]… there was another one, again, you had a very big – I left a big gap… No still nothing, [laugh] I'll count you down to the gap, see if you can get in to it this time (.) Three, two, one… No! Nothing. [laugh][65]

Soon after, the heckler shouts 'bollocks!' as Herring is approaching the punchline to a joke. The following interaction ensues (heckler's interjections in italics):

> I don't know if you've ever tried [to] tell a joke, if you – if you tell a joke and a bloke just shouts out 'bollocks!' in between the feed line and the punchline, probably not gonna work [small laugh]…
>
> *[I can tell a joke]*
>
> You can tell a – go on, tell us a joke then…[66]

There is a pained 'aw' from a male member of the audience while other audience members, clearly irritated with the heckler's disruptive behaviour, mumble their frustration. Herring stands calmly on stage, ready to listen to the heckler's joke:

> *[Alright then. This, this bloke goes to work on a farm, right?]*
> Yeah?
> *[This bloke says right, erm -]*
> Bollocks! [big laugh, applause]… Bollocks! [growing applause, cheers and whistles]… Bollocks! Where you say 'Bollocks'! [applause, cheers and whistles continue] Bollocks! Bollocks![67]

The heckler is clearly very drunk and therefore not on form, but it is not primarily this impairment in his opponent that gives Herring the upper hand. As Herring has already pointed out, the man's interjections are lost under the amplification system, so the inarticulacy of his contributions is relatively unimportant. Herring is taking charge of the heckler's contribution, translating heckles for those who can't hear and importing his own, dismissive attitude onto that translation. What does give Herring the upper hand is his status. The audience grow irritated by the heckler's interjections because they have come to see the show; they have licensed Herring, not the heckler, to engage their attention and try to be funny.

It is not only the situation that places Herring at an advantage. He overwhelms the heckler largely by sheer force of personality. It is Herring who informs the audience that the heckler is bad at heckling, pointing out that the heckler is 'so drunk [he] can't think' and ramming the point home by repeatedly giving the heckler advice on how to heckle. When Herring invites the heckler to tell his joke, at least a section of the audience succumb to the frustration occasioned by the heckler's nuisance behaviour; their reaction is disgruntled muttering. By contrast, Herring is poised, calmly listening and encouraging the heckler. He then generates an explosive and united response from his audience as he completes the prank, repaying the heckler in kind by crying 'bollocks!' repeatedly, instead of allowing the joke to reach its punchline. The gig is a democratic environment in as much as the heckler can feel entitled to shout out and, importantly, it is the mass response of the audience which determines who wins; but we must acknowledge that the comedian's status gives him extraordinary power to be heard, and prioritized. In the final analysis, the 'democratic' practice of heckling really demonstrates just how powerful a status the comedian holds.

The practice of joking provides the comedian both with a licence to engage in dysfunctional and marginal views, and a privileged status that ensures that he is respected and listened to. The inherent power of the comedian's role is expressed in the various theories which surround his subversive social functions with mystique, but originates partly in the simple, practical need for the comedian to control the audience and keep his dialogue with them flowing. It is this which prevents comedians from creating a fully democratic interaction. Part of joking is ignoring both the accuracy and ramifications of the material at which we laugh.[68] The comedian must, of necessity, manipulate this tendency, and can therefore dictate his audience's responses to a striking extent. This is not merely a meaningless game in a marginal reality, but an important instrument in an ongoing social negotiation.

Part Three

Efficacy and Influence

Is Stand-up Comedy an Appropriate Medium for Debate?

Never underestimate the importance of fun. It is easy to dismiss those items of popular culture that are accessed primarily for enjoyment as insignificant: after all, their frivolity is what makes them appealing. Yet those things that are popular will, by definition, reach a large number of people and hence have a large sphere of influence. As Lippmann points out, 'the attempt to see all things freshly and in detail [...] is exhausting, and among busy affairs practically out of the question'.[1] We cannot reasonably absorb or process all of the information available to us, and must necessarily decide what to take on board. We do so partly by selecting and manipulating what information we expose ourselves to.[2] If we are to take an interest in information, it must be presented to us in an appealing and interesting shape, for 'being flesh and blood we will not feed on words and names and gray theory'.[3] Entertainment value makes information more appealing, and thus can cause it to be not only more widely accessed, but also more salient for those who hear it.

Stand-up comedy has a particularly strong position in that it is immensely popular, highly accessible, produced in prolific volume, enjoyable and fundamentally political. Hundreds of live stand-up performances happen across the United Kingdom every week. Television schedules are packed with stand-up comedy. This may come in fairly conventional formats such as the recordings of live, full-length concerts that are released as DVDs, or straight stand-up recorded directly for television such as *Live at the Apollo* (BBC) or *Dave's One Night Stand* (Dave). Stand-up also appears repackaged as game shows such as *8 Out of 10 Cats* (Channel 4) and *Mock the Week* (BBC). Although the format of such quiz and panel shows is very different to the straight stand-up set, they are very effective in building audiences for live comedy.[4] On many panel shows, some of the material presented is drawn directly from the stage acts of the practicing comics who make up the bulk of the participants. The internet provides continuous on-demand access to an enormous range of stand-up, including performances from those who are not famous or moderate enough for television. Some practitioners are big celebrities and household names.

In the live performance and internet arenas, it is difficult for official authorities to police or censor the material offered. Stewart Lee feels that this makes stand-up the ideal medium for the discussion of marginal views:

> Because stand-up needs so little funding and it's so easy to throw together, there's the least interface, probably in any art form, between the writer-performer's brain and the stuff coming out of his mouth. You know, it's not mediated in many ways. And that's both a good thing and a bad thing. Sometimes you can hear someone say something and you think 'what a shame you never had to discuss that with *anyone* before you said it'... *(laughs)*. And other times you think, 'Well, that's such a unique point of view and a unique way of doing it that had that gone to committee it would never have got [through].'[5]

Stand-up comedy is a widespread and dominant form of entertainment, but it is necessarily more than that. As we have seen, stand-up comedy cannot function without commenting on social structures. What each of those hundreds of live, and thousands of recorded, performances are doing is pumping out social criticism to audiences of millions.

Joking and the mob mentality

Comedy challenges established norms and posits alternatives for our consideration. This does not, however, mean that all comedy is driven by the desire for change, nor that it communicates this desire to its audience. In Chapter 1, we met Critchely's idea of the 'comedy of recognition'; some instances of joking may have the effect of 'simply [reinforcing] consensus and in no way [seek] to criticise the established order or change the situation in which we find ourselves'.[6] I argued that a joke cannot function on these terms, as it must necessarily 'criticise the established order' and thereby pose some alternative to it. Critchley's observation is, however, based upon the fair observation that these criticisms spring from differing intentions and are made with different levels of intensity. While some jokes make a vociferous push for real change, others make only a superficial attempt to depose the status quo.

By the end of 2009, Michael McIntyre was firmly established at the top end of the comedy scale, with sell-out gigs at the 02 Arena, his own prime-time BBC show and the fastest-selling stand-up DVD of all time.[7] In an article published in November 2009, Stephen Armstrong describes McIntyre's stage persona as the embodiment of the comfortably off, middle-class experience:

> McIntyre's on-stage persona is the jovial party host. He bestrides the vast O2 stage as if he's stepping between the drinks cabinet and the CD player, delivering his anecdotes and world-view as he waits for his wife to bring the nibbles. His routines are about everyday life: the awkward rituals of men in gym changing rooms, elaborate pretences when trying on shoes, and a sharp deconstruction of restaurant eating.[8]

McIntyre's material is largely observational. It critiques common behaviours and mocks them. Yet it is not generally referred to as 'political'. Comedians such as Mark Thomas, Mark Steel, Robert Newman, Stewart Lee and Josie Long are generally classed in a different genre, where the challenge presented is thought to be more practical and destructive.

It is difficult to describe what, precisely, defines political comedy, separating it from the social critique offered by other forms. Robin Ince sees the difference as, in part, an audience being told what they already know and do versus learning something new. Using the example of Lee Evans, Ince describes the type of joke-laughter exchange offered by observational comedy as a 'call and response'. Ince's theory is that

Evans' material principally represents him calling, 'didn't you all do this?' and the audience responding, 'yes, we all did this' repeatedly for the length of the set. The outcome is that the audience are able to have parts of their lives 'underlined' so that Evans may implicitly affirm that they are behaving correctly, and the audience can find validation.[9] In this sense, the joke which comments upon a shared behaviour could indeed be said to affirm the status quo: it merely tells the audience that their current behaviour is correct and should continue. Observational comedy works by mocking 'normal' behaviours but, even as it does so, it often affirms and promotes a fixed idea of what 'normal' is.

Robin Ince highlights the absurdity of this process, pointing out that hearing what you already know and do repeated back to you should be a dull experience. Surely, he opines, it is more interesting to hear about things you did not already know, or had not already thought of.[10] Stewart Lee emphasizes that this is a matter of personal taste:

> Well, in a club, right, in somewhere like The Comedy Store or Jongleurs [...] there'll be a guy talking about things, and the people in the audience nudge each other going, 'that's what you're like', 'you say that', 'oh, I did that'. Whereas what I like, is I like to be in an audience going 'I would never have thought of that!', or 'I would never have said that!', or 'why would you possibly think that?!' Right? That's what I like, I like to be taken by surprise. So I think it just depends what people want.[11]

Lee concludes, 'I think most people, sadly, like to see their own opinions bounced back at them, and that's why people like McIntyre do so well.'[12]

It was suggested above that stand-up should be seen as politically significant because it is so prolific in its production and mass consumption, but there are aspects in which this mass consumption may be seen to weaken stand-up's opportunity to question social norms. Television may be seen as a force that tends to sterilize and narrow the form, turning stand-ups from uniquely rebellious tricksters into conformists who deliver material according to somebody else's agenda. As John Fiske and John Hartley illustrate, television is a 'conventional' medium which merely articulates and reinforces the dominant culture, demonstrating the agreed value-system and implicating its audience within it. They state that 'television functions as a social ritual, overriding individual distinctions in which our culture engages, in order to communicate with its collective self'.[13] A combative medium like stand-up would necessarily find its claws blunted by such innate conservatism.

Mark Thomas feels that television's adoption of stand-up has had the effect of reducing the range of stand-up comedy with which the general public are familiar, setting narrow expectations:

> When [alternative comedy] started there was something very different about the attitude towards it [compared to now]. And the attitude is about television expectation. [...] Now you go to see stand-ups with a very clear view of what you want to see because you've seen them on telly. [...] So there's a consumerist dynamic within going to see stand-up. [...] Lots of people think political comedy is *Mock the Week*, because [...] that's what they've seen and so they'll go along and they'll go 'I know what to expect'. [...] That's why I sort of think 'that's fine, we'll talk about economic growth right at the beginning just to fucking show we can talk about whatever we want.'[14]

Stewart Lee likewise acknowledges that expectations have been limited by television. For Lee, part of the problem with television is packaging: straight stand-up formats such as *Live at the Apollo* fail to serve any comedians who work outside of the limited range expected, and the panel show format is at odds with anything but short, simple jokes. Like Thomas, Lee feels that there is now a sameness evident in much mainstream comedy, which he suggests is partly due to the limited space that the main TV formats can offer to each comic:

> Most stand-up you see now is, like, tiny jokes on panel shows and then the next joke comes on. Whereas what I like to do is kind of say something, and then wait while it, kind of, settles in, and that pause isn't available on panel shows. That breathing space has gone, so a lot of what I do wouldn't work for that. Also, on those sort of panel show

programmes everyone's pulling in the same direction, whereas I always
feel obliged to go in the other direction, so it doesn't really fit.[15]

Even the exclusive spot available on *Live at the Apollo* may be restrictive;
the relatively short spot could not accommodate the slow-burn
storytelling style of Daniel Kitson, nor Lee's own convoluted arguments
and 'breathing space'. By contrast, Lee's own series, *Stewart Lee's
Comedy Vehicle*, was a hard-won opportunity to address this imbalance
by developing a 'visual grammar' that would serve a wider range of
comedic styles[16]:

> There's loads of people doing different stuff, it's just it doesn't really
> work on television. What I thought might happen with my show,
> because it was well received on the telly, was that they might think,
> 'ooh God,' you know, 'there's all sorts of people you could have on now.'
> But they don't seem to have done that, at all. *(Laughs)*.[17]

At the time of writing, in 2014, British television is perhaps beginning
to recognize the advantage of offering comedians more opportunities
for long-form stand-up. The BBC did eventually commission a second
series of Lee's *Comedy Vehicle*, and Dave has invested in three series of
Dave Gorman's *Modern Life is Goodish*. Panel shows, though, remain
the most prolific means by which stand-ups can access TV audiences.

A further problem is presented by the conventions of interpretation
typically adopted by television audiences. Stewart Lee quotes a
description of live comedy which he attributes to American comedian
and film-maker Paul Provenza:

> I think he said something once along the lines of, 'When you walk in
> to a comedy club, you understand that everything you see is happening
> within a giant pair of inverted commas.' [...] And the audience kind
> of understands that [...] but I think a television audience aren't as
> sophisticated in the same way. Y'know [...] they kind of take it more
> at face value.[18]

Lee suggests that television audiences are less able to use the valuable
operational tool of the 'play-ground', which demarcates the comedy

performance as a marginal bubble in which everything is to be read through the special terms of comic licence.[19] Although stand-up reaches a greater audience through television, both Mark Thomas and Stewart Lee feel that this experience lacks the vitality and efficacy of the live comedy club. Television is seen as an essentially conservative medium, which limits the range of comic material presented, and marginalizes the more revolutionary work that takes place on the live circuit.

Political performers commonly assert that the impact of 'non-political' art is not neutral, but inherently damaging. Baz Kershaw states:

> There is a sense in which even shows that aim solely to promote ephemeral entertainment have long-term designs on their audiences. By encouraging a taste for escapism they may push social and political questions to the background of experience.[20]

Brecht puts a similar idea in very simple terms: 'For art to be "un-political" means only to ally itself with the "ruling" group.'[21] Mark Thomas translates this strand of thought into a practical example: 'In most of the media, impartiality just means not being too critical of the prevalent ruling class perspective.'[22] For Lee, the difference between the brand of comedy that he produces, and the commercially driven populist comedy of performers like McIntyre, is found partly in the integrity of the comedian's role. While many comedians manipulate audiences into believing that their material exists on the fringes of dominant thought, most of it reflects mainstream attitudes:

> I am also aware that to some extent I am actively cultivating a sort of *Independent/Guardian*-reader audience who will like the, sort of, liberal stuff but are also open-minded enough to be confronted with things they don't agree with. That audience really suits me. [...] If you think of, like, [Jeremy] Clarkson or whatever as comedians, what they're very good at doing – that school of comedy – is very good at taking something which is the dominant cultural narrative in British life, the views of all the best-selling newspapers – that there's too many immigrants, that we don't need to worry about global warming and

that political correctness has gone mad – and yet selling this dominant cultural view as if it were, somehow, a subversive minority view. [...] That kind of comedy [...] is able to make its audience feel special. It's like going to them, 'You and me, we think this don't we? They don't, but we think this.' Whereas, in fact, they are the majority, but they manage to give it the flavour of being an interesting, subversive point of view.[23]

Bill Hicks is quoted as saying, 'to me, the comic is the guy who says, "Wait a minute" as the consensus forms. [...] He's the antithesis of the mob mentality.'[24] This is a principle with which Lee heartily agrees:

I think it's the role of the court jester and the clown, historically, to be on the outside. Simon Munnery has a really funny line. [...] 'If the crowd have got behind you, then you're facing the wrong way' [...] and you sort of do feel obliged to take an opposition point of view. [...] You're supposed to be the person asking uncomfortable questions, I think, even if they're about trivial things, rather than the person agreeing with everyone. You shouldn't be agreeing with everyone. You should be disagreeing with them just for the sake of it.[25]

Lee is willing to take this principle to an unusual extreme. Disliking the 'mob mentality' signified when a group laughs in unison, Lee designs his comedy to create uncertainty among his audience about how to respond. As we have seen, successful control of responses in Lee's case is not necessarily about producing regular and hearty laughter:

I don't like consensus, really. I hate that feeling of... well... I just think when there's loads of people laughing at the same thing it just feels nasty. I like the idea that there's some kind of exchange or process going on.[26]

It should be noted that to adhere to his anti-mob principles, Lee must sacrifice the comedian's typical measure of success and so his methodology may differ significantly from that of most comedians. However, the way in which he theorizes his work goes some way to define the difference between the type of challenge present in the work of Michael McIntyre and Lee Evans, and the type of challenge present in the more overtly 'political' comedy presented by the likes of himself and Mark Thomas. Lee purposefully avoids consensus, 'disagreeing […] just for the sake of it'. His preference for avoiding the forms of the Establishment is difficult to maintain, and could become commercially damaging. Yet the anti-mob principle, however impractical its application, has steered Lee into a distinctively oppositional kind of comedy which aims, not for consensus, but to highlight oppositional ideas.

As has been discussed, consensus and the sense of community that Stewart Lee avoids are vital tools in the work of Mark Thomas. Yet consensus has a very particular function in Thomas' work; it is a tool used to recruit people to his ideology, and to impart information which will inspire them to new ways of thinking and, he hopes, action.[27] When asked whether he is forced to sacrifice objectivity and 'balanced reporting', Thomas replies, 'We are the balance':[28]

> If you take the ideas of objectivity, balance and impartiality to their logical conclusion, then I believe you should have the right to reply to every single advertisement. Every time an advert by petroleum companies like Shell or Esso comes on television, then one and a half minutes should be reserved for someone from the public to say what they think about those companies and their environmental records. The idea of objectivity doesn't exist in media – just the veneer of it.[29]

Robert Newman similarly seeks to build consensus in order to move his audience on to a new awareness. He acknowledges that he must necessarily function on the outskirts of his society's thought and experience in order to do this. For example, his 'euro-dollar' theory of the origins of the Iraq war, which suggested that the war could be understood as a 'punishment beating' for Iraq's decision to trade oil in euros rather than US dollars, would not be palatable on BBC *Question Time*. Newman explains that he refused the invitation to appear as a panellist on this major mainstream platform for political comment because if you espouse counter-mainstream views like his, 'you're just

off the spectrum; they can't even hear you [...] there'd be a real danger
that I'd just come across as some sort of anarchist nutter!'[30]

It seems that there is a definable methodology and ideology that
marks out 'political' comedy as something different to that created by
the panel show produced, commercial mainstream. McIntyre's material
may challenge the communal experience of the dominant social group,
but it is this latter group of comedians who challenge dominance itself
and deliberately press for an alternative practice or reality to replace
that which is challenged. The rest of this book focuses upon this more
consciously political strand of the contemporary stand-up comedy
scene. By examining comedians whose work embodies explicit political
aims, we may uncover the potential that stand-up has to persuade.

What comic theory says: Joking and the Establishment

Many theorists argue that comedy is an inappropriate mechanism
by which to effect social change. Stand-up comedy may be part of an
influential popular culture, but some aspects of comic theory imply that
joking is, by its nature, a toothless form of protest. The following is a
discussion of some of the main refutations of joking's ability to function
as serious debate.

1) Joking sweeps contention under the carpet

Some accuse joking of hiding the complexities of important issues:
joking does not always highlight issues for debate, but may rather be
used to sweep them under the carpet. As we have seen, comedy can
involve the use of simple maxims which allow an audience to develop
a straightforward value-system (a manipulated 'map of the world', in
Lippmann's terms) with which to navigate their way through the gig,
pointing them towards the 'correct' response with the minimum of
cognitive effort.[31] Morreall further suggests that humour can be used

as a cynical ploy to settle controversial issues. He has interpreted a joke which occurred during a 1984 debate between presidential candidates Ronald Reagan and Walter Mondale in this light:

> In their first television debate, Reagan had seemed uninformed and confused. Critics pointed out that he was an old man; some suggested he might be suffering from Alzheimer's disease. So Reagan's speechwriters prepared two sentences for the second debate. When someone asked about the 'age issue', Reagan said, 'I will not make age an issue in this election. I will not exploit for political gain my opponent's youth and inexperience.' That made Mondale rather than Reagan look foolish, and for the rest of the campaign the age issue was dead.[32]

In his *Manifesto* show, which is structured around debate of policies proposed by the audience, Mark Thomas regularly uses a related technique to manage the delicate balance of group consensus and genuine debate that is necessary if the show is to function as both entertainment and the means to create a people's manifesto. Where there is a complex debate surrounding an issue or Thomas' own reasoning is two sided, he is able to use short, punchy jokes to reduce complicated issues to simple points and gain consensus for this repackaging of the debate. The show tours during a period of recession; a popular image of rich, fat-cat bankers pocketing billions of pounds in bonuses while steering poorer families into crisis prevails in the public imagination. The 'bonus culture' is widely attacked for rewarding incompetence, and with Members of Parliament also under fire for fiddling expenses, high salaries and generous perks for the elite are becoming an increasingly sore point. Counter to this is the traditional capitalist view that highly skilled jobs which manage important areas of British life must be awarded high salaries in order to retain the most talented personnel.

Thomas reduces the debate to a simple, funny observation which earns the laughter and agreement of his audience: '"pay peanuts, get monkeys": pay bonuses, get wankers!'[33] In itself, the argument is flippant and simplistic, but it is persuasive enough to sweep away the counterargument and form a solid basis for more radical statements. Thomas states that he is in favour of a maximum wage, and relates a conversation with an economist who suggests that this would be best arranged as a formula in which the maximum wage was a fixed multiple of the average wage. Thus, the level of the country's highest pay would be linked to the fate of those on lower salaries. This more radical suggestion would cap potential earnings in Britain, and necessarily mean that there would be higher earning potential for elite professions overseas. Thomas directly acknowledges this criticism: 'If you can't live on two-hundred-and-fifty grand, I'll drive you to the airport myself! [laugh].'

These jokes perform a similar function to those analysed in the discussion of manufactured consensus. They use the evidence of the occurring economic crisis as an unarguable point upon which to convincingly build an argument formed from simplistic evidence. What is important to note for the purposes of this discussion, however, is what happens to the counterargument. By quoting the phrase 'pay peanuts, get monkeys,' and thus acknowledging the maxim that only high salaries may procure talent and experience, it seems as if Thomas has confronted the issue head-on. In fact, he has swerved around the debate altogether. Neither statement really tackles the counterargument, unpicking its complexities or allowing it to have a voice. Indeed, Thomas has made it clear that he considers the idea that such professions really employ the best 'talent' to be spurious in itself. Rather, Thomas makes brief reference to the counterarguments, acknowledging their existence while allowing his audience to enjoy the fact that such points do not get a fair hearing. In fact, his blasé treatment of the old maxim that the current pay structure rewards talent and performance, and thus benefits society at large, implies that he considers this view to be worthless, not meriting serious discussion. The economic crisis is evidence that the system does not work, and those who benefit from it have done so inconsiderately: 'pay bonuses, get wankers'. Those who want to perpetuate that system are a hindrance rather than a help, and their removal is something to be strived for: 'I'll drive you to the airport myself.' It is as simple as that.

Thomas' audience may be fully aware that he has replaced reasoned debate with flippant argument. What is remarkable about the genre of political comedy is that this does not matter. In many political shows, it is likely that the audience are there to learn and to see important issues debated as well as to be entertained; with this show it is a definite and central part of the mission statement. This audience knows that Thomas will campaign upon the policies they choose, so their support in the gig will have an effect in the outside world; indeed, Thomas relates actions that have already been taken in response to policies adopted in earlier shows, allowing the audience to cheer tangible, practical effects. The stakes are therefore high; that this should be so is part of the contract. However, the contract also states that Thomas' work is to be taken as comedy. As such, flippant remarks, shoddy logic and partisan accounts of complicated issues are all considered legitimate. The discrepancy between serious consequences and silly processes is accepted. This provides stand-up with great power.

2) Joking does not urge us to change the wrongs of the world; it gives us the means to cope with them

Some instances of joking could be argued to celebrate or de-stigmatize their topics, rather than exerting a genuine push for change. Critchley provides one such argument in his assertion that most humour comments upon the world without seeking to change it:

> Such humour [...] simply toys with existing social hierarchies in a charming but quite benign fashion. [...] More egregiously, much humour seeks to confirm the status quo either by denigrating a certain sector of society [...] or by laughing at the alleged stupidity of a social outsider. [...] Such humour is not laughter at power, but the powerful laughing at the powerless [...] reactionary humour tells us important truths about who we are [...] humour can reveal us to be persons that, frankly, we would really rather not be.[34]

The comedian does not offer a call to change the situation, but rather provides us with a way to come to terms with its disagreeable elements. While he may adopt the trappings of the dysfunction which Mintz identifies as an important component of the comedian's persona – such as uncontrollable cynicism or abuse of alcohol – he remains representative of the powerful majority.[35] Given the prevalence of white, middle-class males in the current British Comedy elite, the criticism that comedy has become a mechanism by which the dominant, and not the oppressed, express themselves is worth examining.

Morreall notes that amusement is not the only way in which human beings react to incongruity: it can also be perceived as a threat and cause reactions of puzzlement or 'negative emotion' such as fear. Amusement differs from these reactions in that it allows us to enjoy the incongruity.[36] We could therefore suggest that humour is a useful tool for the comedian in his role as exponent of marginal ideologies, as humour provides a mechanism by which incongruous viewpoints, and information which contradicts the hearer's pre-existing attitudes, may be presented in a non-threatening manner. For the hearer, humour is useful in interpreting the incongruity in such a way as to provide pleasure rather than discomfort.[37] The use of humour gives the persuasive speaker an advantage in that his message may be received warmly when it could otherwise have triggered negative feelings or reactance.

However, Morreall's theory also implies a serious disadvantage for persuasion; if the hearer is enjoying the incongruity itself, he is not motivated to change the situation:

> Because we enjoy the incongruity in amusement, our only motivation might be to prolong and perhaps communicate the enjoyable experience; we do not have the practical concern to improve the incongruous situation, nor the theoretical concern to improve our understanding of it.[38]

Morreall interprets 'humorous amusement' as a reaction to incongruity that eliminates the motivation either to resolve the incongruity or to adapt the factors that create it. He acknowledges that this idea does not sit comfortably with the theory of cognitive dissonance, which is the leading explanation for opinion change offered by social psychology.[39] Cognitive dissonance theory states that when an individual has conflicting opinions, or is exposed to information which contradicts his current world view, this creates a state of psychological tension which he will seek to resolve by adapting or reinterpreting the existing cognitions until they achieve consonance. A change in attitude is an important method by which this can be achieved; thus it is discomfort caused by the perception of incongruity which motivates attitude change.[40]

Morreall criticizes the cognitive dissonance theory for failing to take into account the instances in which incongruity may be enjoyed.[41] There is a type of humour in which our inability to achieve consonance forms the basis of the joke. Morreall gives the example of the nonsensical question, 'What's the difference between a duck with one of its legs both the same?' which is funny precisely because none of the schemas into which it should fit can make it sensible.[42] We could also interpret Stewart Lee's IRA routine through this model; the joke draws humour from the embarrassment caused by a socially awkward situation, which is created by trapping the audience in a difficult cognitive conundrum. On the one hand, applauding the IRA for their terrorist acts is definitely wrong; on the other, Lee has given an ostensibly logical reason to do it (the 'gentleman bombers' suggestion), and, most important of all, it is only a joke. The routine purposefully creates dissonance which is not supposed to be resolved, but enjoyed. As Lee himself has stated, the cognitive challenge is part of the fun.[43] Thus a comedy audience, arguably, cannot be motivated to resolve incongruities through puzzlement or the need to resolve dissonance.

Negative emotion is similarly dismissed as a potential motivator. As we have seen, it is widely acknowledged within comic theory that laughter involves emotional detachment. This idea is expressed in Morreall's model of 'practical disengagement', and in Bergson's oft-quoted maxim that 'laughter has no greater foe than emotion'.[44]

Neither Morreall nor Bergson claim that we lack the ability to laugh at things which inspire negative emotion – our sympathies need only be temporarily suspended – but the fact remains that sympathy is deemed to be incompatible with laughter. If this is so, and if joking is not concerned with normal standards of morality and decency, then it follows that an appeal to the hearts of audience members will go unheeded. As Morreall notes, reacting with humour to a situation that causes someone pain is often counterproductive:

> Humour can be irresponsible, for example, by supplanting some action which we should have taken to remedy a serious problem. [...]
>
> Even when it does not block actions to remedy a problem, humour can be objectionable by showing insensitivity or cruelty toward a person who is suffering from a problem.[45]

Morreall suggests that humour makes a positive contribution by promoting critical thinking, helping us to deal constructively with mistakes and decreasing stress in unpleasant situations. In the latter two instances, humour deals with the issue of negative emotion: through humour we are able coolly to analyse our mistake unencumbered by feelings of remorse or misery, and can use practical disengagement to divorce ourselves from the negative emotions inspired by a stressful situation, boosting our morale.[46] Crucially, Morreall traces all the benefits of humour back to its capacity to 'block' emotion, and does not concede that the negativity highlighted in a joking register can, itself, motivate change.

We must be careful, however, not to confuse the willingness to suspend practical concern with a universal inability to care. Practical disengagement is not best understood as a universal element or defining feature of joking. It is a more helpful model if we see it as a tool that joking uses profusely, but somewhat selectively. Experience tells us that the separation between our amusement and our sympathetic response can feel very insignificant. In his *Dambusters* show, Mark Thomas relates the experiences of Kurdish human rights expert Kerim Yildiz. Thomas explains that Kerim has a habit of beginning his stories with the words 'was hilarious!' This becomes Kerim's catchphrase, and sets up a joke which plays on the incongruity of his overly positive attitude to his past, for, as Thomas states; 'I quickly [...] found out whenever he said "was hilarious," I'm about to hear something really fucking bad.'[47]

Thomas explains that Kerim was arrested on a false pretext, and celebrates the victory of Kerim's cunning over the dull-witted attempts of the Turkish police to extract false confessions. Kerim confesses to twenty-three murders under duress, but the court case becomes a farce when he demonstrates that he could not have killed any of his supposed victims: in some cases they died before he was born. Thomas achieves some enthusiastic laughs in response to the description of the corrupt judge's increasing frustration, the police's stupidity and Kerim's incongruous but admirable insistence upon describing the experience as 'hilarious'. When he cannot be found guilty, Kerim is not released but imprisoned again, this time solely on the grounds that he is a Kurd. In the following, Thomas relates a conversation in which Kerim continues the story (italics denote Thomas' characterization of Kerim):

> '*Was hilarious!*' [laugh] '*There were ten of us in the prison cell and we decide that when the prison guards come to collect us to take us away to torture us, we will attack the guards and beat them up!*' [laugh]...
>
> 'You fucking nutter!' [big laugh]...
>
> '*No, no, no – no, was psychology 'cause we attack the guards, the guards get very cross, when they are cross they cannot torture properly, you pass out quickly, doesn't matter what they do to you!*' [laugh]...
>
> 'Fuck!'
>
> '*Was hilarious!*' [laugh][48]

This section, like much of Thomas' material, is unusual among stand-up performances for the emphasis it places upon truth. While much comedy places the importance of the gag above factual accuracy, this audience know that Kerim's story really happened, and cannot tell themselves that it is 'only a joke'. This means that even as they laugh at Kerim's catchphrase and the hyper-logical solution of physically assaulting the torturers, the audience are simultaneously being given some harrowing information.[49]

Thomas makes it easier for the audience to laugh by employing various techniques which allow them some detachment from the story. He does not relate events directly, taking the audience to the moment at which the atrocities were committed, but rather relates a conversation between himself and Kerim. This provides an extra layer of distance, and shows that Kerim is alive, well and laughing at his oppressors. Thomas filters the story back via the character of his past self, and thus directs and segments the audience's reaction. When the Thomas-character says 'you fucking nutter!', he directs the stand-up audience towards the incongruity of the prisoners' plan, prevents them from becoming overwhelmed with sympathy towards Kerim's ever-worsening predicament and reassures them that it is acceptable to laugh. Similarly, once it has been established that laughter is an appropriate response despite the difficult nature of the material, the Thomas-character is used to acknowledge the audience's shock at Kerim's explanation and its implications ('fuck!'), voicing both the audience's sympathy and the incomprehensible awfulness of the information. The audience are quickly given the means to release the tension that this creates through the reappearance of the catchphrase, which provides the opportunity for an easier laugh.

There is a sense in which the Thomas-character is used to promote practical disengagement, and this is vital in allowing the audience to laugh. However, this does not mean that Thomas' message loses its power. *Dambusters* exists to raise awareness, and this is one of many routines within it, designed to convey shocking information and capitalize upon the audience's response.[50] If the audience are incapable of appreciating the practical and emotional implications of what they are hearing, the educational purpose of the show is lost.

However, the audience are clearly capable of engaging their empathy with the topic at the same time as they disengage from the social imperative to demonstrate empathy which would make laughter an inappropriate response outside of a joking situation. The quality of the laughter in this section is distinctly different to the section that precedes it, in which Thomas relates the more comfortable experiences of British human rights campaigners. When Thomas relates the story of his friend Nick, who cleverly finds a way to expose and humiliate an undercover police officer in a public meeting, the laughter is an enthusiastic and celebratory burst. The laughter accompanying Kerim's story is comparatively muted and restrained. We could make sense of this by applying the theory that laughter is incompatible with negative emotions; in this case our pity and anxiety for Kerim. However, the audience are still laughing. The material is not less funny, but differently so. What the more muted reaction signifies is perhaps a sense of respect for Kerim's suffering, and, crucially, that even while they laugh, the audience are indeed cognizant of the practical and emotional implications of the material.

To say that enjoyment of incongruity removes the wish to change the situation is to deny the complex and layered reactions that audiences may experience simultaneously in response to a single event. The audience enjoy certain incongruities of Kerim's story, but to say that this removes the motivation to change the situation is to believe that they are left accepting of Kerim's brutal treatment – or even pleased that it occurred, so that they may enjoy the story. This, of course, is not the case. The audience laugh, but their laughter heralds increased awareness of, and passion for, the need for change. If the jokes encourage the audience to separate the incongruities presented from their negative emotions, then that separation is rather insignificant. The fact that the information is presented in a humourous forum does not remove the wish to change the situation.

3) Joking is a harmless form of protest which just keeps the oppressed happy

The third accusation is related to the second: while the joke certainly issues challenges, these bolster the Establishment which they purport to attack. Zijderveld makes reference to Wertheim's theory that joking is an expression of resistance to the dominant hierarchy. The oppressed use jokes to express their latent hostility to the powerful. In the institution of the court jester, the royal ruler finds a means of subsuming this force into his own domain, allowing the attack and protest but in a harmless, authorized form. According to Zijderveld, if the Establishment is clever, it will consciously turn the challenge to its advantage:

> The social sublimation of protests and conflict by means of joking, therefore, is not just a relief from the social frustration of those who are dominated, but may also be a technique manipulated by the powerful in order to keep protest and conflict within certain limits and to provide society at the same time with a possible outlet. Joking in this case functions as a safety valve, installed on society by those in power [...] Brecht's statement, 'one should not fight dictators, one should ridicule them,' therefore holds true only in those societies in which the powerful leaders are still not acquainted with the possibilities of a manipulatory use of joking.[51]

Such mastery is, however, difficult to achieve:

> Joking, it seems to us, appears to be a much more appropriate weapon for the Establishment than sticks, clubs and tear gas [...] the art of good joking admittedly is infinitely more difficult to master than the handling of clubs and guns.[52]

Zijderveld states that the opposite situation can also occur; where the Establishment fails to use joking as a weapon on its own terms, the joke can be an empowering form of rebellion. Franca Rame claims to have experienced both sides of this paradox. When performing in Italy's traditional theatres, she had provided a boost to the audience she had sought to attack:

> We [...] realised that, despite the hostility of a few, obtuse reactionaries, the high bourgeoisie reacted to our 'spankings' almost with pleasure. Masochists? No, without realising it, we were helping their digestion. Our 'whipping' boosted their blood circulation, like some good birching after a refreshing sauna. In other words we had become the minstrels of a fat and intelligent bourgeoisie.[53]

However, the problem was not the material, but the forum:

> This bourgeoisie did not mind our criticism, no matter how pitiless it had become […] but only so long as the exposure of their 'vices' occurred exclusively within the structures they controlled. […] We had to place ourselves entirely at the service of the exploited, become their minstrels. Which meant going to work within the structures provided by the working class.[54]

For Rame, the move from performing in the traditional, bourgeois theatre to the workers' clubs was the equivalent of giving up the King's patronage and protection and allowing the Jester's jibes to become weapons in the hands of the people.

Zijderveld's model of joking as a gentle release of social tensions fails to reflect the reality of Rame's experience. Even when working in the traditional theatre, Rame and her colleagues were confronted with censorship; she even relates an incident where they were physically assaulted, 'just at the moment when, by a strange coincidence, the police had disappeared'.[55] In 1973, Rame was kidnapped, beaten, mutilated and raped by neo-fascists. Many years later, evidence was uncovered which suggested that the attack had been ordered by senior police officers, themselves following orders from the upper echelons of government.[56] In these instances, the Establishment was using 'sticks, clubs and tear gas', rather than effective manipulation of joking, to control the counterculture.[57] Rame's experience does, however, demonstrate that in some cases comedy is not a gentle poking at the opposition, but war. Comedy may be mobilized by either side – it can be used as a weapon to challenge the status quo, or to bolster it – but the instances in which it triggers violent reprisal suggest that it is anything but toothless.

Stand-up comedy can make an important contribution to social change. It is one of the catalysts which enables renegotiation of attitudes, and the dissemination of new ideas, to occur. For a medium to communicate to the mass of people it must, by definition, be popular. With so much stand-up comedy being produced, and with the incentives of fun and laughter to encourage its wide consumption, this medium of debate is well placed to play a vital role in formulating the ideas and attitudes of its society. When comedians choose to place their own views in serious contention, they necessarily make a contribution to the wider social debate. In the next chapter, we turn to the question of how effective this contribution is likely to be in influencing individuals' attitudes, and in shaping public opinion.

How Stand-up Matters

In a 2005 article for the left-wing political magazine *New Statesman,* John Oliver and Andy Zaltzman wrote:

> Does political comedy change people's minds? There are two answers to that – a short one, and a slightly longer one. The short one is: no, it doesn't. The slightly longer one is: no, of course it doesn't, don't be ridiculous.[1]

Four years later, in the same publication, Lucy Porter took a similar stance, saying that 'the difficulty with political comedy is that it doesn't really endure'.[2] That comedians writing in a magazine specifically for a progressive, politically orientated audience could be so dismissive of comedy's impact seems rather damning.

For all that comedy is theorized as a challenging, norm-subverting practice, the idea that a comic performance could go so far as to 'change people's minds' appears ridiculous to many. We know from experience that sudden and dramatic conversions from an intensely held opinion to its opposite are not the norm at comedy nights. Comedians typically avoid playing to incompatible audiences precisely because audiences do not display this kind of adaptability. It is perhaps discomforting to think that a change in opinion could be sparked by something as frivolous as a comedy performance. Such a possibility could be stifling for both comedians and audiences; the sheer weight of responsibility would ruin everyone's fun.

All in all, it is difficult to conceive of stand-up comedy as something that changes people's minds. It is probable, however, that this is due more to a misunderstanding of what it means for a person's mind to be changed than any real evidence of stand-up's impuissance. If we look for total conversions from one extreme of opinion to another, or for statistical evidence demonstrating uniform and tidy shifts of attitude in audiences, then we will probably be disappointed. Opinion change simply does not work in this way. A more helpful starting point may be to ask how opinion change really works and how it becomes socially significant.

The aim of what follows is not to demonstrate quantitative changes in individual or public opinion, but rather to apply existing knowledge of how people come to change their minds to stand-up performance. A selection of established sociological tools are mobilized to demonstrate that it is stand-up's nature as a social interaction which gives it this potential to influence. The examples of stand-up that are chosen are all taken from political comedy shows in which the comedian explicitly communicates how and why they would like to influence audience attitudes. The aim is not to present an exhaustive list of the ways in which stand-up's potential for influence may be understood, but rather to propose a new way of thinking about and articulating stand-up's impact; a new approach that may be used to interpret the potential for influence across a wider range of performances and using a wider range of sociological tools. When we apply knowledge of the way our opinions behave to the way we behave in a stand-up performance, it seems likely that stand-up really is changing your mind.

How opinions behave

We have already seen that comedians can persuade audiences to agree with controversial or poorly evidenced ideas in the short term in order to facilitate the smooth running of the performance. This is at play when audiences demonstrate cognitive and practical disengagement with the comedian's material, and in cases where they deliver responses that would not usually be deemed socially acceptable; Stewart Lee's audience applauding the IRA and Dan Atkinson tricking an audience member into high-fiving paedophilia are dramatic examples.[3] While these instances demonstrate that audience members can be persuaded to outwardly demonstrate an attitude contrary to their 'real' or everyday beliefs, it seems unlikely that either manipulation will have led to those attitudes becoming fixed in the minds of the audience. The manipulation is impressive, but short term, and in itself may demonstrate a mere willingness to facilitate the gig.

Anyone who seeks to alter attitudes and opinions in the long term is faced with a considerable challenge. Even the most logical and well-founded arguments will come up against fearsome competition if they seek to replace those opinions that the individual already holds. According to Lane and Sears:

> Opinions are often learned as mere affective tendencies, as 'pro' or 'con' feelings, without adequate informational support. They are formed on the basis of biased exposure to information, and selective perception and selective learning […] most citizens are not […] notably 'rational' in their political thinking. Their main interest lies in defending emotionally derived and poorly considered opinions – opinions based on early imitation of parental beliefs, partisan adherence to the norms of various groups, and selfish economic or personal interests.[4]

Analysis of the process by which people develop, use and change their attitudes and opinions is complicated by the fact that not all people, attitudes or opinions behave in the same way. Individuals are subject to different influences, hold different things to be important, and are educated to assimilate new information in different ways.[5] Individuals also hold the opinions they have with differing intensities; some opinions are not important and are therefore more easily altered or discarded, while others are of fundamental importance to the individual's understanding of both themselves and their environment.[6]

Attitudes and opinions have some characteristics which most experts agree to be universal. First, opinions, especially intensely held ones, are rarely arrived at or altered by a cool process of balanced reasoning in the light of fairly judged evidence. We seek little factual evidence on which to form an opinion, and it is usually after we have decided on an attitude to take that we develop supporting cognitions.[7] We allow ourselves more exposure to, and take more notice of, the evidence that supports our decision and ignore, avoid or otherwise disregard information that may contradict our viewpoint. Oswald and Grosjean add that, even when we allow ourselves to be exposed to, and take on board, evidence that contradicts our current hypothesis, we tend to assume that such evidence is less relevant than that which confirms it.[8] In summary, Lane and Sears rather pessimistically conclude that 'it is one thing to be informed and something else to have an opinion'.[9]

In 1922, Walter Lippmann put forward a similar and influential idea, identifying what he called 'stereotypes' which enable us to interpret a world that is too complex to comprehend in full and in which we cannot expose ourselves to every relevant piece of information. Stereotypes precede the formation of opinion, intervening at the very moment in which the individual first receives and interprets information from their surroundings, manipulating the individual's experience even before a value-judgement is made. Stereotypes appear in many different guises in writings about opinion and prejudice, and are similar to what psychologists call 'heuristics': 'simple and approximate rules' which allow us to interpret the world with the necessary efficiency, but which sometimes cause us to interpret it incompletely or inaccurately.[10] According to Lippmann, people are deeply motivated to defend their stereotypes against contradictory evidence:

A pattern of stereotypes is not neutral. It is not merely a way of substituting order for the great blooming, buzzing confusion of reality. It is not merely a short cut. It is all these things and something more. It is the guarantee of our self-respect; it is that projection upon the world of our own sense of our own value, our own position and our own rights. The stereotypes are, therefore, highly charged with the feelings that are attached to them. They are the fortress of our tradition, and behind its defenses we can continue to feel ourselves safe in the position we occupy.[11]

Each individual has a commitment to their own series of opinions and beliefs, and is motivated to defend them. Any heavy-handed attempt to change a strongly held attitude, opinion or stereotype is likely to lead to 'reactance', where the individual responds to the message by thinking or doing the opposite of what was asked. Gross points to the example of smokers who know that smoking is dangerous to their health and yet develop cognitions to support their behaviour. The smoker may, for example, decide that the mass of evidence which shows smoking to be dangerous is flawed; associate with healthy people who are also smokers in order to provide evidence for the view that smoking is not damaging; convince him or herself that smoking is an important recreational activity, or perhaps reinterpret the behaviour as indicative of a romantic, 'devil-may-care image'.[12]

In a BBC video designed to give practical advice on improving persuasive speaking, Alastair Campbell offers the following summary of his experience as a political speaker and speech-writer:

> Maybe this is a bit naive, but I have quite an old-fashioned belief that most people will listen to a well-constructed argument. So if you make a case founded on factual analysis, values, your own experience, history, colour, bringing in human stories and so forth [I think] you can [...] usually persuade somebody closer to your case, even if, ultimately, they're not going to necessarily agree with you. [...] Sometimes you're never going to persuade somebody. What you might be able to persuade me is actually 'you've got a point I hadn't thought about – you made the case rather well.' So [...] you're not always persuading somebody to go from A to Z, you might be persuading them to go from, kind of [...] G to J.[13]

Campbell's experience supports the idea that persuading any individual to change their mind is difficult and often impossible. The evidence suggests that Campbell's belief in 'factual analysis' and 'a well-constructed argument' is indeed naive, and it is interesting that Campbell himself goes on to bury this strategy beneath a heap of techniques designed to play upon the audience's emotions and partisan tendencies such as 'values' and 'human stories'. As the logic of Gross' smoker demonstrates, human beings are adept at resisting logic when it conflicts with their perceived interests and established, comforting world view. Far from weighing up facts against each other and making a cool judgement, we will go to extremes to defend those attitudes and opinions that are important to us, and are even willing to counter overwhelming evidence with beliefs that range from the bizarre to the ridiculous. This could be a serious disadvantage for the speaker who wishes to persuade by sensible logic; for the comedian, it only serves to bring the fight on to home ground.

To change an individual's opinions, the best strategy is to go gently, slowly shifting the points of reference by which they define themselves and interpret their experiences. In performance, sudden and dramatic opinion change is the province of psychological illusion. If we are looking for good, honest, long-term opinion change, then we are looking for small, incremental changes.

Preaching to the converted: The power of the reference group

Political stand-up comedy is commonly dismissed as mere 'preaching to the converted': an insular activity that can have little impact on those who do not already identify with the political persuasion of the performer. This interpretation is based on the fair assumption that audiences do not attend overtly political shows unless they expect to broadly agree with the ideology offered.

One way in which a political comedian might access a wider audience is on the circuit, particularly in those clubs that attract an audience more by virtue of the night's reputation or location than by the names on the bill. Performing his own show at the Gardner Arts Centre, Mark Thomas offers a vivid picture of the problems inherent in delivering political material to a more generalized audience. Such are the demands of Thomas' typical Friday night Comedy Store audience that, by two o'clock in the morning, he would be 'just shovelling off knob gags to stay afloat' (Thomas' impersonation of audience members in italics):

> What I'd do is I'd talk about, sort of like, knob gags for about nineteen minutes (.) just so I could speak about East Timor for thirty seconds. [Small laugh]… And that was the trade off – do you know what I mean? So I'd be up there going 'Knob gag' – and they go *'Knob gag!'* [Small Laugh]… 'Knob gag' – *'Knob gag!'* [Laugh]… 'East Timor!' – *'Eas' Ti'*– *What the fuck? I don't know what the fuck that is* – [laugh] *do you know what the fuck tha-'*, *'I dunno, I think it's by the clitoris.' 'Is it? Marvellous!'* [Big laugh] *'Very good'*… Like knob gag by default, really [Small laugh].[14]

Thomas goes on to jest that his audience at the Gardner Arts Centre have their own foibles:

> you nearly fell into the trap at the beginning (.) Classic arts centre trap. Nine times out of ten you get to an arts centre you jump on stage and go 'Hello everyone', they go *'what does he mean by that?'* [Big laugh][15]

The audience's behaviour and interpretation of the material is shaped by the nature of the gig they are attending. Thomas' audience recognizes this truth, laughing at the contrast between the drunken, disinterested antics of the Comedy Store crowd and the overly analytical, slightly pompous social concern of the well-behaved Arts Centre audience. Political crowds like those who attend Thomas' solo shows have opted in to a particular code of behaviour and interpretation; the problem with addressing political material to a generic crowd is that they have not.

In the majority of cases, then, the successful political comedy show will be delivered to an audience of the converted. Even if an audience member who strongly disagreed with the comedian's political code were to attend, that audience member would be highly unlikely to have his or her mind changed. It seems fair to say that comedians do indeed preach to the converted. This does not, however, mean that the performance will be politically neutral. Double defends the importance of such collective, in-group activity:

> The point of the phrase is that preaching to the converted is a useless activity, because they're already converted. This ignores the fact that a sermon is partly about sharing and celebrating common beliefs to send the flock out into the wicked world with a strengthened faith.[16]

Far from being a sign of impuissance, the way that stand-up functions as an expression of in-group unity may be seen as one of its most effective political features. This interpretation finds support in the notion of the reference group.

Robert Merton, one of the most influential writers on reference group theory, acknowledged that 'sociology... has always centred on the group determination of behaviour'.[17] That people decide what to think and what to do based on the social norms imparted to them by the community with which they identify is an essential tenet of the social sciences. Merton claims that reference group theory is distinctive in acknowledging 'the further fact that men frequently orient themselves to groups *other than their own* in shaping their behaviour and evaluations'.[18] As Lane and Sears state:

> When a group's norms serve as reference points for an individual, the group may be described as one of his *reference groups*. A reference group may be positive, with the individual adopting its norms as his own opinions; or negative, with its norms telling him what *not* to think. [...] Clearly, a person does not have to be a member of a group for it to serve a reference function for him.[19]

Joel Cooper acknowledges that entertainment and relative frippery can form a basis for strong group identification. He cites the example of strong in-group feelings shared by the supporters of sports teams, and highlights the significance of such group dynamics:

> When we share group membership with someone, we take on part of that person's identity and they take on part of ours. [...] Our

membership in social groups affects our very identity as human beings and puts us in unison with others who share that identity.[20]

When an individual chooses to be in a particular comedian's audience, they usually do so because they already feel some affiliation with that comedian. They know that other audience members will be doing the same. Hence, when we go to see a specific comedian, we opt in to a like-minded group. At the overtly political gig, the notion of group membership is highlighted, because the nature of such events causes audiences to be cognizant that they are getting together with people who share their values. This forms the basis for a potentially powerful, positive reference group.

Comedians often play upon the human tendency to draw on reference groups, both positive and negative. Sometimes the approach is blatant. In *The Night War Broke Out*, Mark Thomas encourages his audience to counter government 'propaganda' supporting the invasion of Iraq by the UK and the United States. He suggests that, whenever they see British Prime Minister Tony Blair or US President George W. Bush on the television, they should hum *The Imperial March* from *Star Wars* to themselves; when the loose association of peace activists whom Thomas refers to as 'us lot' appear, they should hum a riff taken from the *Star Wars Main Theme*.[21] To support Thomas is to maintain allegiance with the Galactic Republic and to support the Iraq war is to join the dark side: Thomas equates his current political situation with one of fiction's most clearly demarcated sets of heroes and villains.

The drawing of reference groups can be more subtle. Josie Long's 2006 show *Kindness and Exuberance* is, perhaps, less overtly political than some of her latter work. It has none of the direct assault on government actions and ideals that is explicit within her 2012 show, *Romance and Adventure*.[22] However, Long sees her approach, and hence her early work, as inherently political.[23] Broderick Chow identifies Long as one of a group of relatively young comics who had, by 2007, established a new sub-genre of stand-up which addressed social and political concerns pertinent to their generation: the 'new alternative' known as DIY comedy. It opposed the commercialist ethos that had come to dominate alternative comedy and responded to an 'increasing sense of purposelessness and loneliness among young persons in Western society'.[24] Chow argues that, like the alternative comedy revolution of the late 1970s and 1980s, DIY comedy had its own, timely social and political mission: 'While DIY comedy may not express a prescriptive morality in its content, it expresses an important humanist morality of inclusion and human agency'.[25]

Long's career has also been shaped by another artistic and, arguably, political determinant: the wish to embrace positivity over cynicism. That this was a deeply countercultural approach on the stand-up circuit is evidenced by the comment and criticism that this decision raised. In his 2007 review of *Trying is Good*, the show that became Long's first commercially released DVD, Brian Logan said: 'That's the truism: that comedy thrives on pain, discomfort, failure [...] can you be funny while being unremittingly upbeat?'[26] Logan's assessment is fairly damning. He gives the show a relatively meagre two stars and comments: 'The question is: is it funny? The answer is: sometimes. [...] I heartily welcome any challenge to cynicism in comedy. But, at least on this occasion, Long's combination of relentless positivity and cuteness had me desperate for someone to get hurt.'[27] Long may not have been addressing overtly political topic matter, but the show may be seen as profoundly political and norm-defying in that it addressed fundamental precepts regarding the way we live our lives, and sought to challenge a prevailing 'truism' attached to her chosen form.

At the start of *Kindness and Exuberance,* Long explains the show's title: 'I decided to call the show *Kindness and Exuberance* because, I think, pretty much that's the perfect distillation of how I think you should live your life.'[28] This makes explicit the show's mission of imparting positivity, generosity and enthusiasm. Audiences at the show were given a slip of paper and asked to write or draw their 'favourite small thing'.[29] This began a process of encouraging the audience to buy in to Long's ethos, establishing positivity and enthusiasm as group norms. In the show's Edinburgh run, these were pinned up at the side of the auditorium, creating a literal display of the group's adoption of these ideals. A few minutes in to the show, Long explains why she asked audiences to share their favourite small thing:

> I've kind of fallen in love with asking crowds it, 'coz people come in with a real attitude of like, *"well the thing is you're not even gonna entertain me, so I don't even know why you're bothering"* [small laugh]…

As Long delivers the lines attributed to the representative, stroppy audience member, she crosses her arms in a sullen pose, adopting an aggressive, belligerent tone of voice. However, the imagined audience member soon changes their attitude, smiling and raising their hand in a spirit of overexcitement:

> And then (.) you give 'em that slip of paper and they turn into someone who's like, *"um… I really like drinking water out of sponges!"* [big laugh]… I've got you, weird […] girl, I've got you! [laugh]

Long bounces over to the display of audience members' 'favourite small things', which have been collected across the show's run:

> Right, check this out. Um, this is my favourite one to date. […] Gemma says, 'I like thinking that boys in gangs are holding hands.' [Laugh]… Beautiful![30]

In referring to the favourite small things exercise, Long not only defines the characteristics of the in-group; she also gives shape to a negative reference group. While it is feasible that some audience members would not have been familiar with Long's work before attending *Kindness and Exuberance*, the show's title and publicity clearly advertised its social message and DIY ethos. By choosing to attend this event, the audience are opting in to Long's philosophy. They came primed to accept those present as a positive reference group. Long's discussion of the favourite small things then establishes enthusiasm and positivity as norms for that group.

Long also establishes negative reference points. She begins her show by equating superslick stand-up performances with an aggressive, domineering approach. She explicitly states that she does not aim for this kind of success, preferring the show to be 'a bit creaky'.[31] The cynical, confrontational approach initially adopted by the exemplar audience member, which interprets stand-up as a battle, is not appropriate at Long's gig; that kind of audience serves a negative reference function in this context. Thus Long tells her audience that such behaviour is not appropriate here, and should be avoided. The audience's laughter expresses their acceptance of this premise.

As the show develops, Long makes positive reference to instances of kind and exuberant behaviour. She celebrates the commitment of an imagined individual for whom running an unsuccessful pub quiz with undue enthusiasm is 'their sunshine', and a couple who embody the principle of enjoying small pleasures and excitements in any context by suddenly beginning a game of rock-paper-scissors on the London Underground. By laughing and supporting Long, the audience affirm the attitudes that she is promoting. The group adopts a new norm: that 'kindness and exuberance' should be used as guiding principles for life and behaviour. This may create a powerful reference group effect for each individual.

It should not be assumed that audience members cease to utilize the reference group once the show is over. At performances of *Trying is Good*, Long asked audience members to send in handmade pictures of odd people after the show, celebrating their eccentricity and effort. We know that audience members did respond, as there is a gallery of contributions included on the *Trying is Good* DVD.[32] Participation in this exercise indicates ongoing involvement with the reference group, and hence that the values celebrated in the gig still have some sway over the individual's daily decisions and thought processes. More commonly, comedians gather fan bases or cult followings. As Merton identifies, reference groups can have varying degrees of clarity, formality and unity in their formation, and membership of a group does not necessarily presuppose intense engagement with it.[33] Identifying oneself as a 'fan of', or more simply as someone who 'likes' or 'follows', a comedian like

Long would be a way of expanding both the scope and longevity of the reference group.[34]

When a comedian brings an audience together, they create, cement and instruct a reference group who have a potentially powerful impact on the processes by which future opinions and behaviours are determined. The community and kinship that comes with laughter, allied with the relative homogeneity of most comedy audiences, gives stand-up potency as a method to shape and change attitudes, and to influence behaviours. 'Preaching to the converted' is not a meaningless activity; it is a compelling one.

Opinion change as dissonance-resolution

In the 1950s, Leon Festinger proposed that human beings find contradictory ideas inherently uncomfortable. Thus, if a person is put in a situation where, for example, their behaviour conflicts with their attitudes, or where new information clashes with old preconceptions, they will mobilize mental efforts to achieve consonance: a more comfortable state where ideas work in harmony with one another. Festinger's theory has been evolved and enhanced but never debunked, and cognitive dissonance remains a leading concept describing how and why people change their minds.[35]

Festinger's own experiments demonstrated that 'if a person is induced to act in a manner contradictory to his private belief [...] the person will later tend to bring his private opinion closer to what he has overtly and publically [*sic*] said'.[36] Cooper notes that 'the most direct way to reduce the dissonance is to change your future behaviour to make it consistent with your attitude'.[37] Individuals are driven to act in a way that supports, rather than contradicts, the opinions they have expressed in public. Cooper cites experimental evidence demonstrating that this tendency can be manipulated to cause changes in other people's behaviour.

It seems plausible that such a process might occur for stand-up comedy audiences; indeed, a stand-up comedy gig is potentially an ideal environment in which to subject individuals to this kind of persuasive power. Take, for example, the following gag. This is delivered by Robert Newman in his show *History of Oil*.[38] The performance was filmed in front of a live audience in London, and first broadcast in edited form on British television channel More4 in 2006. The show serves as both entertainment and informative lecture, as Newman attempts to persuade audiences that industrial society faces imminent doom, and that Britain is and has been a much more dastardly player on the world stage than either their school textbooks or current media machine would have them believe. It's a master class in persuasion. He incorporates impressively detailed, factual information, carefully orchestrated into a logical and convincing argument. Along the way, though, there are some pivotal moments in Newman's argument which rely not upon fact and reason, but upon joking logic. At one point, he recalls a sound bite which he heard broadcast repeatedly on Radio 4's flagship *Today* programme: 'The G8 has today endorsed an American plan to bring democracy to the Middle East.'[39]

With the air of a man who cannot believe the audacity of falsehood in what he is hearing, he cries:

> The level of naivety necessary before you can talk about 'an American Plan [small laugh] to bring democracy to the Middle East', you will not find that level of naivety anywhere outside of 1970s porno films [big laugh]... 'Gee Mister, you mean the time machine only works if I take off *all* my clothes?' [laugh][40]

We might reasonably expect Newman's audience to find this gag very palatable: British left-wing audiences of the mid-2000s were highly sceptical about Western, and especially American, motives in the Middle East, so acceptance of his idea does not involve a big ideological sacrifice for them. Yet any audience member who stops to think could easily discern that Newman has not addressed the issue's complexities. Whatever the audience's beliefs or interpretation of events, they would logically have to acknowledge that the notion of '[bringing] democracy to the Middle East' was a pervasive one, reported by many seemingly authoritative sources, and could coexist alongside less idealistic motivations. The issue is complex, and defies tidy, linear interpretation.

Newman's project within this show is to 'put oil centre stage';[41] his argument is founded upon the belief that Western intervention in the Middle East constitutes a set of geopolitical manoeuvres which have been motivated by the wish to acquire economic and strategic advantages for Western nations, not for the benefit of the Middle East's resident populations. The joke is a shortcut which makes this argument without the support of factual information. Indeed, Newman's joke stands in for the facts, constituting the entirety of the evidence offered to support the discounting of a pervasive 'truth'. This relies not upon reason, but upon a comparison between the *Today* programme's announcement and the flimsy plot points of 1970s pornography; an enjoyably cheeky and incongruous link which both Newman and his audience know to be symbolically telling but empirically flawed.[42]

Having publicly agreed with Newman's idea, the audience will be faced with cognitive dissonance when asked to acknowledge that the debate is more complex than Newman's tidy gag suggests. Festinger identified that, for dissonance to resolve itself in a shift of opinion, the individual's inducement to act (i.e. to express support for an opinion they did not really agree with) must be relatively small.[43] Later experimenters added that individuals must also feel that they had some freedom in deciding to act, and that their action could produce some adverse consequence.[44] If, for example, the individual were offered a very large financial reward, acted under threat of violence, or thought that no one would ever find out what they had said, it would be easy for them to justify or excuse their own dishonesty without shifting their opinion. To some extent, the ideas expressed and affirmed in joking are understood to be transitory, and Newman's audience are arguably coerced into agreement by the social pressure to show that they get the joke.[45] However, despite the incentives to laugh, Newman's audience can hardly tell themselves that they were *forced* to express agreement.

Nor can the defence that 'it was only a joke' carry much weight in a show like this one. Newman's reputation and the show's marketing both emphasized the political nature of the interaction, so the audience knew that their attendance and participation was supportive of Newman's political ideology.

Hence the evidence suggests that when these audience members are confronted with the real complexities of the issue, their thinking will have shifted a little closer to Newman's. They have publicly supported his idea; thus they will be motivated to resolve any cognitive dissonance, and lessen their own perception of their own hypocrisy, by shifting their private opinion closer to the one they expressed. The change is small and incremental; but the experimental evidence as produced by Festinger, Cooper and others suggests that it will be real. The rules of joking excuse Newman from the need to be factually accurate, and yet the dodgy, joking logic seems to function as powerfully as a well-evidenced fact.

Lane and Sears describe a simpler model of dissonance-resolution designed particularly for 'influence situations'. This conceives of dissonance as a battle between three sets of cognitions:

> In any influence situation, someone ('the source') is attempting to persuade someone else (the 'influencee' in the audience) to adopt a given position. [...] In a simple influence situation, the influencee has three basic sets of 'cognitions' or 'thoughts': his *evaluation of the source*, his *judgement of the source's position*, and his own *opinion* on the issue.[46]

The influencee's cognitions may easily clash, creating cognitive dissonance. For example, a source that the influencee is predisposed to like may say something that the influencee does not agree with, or vice versa. Equally, a positively evaluated source may deliver a positively evaluated message that contrasts with the individual's own opinion.[47] Lane and Sears state that the dissonance is resolved by altering whichever cognition can most easily be changed.[48] Thus a persuasive message has the greatest chance of achieving the desired effect upon its audience if it comes from a source who is liked or respected, and is itself palatable and well argued. Only under these circumstances is the influencee likely to resolve the dissonance by altering the opinion to accommodate the message.

If a comedian is to influence his audience through stand-up comedy, we have a situation where one speaker (the comedian) delivers a persuasive message to a group of individuals (the audience). If the equivalent situation occurs in a stand-up show, the audience may, of course, choose to resolve the situation by negatively evaluating the comedian. This can and does happen, as in the example of Bruce Devlin, whose reviews on the *Chortle* website in November 2008 contain a mixture of praise and vicious outrage. Devlin is called 'vile' and 'one desperately unfunny and eyebleedingly unpleasant compere', and it may be assumed that writers were not disposed to agree with whatever sentiments Devlin expressed when they saw him perform.[49] However, in a case where the positive feelings towards the leader outweigh any contradictory feelings about what the leader says, the affection or respect that the influencee holds for the leader will bring the influencee into agreement with them. It therefore follows that a leader who is funny and exciting, in a position which usually inspires affection, will find himself at a distinct and important advantage when it comes to exerting influence and persuading an audience.[50] An example of this tendency might be Josie Long, whose charm and indi-cool persona are surely the main reasons why her audience are willing to accept, and even share, her admiration for the rather dull and eccentric career of nineteenth-century Quaker artist Edward Hicks.[51] Long celebrates the fact that, in his whole career, Hicks painted 'a hundred versions' of his *Peaceable Kingdom*, 'and nothing else', for fear that he would become decadent and ungodly. Hicks could easily be dismissed as a 'religious zealot', 'mad', 'stupid' or plain 'boring', but Long manages to establish respect among her audience for his achievements.

Yet the greatest protection for the comedian's status in this situation is perhaps the influencee's tendency to distort the perception of what was said or meant by the leader. We instinctively give jokes immunity;

hence the 'it was only a rumour' of Lane and Sears' example could easily be substituted for the most robust of get-out-clauses: the audience member tells themselves that 'it was only a joke'.[52] This could be seen as a problem for influence: if audience members use distortion to make the comedian's message more palatable then they are not taking the intended message seriously, and are unlikely to be persuaded to adopt it in the long term.[53] From this point of view, distortion is helpful to the comedian as protection from negative evaluation, but not for influence. Yet it is worth remembering what laughter does: whether the laughter signals genuine agreement, misinterpretation or is a deception by the audience members, designed to make themselves appear socially competent, the laughter serves to legitimize the joke's premise among the audience as a whole.[54] This public act of support for the idea presented thus has implications not only for the individual, but also for the other members of the audience.

The diffusion of innovations: Comedian as change agent

In the first of his Radio 4 lectures in his 1998 *Revolution* series, Mark Steel aims to persuade his audience to change their view of the French Revolution.[55] He begins by outlining the problem with the typical British perception:

> On the whole, I don't think we're supposed to like the French Revolution because usually it's portrayed as this period in French history when, for some reason, people just couldn't help guillotining each other. People would just invite round their friends and say:
> (French accent) *'ah, Henri, Marianne, so nice to see you, how are you?'*
> Woosh! [laugh]...
> *'Henri, I'm so sorry, I have guillotined your wife!'* [laugh][56]

Steel explains that this perception is based on the Terror, a vicious and dysfunctional aspect of a revolution which was really about progressive social change. Around twenty minutes into the show, he comes to explaining the changes that occurred during the Jacobins' first year in charge. This was 'the most radical year of the Revolution'[57]:

> Spurred on by all that had happened, the Jacobins imposed a maximum price for bread; plans were made for the first ever welfare state; payments were made to the relatives of injured soldiers; a national plan was drawn up for comprehensive education; and as far as I know Robespierre was not caught sending his own son to a selective school in Hammersmith [laugh]

Steel's list of Jacobin reforms paints a picture of a progressive society; these are measures which provide security and education to the poor, and are likely to appeal to a broadly leftist, 1998 audience who themselves grew up with a welfare state. Indeed, the comparison of Robespierre to the audience's Prime Minister, Tony Blair – who had claimed to prioritize the comprehensive education system but chose not to put his own child in to it – suggests that the Jacobins were more genuinely progressive than the audience's own government.

On the whole, Steel's audience is unlikely to demonstrate much reactance against the change in opinion that he suggests. The idea that the French Revolution represents violent mass murder is pervasive and has emotive implications, but the audience's commitment to that opinion is unlikely to be intense. The horror of the events is dulled by their distance in time, and the opinion is unlikely to be one of the 'pattern of stereotypes' which Lippmann sees as an important 'guarantee' of our sense of self and our place in the world.[58]

Steel does face a substantial challenge, however. His argument relies upon understanding the humanity of the historical persons he talks about. The distance of time and popular myth-making that separates Steel's audience from the personalities involved makes that humanity relatively inaccessible. Robert Newman faces a related problem in his *History of Oil*. He is dealing with recent and current events, but is addressing aspects of them which are, as he says, 'off the spectrum' of mainstream thought.[59]

The difficulty lies in translating historical data into a story that the audience can relate to. Lippmann defines the problem:

> We cannot be much interested in, or much moved by, the things we do not see. Of public affairs each of us sees very little, and therefore, they remain dull and unappetizing, until somebody, with the makings of an artist, has translated them into a moving picture. [...] Not being omnipresent and omiscient [*sic*] we cannot see much of what we have to think and talk about. Being flesh and blood we will not feed on words and names and gray theory. Being artists of a sort we paint pictures, stage dramas and draw cartoons out of the abstractions.
>
> Or, if possible, we find gifted men who can visualize for us.[60]

Both Steel and Newman meet this need by translating their dense material into structures that their audiences can relate to, translating the 'gray theory' into vivid pictures which allow their audiences to completely understand the information offered.

In order to translate dry, historical information into material that the audience can vividly picture, Steel draws several comparisons between events in the French Revolution and their imagined equivalents in Britain in 1998. Steel tells his audience that King Louis XVI was forced to wear the Cap of Liberty, a symbol of the revolution, as he travelled from his palace at Versailles to Paris. In itself, this is a fairly dry fact which does not encourage the audience to make the imaginative leap necessary to understand the depth of humiliation and absurdity that Louis would have experienced. In order to communicate this, Steel translates Louis' predicament into a picture that the audience can more readily understand, using a high-profile Conservative politician:

> The King was eventually taken back to Paris and made to wear the Cap of Liberty *en route* (.) Which would be like making Michael Heseltine walk from Henley to Westminster selling copies of *Socialist Worker* [laugh]

By translating the experience of King Louis XVI across to a contemporary equivalent, Steel is able to bridge the gap of two centuries and give his audience a vivid picture of the experience of a key player in this historical event. That the audience now engage with the full implications of this concept is illustrated by their somewhat derisive laugh, which expresses satisfaction at the idea of inflicting so pitiless an incongruity upon an individual.

Steel uses this technique to emphasize that the figures who drove the revolution were real people, driven by similar motivations and as prone to mistakes as the modern-day audience. Explaining Louis XVI's unwise trampling of the Cap of Liberty at a party as a drunken misdemeanour, Steel imagines a universally recognizable scene: 'The brilliant thing is, the next morning he must've woken up on the floor and gone, "*(groan)* there's the Cap o' Liberty, oh I never did I?" [laugh].'[61] Steel also emphasizes the humanity of the mass of French people. He explains that the representatives of the Third Estate, having declared themselves to be the French Parliament, called a mass meeting to ask that each district provide two hundred men to fight in a revolutionary army:

> In truth, this meeting was probably as chaotic as any mass meeting. There'll have been some people going, 'well maybe if we just talk to the King politely', and there'll have been some getting over-enthusiastic and going:
>
> *(Cockney) 'ere, my brother, 'es a builder – maybe 'e can knock us up a castle'* [laugh]
>
> And then some hippy going:
>
> *(Droning) 'I'm no good at fighting but I can play the flute'* [laugh].

By importing language and reasoning that the audience recognize from their own time on to the revolutionaries, Steel translates the dry history into a story about real people with whom his audience can empathize.

Robert Newman similarly acts as a bridge between the dense theory upon which he draws and the audience's prior experience. Having established that 'bringing democracy to the Middle East' is not a credible explanation for the motivations behind the Iraq war, he presents his 'Euro-Dollar' theory as one of the genuine reasons for the conflict. The Euro-Dollar theory states that the war was a 'very public punishment beating' which attempted to prevent other nations from following Iraq, Iran and North Korea in trading their oil in euros rather than US dollars. Such a decision would have meant that the billions of dollars that were safely tied up in oil trading would have been released and the value of the dollar would collapse; thus the 'beating' of Iraq was a way for the United States to demonstrate its strength and threaten similar aggression against any other nation which tried to damage its interests.

In order to fully and clearly explain his Euro-Dollar theory, Newman needs his non-expert audience to understand the laws of economics which make the US dollars harmless while tied up in oil transactions and destructive when released. He must also help his audience to visualize so large and far-reaching an event as a war as a straightforward 'punishment beating'. Newman begins by describing the dollar as used in oil trade as a 'magic chequebook'. He illustrates this by reference to Salvador Dali's practice of drawing sketches on the back of his cheques: with so valuable a piece of art upon it, the cheque, although legitimate, would never be cashed and so Dali would never have to pay for the extravagant habits in which he indulged. The release of the US dollar, Newman explains, is equivalent to all Dali's cheques being cashed at once. Newman makes the example vivid, playing the character of Dali and, in the version edited for television, including a sketch in which we see Dali write out his cheque, draw on the back of it, and look at the camera with a cunning smile as the restaurant owner says, 'Signor Dali! You do me a great honour! A signed original from the Maestro? I will never cash this cheque!' A canny laugh from the audience illustrates that they follow the logic.

The idea of the Iraq war as a punishment beating is made similarly vivid. Newman acts out a metaphorical tale in which the world is a Bronx housing project and the United States is 'the number-one crack dealer' and local bully, trying to keep control of other nations and quash dissent. Iraq is violently beaten by America and Britain for continuing to sell crack, as an example to others who may be tempted to challenge their authority. Venezuela looks on, disparagingly teasing America, no longer impressed or threatened by his power: America is growing increasingly desperate. Like Steel, Newman acts as a bridge between the audience's understanding and a theory that they may find inaccessible owing to lack of interest or expertise.

Everett M. Rogers analyses the successful spread of new ideas as the 'diffusion of innovations'. An innovation may be 'an idea, practice or object'.[62] In Steel's case, the innovation is mainly an attitude: the item that he is trying to disseminate is a more positive or balanced view of the French Revolution. For Newman, we could see a better understanding of history and the current situation as the intended innovation. More importantly, however, the *History of Oil* show seeks to urge a change in behaviour: Newman wants the audience to adopt the innovation of action to rectify the fuel and climate crises.

Rogers identifies that many innovations spread with the assistance of 'change agents'; 'an individual who influences clients' innovation-decisions in a direction deemed desirable to a change agency'.[63] Relationships between change agents and their 'clients' vary, but the purpose of the change agent is broadly to facilitate the process of diffusion on the popular level. Successful change agents are usually those who work in a client-centred way; they use empathy, understanding the factors that may cause barriers to adoption of the innovation as well as those that may motivate the client to adopt. They are more likely to be successful if they are fairly homogenous with their client group, and particularly if the client group do not perceive that the change agent has an ulterior motive for persuading them to adopt the innovation. Indeed, change agents may work alongside 'aides' who are more homogenous with the client group because they have no formal relationship to the innovation, or have a comparative lack of expertise. Aides 'have the special advantage of *safety credibility,* the degree to which a communication source or channel is perceived as trustworthy. Because an aide is perceived as a near peer by clients, they are not likely to suspect the aide of having selfish motives or manipulative intentions.'[64]

Although Rogers' language is perhaps more appropriate to the diffusion of technologies, where a 'change agent' could be a direct employee of a government or corporation which wishes to promote the use of a specific product, he states that the theory is equally applicable to the diffusion of attitudes. He cites teachers, as well as consultants, public health workers and salespeople, as change agents.[65] Comedians may also work in this way. For Steel and Newman, the change agency is unlikely to be a cohesive group but is rather a body of ideologically charged political opinion. Steel and Newman each perform all of the roles which Rogers cites as the function of a change agent.[66] They identify the difficulties that their audiences ('clients' in Rogers' terms) face in adopting the innovations, and offer solutions. They make their audiences aware that they need the innovation, and develop a relationship with the audience which allows them to persuade the audience to adopt the innovation. Like commercial change agents, the comedians aim to 'stabilize' the audience's adoption and 'achieve a terminal relationship', meaning that they hope that the audience will adopt the innovation in the long term, and that the innovation will continue to influence the audience once contact with the comedian has ceased.

The fact that Steel and Newman operate as stand-up comedians allows them to combine many of the characteristics of successful change agents. The audience know that the comedian is trying to persuade them towards his own point of view, but the audience rightly assume that he is motivated by conviction and not by personal gain (as might be the case if the change agent were a salesman working on commission, for example). The relationship is founded on informality and, as has been noted, relative homogeneity: audiences opt to see comedians whom they feel represent them. Although neither Steel nor Newman advertises any particular professional credential qualifying them as an expert on their topic, the use of dense factual information and an authoritative persona indicates that they have amassed significant knowledge relating to their chosen topics: they demonstrate that they know what they are talking about. The comedian is well placed to act as a good change agent or, perhaps, aide. As Rogers states, 'An ideal change agent would have a balance of competence and safety credibility.'[67]

By seeing the role of political comedian as that of change agent, we discover the importance of the comedian's role in galvanizing social change: performing in an accessible and popular medium they diffuse their particular political ideals. As we saw in the previous chapter, such innovative views do not operate in a vacuum, but rather form the 'balance': the existence of that which operates outside of the mainstream viewpoint is an important check and counterweight which broadens and enlivens social negotiation. As Rogers shows, the diffusion of innovations is also a necessary and decisive part of behavioural change. Recognition of the comedian as change agent is one way in which we might begin to articulate the place of stand-up in the development of genuine, concrete social changes.

What is the practical impact?

Discussion of stand-up comedy is littered with small examples of behavioural change that are credited to the intervention of an individual comedian. Mark Watson states that he once spent a large part of a performance ranting about L'Oreal, and was proud when he received an email from an audience member saying that they had ceased purchasing L'Oreal skin creams as a result.[68] In an interview for the DVD extras released with her show *The Good Life*, Lucy Porter is asked whether her show has 'worked'. Porter responds in upbeat tones: 'Yeah, I've had a bit of feedback from people saying that they have, er, embraced environmentalism, vegetarianism and, er, clean living... which is quite ironic, 'cause I haven't.'[69] Evidence of such behavioural changes, reflective as it is of private habits among a disparate group of people, is necessarily anecdotal. Yet it is evidence that stand-up can cause audience members to change their behaviour.

However, the anecdotal evidence suggests that behaviour changes are likely to be a modest part of stand-up's impact. They point to actions by isolated individuals which, although impressive in themselves as indicating real impact, are unlikely to change the world in themselves. Yet these sorts of specific, personal behavioural changes are only one form of impact. If, as has been argued, stand-up is in a strong position to shape individual opinion, it is productive to examine what this might mean for public opinion at large.

In 1995, Radio 4 series *The Mark Steel Solution* put forward the ludicrous idea that 'everyone should have to be gay for two years'.[70] The show proposed that such a decree would make people more comfortable with their sexuality and increase freedom by eliminating homophobia. Steel contributes to the current debate by deconstructing stereotypes about homosexuality and highlighting the ridiculousness of homophobic attitudes (characterizations in italics):

> And then there's this paranoia that people have:
>
> *(Cockney wide-boy) 'ere, here's that poof. Watch yourself!'*
>
> Like, do these people honestly think that if they're not careful this gay bloke's gonna come in the pub and think, 'ooh, good, they're off their guard, I'll 'av the lot o' them' [big laugh]…Just because someone's gay doesn't mean they want to have sex with *you*, ya slob! [laugh]… These blokes must think that gay men are like a sexual version of the Terminator, an unstoppable force:
>
> *(Arnold Schwarzenegger) 'Gender (.) Male (.) Mission (.) Have sex (.) Hasta la vista Duckie!'* [laugh][71]

The audience's laughter signifies that they recognize such homophobic attitudes as something they genuinely encounter. The 1980s had seen an atmosphere of overt homophobia, typified by the linking of AIDS paranoia to homosexuality and open declarations by Manchester's Police Chief James Anderton that homosexuality should be criminalized.[72] In 1995, the same year that Steel's show was first broadcast, the Appeal Court refused to view the dismissal of four servicemen on the grounds of homosexuality as unlawful. *The Daily Mail* ran an article stating that the government had indicated that the ban would 'never' be lifted, quoting the then defence minister, Nicholas Soames, as saying:

> We are absolutely delighted. The Armed Forces do not go along with politically correct claptrap. Homosexuality and its practices are simply not compatible with service life and that policy has now been vindicated by two courts in Britain.[73]

The ban was finally lifted in 2000. Comments attributed to the judges who heard the case suggests that attitudes were changing even by 1995: 'The judges rejected accusations that the policy was "absurd, outrageous, perverse and impossible to justify," although one did say it was "ripe for reconsideration." '[74] That the ban was upheld by the legislature, but considered 'ripe for reconsideration', gives a picture of Britain c.1995 as a society evolving from a dominant attitude of homophobia towards a greater degree of acceptance. Attitudes towards this issue were evidently in flux for Steel's 1995 audience.

Steel begins his show by summarizing the awkwardness and difficulty that surround sexuality, highlighting the need for change. He then announces:

> So, what's needed is a whole new approach to sexuality that would make everybody content with the way they are, which is why tonight's solution is: *(fanfare)* that everyone should have to be gay for two years.[75]

From the moment that Steel announces his 'solution', it is clear that the audience are on side. Although the announcement is delivered without excitement, Steel's matter-of-fact tone upholding the premise that the ludicrous solution is intended as a serious suggestion, it is greeted with an immediate, loud, surprised laugh, followed by applause and cheering which lasts for a full seven seconds. This is, perhaps, not surprising. It is likely that the majority of the live audience are familiar with some of Steel's previous work and have chosen to come to his show specifically to see him; they are likely to be in agreement with his world view, and his liberal attitudes towards sexuality. We might certainly expect the majority of people who knew that they were unlikely to agree with Steel to avoid the performance, both live and on the radio.

Yet, even if we take the view that Steel's broadcast is aimed at like-minded people, this does not preclude it from constituting important debate. Twenty years on, it is clear that social attitudes towards homosexuality have progressed somewhat since the original broadcast of this show in 1995. In 2000, the age of consent for gay sex was lowered from eighteen to sixteen, bringing it into line with the heterosexual equivalent. In 2002, the government repealed Section 28, which had prevented schools from 'promoting' homosexuality.[76] In 2004, Civil Partnerships were introduced in order to make the rights available to married, heterosexual couples available to same-sex couples, followed ten years later by same-sex marriage in England and Wales, then in Scotland. This is not to say that homophobia has been eradicated, but British social norms have certainly evolved.

Steel's show did not orchestrate debate between differing factions in his audience, but was part of a debate on a wider social scale that was building towards a change in norms and attitudes that culminated in the changes in legislation listed above. In the performance of Mark Steel, and his colleagues across the alternative comedy scene, a developing norm found a voice. Supporters of that developing norm were brought together and bolstered, individuals were pushed to adopt the new reference point, and the attitude was affirmed. Slowly, incrementally, that norm became prevalent. Of course, neither Steel's show nor the efforts of alternative comedy at large are the sole reason for progression in attitudes, but there surely would have been no change in social attitudes without forums in which that norm could develop. The comedy gig fills a particular niche in this respect. It is a popular form which is licensed to test attitudes and has particular strengths in persuading its audience to shift their reference points.

To take this wide view could perhaps feel less satisfying than the idealistic notion that a single gig might convert the masses. Yet the fact that the process takes time, and that it is widespread and democratic, does not make the result any less real. The contribution of any one gig, or any one comedian, may be subtle and incremental but this is not the same as being trivial. Stand-up not only shapes individual opinions, it shapes public opinion too. This is impact, and it is important.

Can Stand-up Change the World?

Joking's influence

Many comedians are cautious about the idea that their material has an ongoing effect. Joe Wilkinson states that stand-up is no more likely to lead to the adoption of a new idea than is participation in any conversation where the individual is exposed to new information.[1] Dan Atkinson emphasizes that stand-up is intended as entertainment, stating that, although stand-up may produce other valuable effects, 'you're there to entertain people, and that's the job'.[2] Even Mark Thomas, the master of efficacious stand-up, agrees that many comedians fail in this area:

> There is this thing that people say 'oh comedy can't change anything'. And I just think, well […] the thing is, it sounds terribly egotistical but I just think, 'well your comedy can't.'[3]

However, stand-up can contribute to real, concrete change. Speaking in 2008, Thomas is able to pinpoint several examples effected by himself and his associates:

> You know, that you can look at conditionally exempt works of art which I did, like, three programmes on and they changed the law on, you can look at Nestlé product stuff that they changed the packaging stuff on, you can look at the Illisu Dam which we collapsed the British end of the deal, you can look at the stuff we're getting through at the moment which is on the back of the arms trade stuff where they're looking at changing laws [in response to] stuff that we mooted. […][4]

Thomas' achievements are impressive, and are evidence of comedy's potential to produce real and significant change. It is important to note, however, that it is not only stand-up but the whole body of Thomas' work that has had this influence. The protests and the pranks, and the links with official campaign groups, are vital to his efficacy: although his activism tends to take the form of comedy, he does not operate solely through stand-up.

Thomas is, furthermore, a special case. The contribution that most comedians make to social change is, perhaps, more ethereal. In the last chapter, I argued that pieces of political stand-up, such as Josie Long's *Kindness and Exuberance*, Robert Newman's *History of Oil* and Mark Steel's radio programmes 'The French Revolution' and 'Sexuality', have made an influential contribution to the renegotiation of opinions and attitudes, and thus of societal norms. The remaining difficulty is that such effects are not unique to stand-up. Many of the manipulative techniques which have been identified are available to other types of communication. This begs the question of whether stand-up really has any special powers of manipulation or influence.

Christie Davies makes the case against the efficacy of joking as influence:

> Jokes are both very important and very unimportant [...] Jokes are important because they are one of the few independent items of popular culture that exist. They are created by the people for the people and they are of the people. [...] Jokes are intensely pleasurable. [...] Yet jokes are also unimportant. They have no significant material consequences. Vigorous political rhetoric, a stirring sermon, a persuasive advertisement, a well-placed lie, a piece of malicious gossip are all uses of words that are infinitely more powerful than jokes. When jokes are used in the pursuit of particular ends they are merely ancillary. They are added to the main message to make it more interesting, appealing and entertaining; they do not achieve anything that could not be attained in other non-humorous ways. Wit is not a weapon; it is merely the artistic decoration on the scabbard. Jokes are neither tiny revolutions nor an important safety valve for keeping the discontented passive. Jokes are not important.[5]

Davies claims that professional comedians and scriptwriters are part of this process, for they are 'dependent on collecting and massaging jokes that are already in circulation.'[6] According to Davies, therefore, comedians may serve an important function by utilizing a tool which grants us freedom (although he implies that it is in the hands of the lay joker that jokes truly perform their most liberating function as 'independent items of popular culture'), but joking is an inappropriate medium for influence. Davies gives two main reasons for this: first, joking is less effective at persuasion than other mediums of communication and, secondly, jokes are merely the 'decoration' upon a proper argument and do not, themselves, carry influential messages.

On the DVD recording of his show *41st Best Stand-up Ever*, Stewart Lee delivers the following routine in defence of political correctness:

> Now one hesitates, in the current climate, to make a joke on stage about the Muslims, right. Not for fear of religious reprisals, right – when's that ever hurt anyone? [laugh, one person claps] – but… but because of a slightly more slippery anxiety, which is, like, basically, when you do like, stand-up in a small room it's like er, we're all friends – hooray – and we can make a joke but you don't really know – you don't really know how a joke's received and it could be that it's laughed at enthusiastically in a way that you don't understand and particularly *(Lee turns to face one of the cameras at his side and points towards it)* out there – you don't know who's watching in television. I mean, if it's *(Lee turns to face the live audience)* on telly on Paramount, probably someone horrible, an idiot [big laugh]… erm… *(turns to camera)* The kind of person who's awake at (.) five in the morning. *(turns to live audience)* Who [laugh] knows what. […] The problem is, eighty-four percent of people, apparently, of the public, think that political correctness has gone mad. Now, [some giggles] erm, I don't know if it has, people still get killed, don't they, for being the wrong colour or the wrong sexuality or whatever. And what is political correctness? It's a – it's an often clumsy negotiation towards a kind of formally-inclusive language, and there's, there's all sorts of problems with it, but it's better than what we had before…But eighty-four percent of people think political correctness has gone mad, and you don't want one of those people coming up to you after the gig and going, 'Well done mate' (.) er, 'Well done, actually, for having a go at

the fucking Muslims' [laugh]… 'Well done, mate. You know, you can't do anything in this country anymore, mate. It's political correctness gone mad. D'y'know, you can't even write racial abuse in excrement on someone's car' [big laugh]… 'without the politically correct brigade' [laugh]… 'jumping down your throat'.[7]

Lee demonstrates that he is aware of the potential for his jokes to be interpreted in a way that he did not intend, and that this matters to him. He states that he is anxious about the possibility that such jokes could be misinterpreted as attacks; that is to say that he is worried that the jokes' content could do damage. Lee does not explain why this result should be considered damaging: he sees inherent harm in spreading racial abuse and in encouraging others to hold such views. Surely this is a legitimate concern in and of itself. If further justification were needed for Lee's squeamishness, then this may be found in the ability of racist humour to form and cement societal prejudices. As we have seen, the process of laughing at a comedian's joke – of expressing enjoyment and approval in a public forum – endorses its inherent ideologies and exercises peer pressure. If someone misinterprets Lee's humour as genuinely anti-Islamic, then Lee may be unintentionally responsible for validating and spreading an ideology that he finds harmful.

The climax of this routine is the gag in which Lee impersonates a hypothetical, racist audience member saying, 'D'y'know, you can't even write racial abuse in excrement on someone's car…'. This joke is used 'in the pursuit of particular ends'. Lee aims to provide a counterargument to the claim that 'political correctness has gone mad' and to demonstrate that, for all its clumsiness, political correctness is 'better than what we had before'. Of course, these points could be communicated through means other than joking. Indeed, in the section transcribed above, Lee builds up to the final set of jokes by putting forward his argument as a statement of opinion without jest or irony, creating a comparatively long section which has no gags at all but in which the point is conveyed. Davies is clearly correct in saying that other 'uses of words' could serve the purpose.

Davies is, however, wrong in claiming that such alternative methods would be 'infinitely more powerful'. When Lee ironically bemoans the fact that 'you can't even write in excrement on someone's car' he provides a vivid and concise summary of the problems with anti-PC attitudes. The laughter of the audience confirms the validity of Lee's point for the assembled group. This makes the point for the audience who witness Lee's delivery of the gag, and also provides them with a way of spreading the idea further afield. As Davies himself notes, people enjoy jokes and they like to pass them on. Lee's joke provides each audience member with a handy package that they can use to argue this point in future.

The joke is not 'merely ancillary' to the argument. The build-up explains Lee's point, but it is within the joke itself that his point is expertly crystallized into a deft statement with all the advantages for persuasion mentioned above. Contained within the joking statement is a complex set of points that support Lee's argument. In that one, concise phrase, Lee connects anti-PC attitudes to vicious racist action, questions the practical motivations of people who deny the importance of being inclusive and kind with their language and shows how spuriously the accusation of 'political correctness gone mad' has been applied. If comic licence was not in force to protect Lee's statement from accusations of inaccuracy, the link between racist acts and the rejection of political correctness would be too tenuous for the statement to be taken on board; they are not the same thing, and it is only the unacceptability of attacking jokes on the grounds of inaccuracy that prevents this from becoming a salient issue. Similarly, comic licence allows the audience to focus on the point itself, rather than practical concern for the potential victim of the racist act, or anger towards its perpetrator.[8] It would be difficult to make such a statement appear acceptable outside of a joking context.

Lee's joke does not decorate the message: it is the message. The joke form does not make the message less powerful, but rather brings advantages in terms of influence. Joking makes the point vividly and forcefully, while also providing the opportunity both for the audience as reference group to approve the message, and for individual influencees to package it up and pass it on.

The importance of ethereal changes

This book has argued that all comedians participate in a process which challenges and renegotiates societal norms, whether or not they, themselves, intend or acknowledge it. Stand-up plays its part in determining attitudes towards subjects drawn from all levels of human experience – we have seen examples of material on climate change, revolution, terrorism, homosexuality, abortion, body image, frogs and the inefficiency of the home shower. Through live performance, television, commercial recording and the internet, stand-up participates in the process of renegotiating these norms for millions of people every day. These negotiations are not merely meaningless theoretical exercises, but have a genuine effect on the concrete world. As Walter Lippmann notes, our thoughts, feelings and actions 'operate not in the pseudo-environment where the behaviour is stimulated, but in the real environment where action eventuates'[9]: although such a process may appear ethereal, the conclusions offered by these negotiations guide our actions. In this important sense, stand-up does indeed play its part in changing the world. As Mark Thomas has stated, 'Change occurs all the time. It's about whether you can shape or change or influence its direction.'[10]

Stand-up combines genuine challenge with a relaxed approach to the concern for truth and a relaxation of everyday standards of decency. This delightfully irresponsible combination both allows the opportunity for nasty ideas to slip past our usual constraints, to be released and enjoyed, and broadens the scope for debate beyond the confines of 'normal' viewpoints in a way that has been helpful to the progression of societal attitudes. As discussed in Part 2, stand-up has developed mechanisms that enhance this freedom by ensuring that all elements of the event, including the venue, the delivery of the material and the persona through which it is presented, are skilfully arranged to manipulate the audience into laughing. Stand-up creates a playground, in Huizinga's sense, both physically and ideologically, which operates in accordance with joking's rules of challenge and negotiation. This is both a force for societal good and a potential source of harm. If we are too ready to excuse the validation of nasty ideas with reference to comic licence – to say 'but it was only a joke' – then we risk allowing harmful ideas to reproduce and perpetuate. This is not to say that we should ruin our experience of comedy by over-analysing every joke before laughing at it – such an approach would clearly ruin the form and produce no helpful impact – but it is to say that we should approach joking with the understanding that it does have significance. We are generally willing to admit that a critical approach to other kinds of discourse is useful and necessary; we must be willing to extend the same respect and awareness of our own responsibility to stand-up.

This book has demonstrated that stand-up is well placed to have a long-term effect on attitudes and opinions. I have shown that stand-up performs an important function in representing marginal views, and is an ideal medium in which to conduct debate and negotiation. I have also demonstrated that joking is not incompatible with 'serious' opinion change, but is rather an example of the very type of interaction most likely to have a lasting influence. Davies states that joking cannot function as anything more than the decoration on a solid argument: I argue that the joke itself has the power to make the argument forcefully, memorably and downright sneakily. Mark Thomas knows from experience how important stand-up comedy is as a platform for negotiation and influence:

> The point is actually jokes do create change. Comedy clubs and toilet walls (often they are perilously close in proximity) are two of the few places where freedom of speech [exists]. Prime Ministers can control MPs, enquiries, appointments and patronage of power – just

as the press can control the agenda for news. BUT the one area they cannot control is a stand up gig. […]

So actually we have a huge amount of power if [we] choose to use it. […]

We can be cheerleaders for change and we can confront taboos, comedy naturally lends itself to that. Culturally we can inflict (and I use the word carefully) huge change.[11]

Endnotes

Introduction

1 *The Paperback Oxford English Dictionary*, edited by Catherine Soanes, 6th edn (Oxford: Oxford University Press, 2006). [My emphasis].

2 Stewart Lee, Interview, The Leicester Square Theatre, London, 16 December 2009.

3 Josie Long, 'Kindness and Exuberance', in Josie Long, *Trying is Good. Real Talent*. 2008. DVD.

4 I am focusing on jokes told verbally, here, but the same principle applies to jokes that are written down. In these instances the hearer – or reader – utilizes the context in which the joke is presented to frame the gag, and this process is equivalent to the performance of the joke. A Christmas cracker, for example, sets up a specific frame of reference for the joke it contains, as well as expectations about the joke's quality.

5 M. Douglas, 'Jokes', in M. Douglas, *Implicit Meanings: Selected Essays in Anthropology*, 2nd edn (London: Routledge, 1999), pp. 146–64.

6 O. Double, *Stand-Up!: On Being a Comedian* (London: Methuen, 1997).

7 Dan Atkinson, Interview, by telephone, 29 September 2008.

8 See, for example, J. Carr and L. Greeves, *The Naked Jape* (London: Penguin, 2007), p. 113.

9 Jason Byrne, *The Jason Byrne Show*, BBC Radio 2, Episode 2, 19 July 2008. Radio broadcast. Robert Newman, *History of Oil*, Tiger Aspect Productions. 2006. DVD.

Chapter 1

1 O. Double, *Getting the Joke: The Inner Workings of Stand-up Comedy*, 1st edn (London: Methuen, 2005), p. 106.

2 Double, *Stand-Up*, p. 5.

3 Tony Allen, quoted in D. Brazil, 'How to Talk Dirty and Get Arrested', *The Leveller*, December 1979, p. 14.

4 Jack Dee, *Jack Dee Live*. WEA International/ Channel 4 Television. 1992. DVD.

5 S. Lockyer and M. Pickering, eds, *Beyond a Joke: The Limits of Humour* (Basingstoke: Palgrave, 2005), p. 3.

6 K. Lash, 'A Theory of the Comic as Insight', *The Journal of Philosophy* 45 (1948): 113–21 (p. 113).

7 W. F. Wertheim, *East-West Parallels: Sociological Approaches to Modern Asia* (The Hauge: W. Van Hoeve, 1964), p. 26.

8 A. C. Zijderveld, 'Jokes and their Relation to Social Reality', *Social Research* 36 (1968): 286–311 (p. 311).

9 Douglas, 'Jokes', p. 155; p.152.

10 Ibid.

11 A. Schopenhauer, 'The World as Will and Idea', in *The Philosophy of Laughter and Humor*, edited by J. Morreall (New York: State University of New York Press, 1987), pp. 51–64 (pp. 52–3).

12 Ibid., p. 53.

13 Ibid., p. 62.

14 L. E. Mintz, 'Standup Comedy as Social and Cultural Mediation', *Amercian Quarterly* 37 (1985): 71–80 (p. 77).

15 S. Freud, *Jokes and their Relation to the Unconscious* (London: Routledge & Kegan Paul, 1960), p. 90.

16 Ibid., p. 96.

17 Tim Vine, *Live at the Apollo* (BBC), *YouTube*, http://www.youtube.com/watch?v=VPaZfeAYUyk [accessed 20 April 2010].

18 J. Morreall, 'Humour and the Conduct of Politics', in *Beyond a Joke: The Limits of Humour* (see Lockyer and Pickering, above), pp. 63–78 (pp. 65–8).

19 T. Hobbes, 'Human Nature', in *The Philosophy of Laughter and Humor* (see Schopenhauer, above), pp. 19–20 (p. 20).

20 J. Morreall, ed., *The Philosophy of Laughter and Humor* (see Schopenhauer, above), p. 6.

21 H. Spencer, 'The Physiology of Laughter', in *The Philosophy of Laughter and Humor* (see Schopenhauer, above), pp. 99–110.

22 Freud, *Jokes and their Relation to the Unconscious*.

23 Ibid., pp. 118–19.

24 Ventriloquism presents a similar situation to stand-up comedy. Like stand-up, Dunham's ventriloquist act involves a solo performer addressing an audience directly with the intention of making them laugh. This is in line with Oliver Double's first definition of stand-up comedy (Double, *Stand-up*, pp. 4–5); his later definition, which states that the comedian communicates with his audience through 'personality' and 'direct communication', and in the 'present tense', may also be applied to ventriloquism (Double, *Getting the Joke*, 1st edn, pp. 18–19). Indeed, ventriloquism could be claimed as a sub-genre of stand-up, if we view the puppet merely as a device through which a stand-up comedian works. Either way, what may be learnt from this example is applicable to stand-up.

25 Jeff Dunham, *YouTube*, http://www.youtube.com/ watch?v=1uwOL4rB-go [accessed 21 April 2010].

26 'Comments on Jeff Dunham Video', *YouTube*, http://www.youtube.com/ watch?v=1uwOL4rB-go [accessed 21 April 2010].

27 B. Logan, 'Laughing in the face of terror?', *Chortle*, 3 April 2009, http:// www.chortle.co.uk/interviews/2009/04/03/8675/laughing_in_the_face_ of_terror%3F [accessed 17 June 2009].

28 Ibid.

29 Spencer, 'The Physiology of Laughter', pp. 106–7.

30 Freud, *Jokes and their Relation to the Unconscious*.

31 G. W. Allport, *The Nature of Prejudice*, 25th Anniversary edn (Cambridge, MA: Addison-Wesley Publishing Company, 1954), p. 8.

32 Logan, 'Laughing in the face of terror?'.

33 S. Critchley, *On Humour* (London: Routledge, 2002), p. 1.

34 A. C. Zijderveld, 'Jokes and their Relation to Social Reality', *Social Research* 36 (1968): 286–311 (p. 290).

35 Zijderveld, 'Jokes and their Relation to Social Reality', p. 301.

36 Mark Thomas, *The Night War Broke Out*. Laughing Stock. 2004. CD.

37 Zijderveld, 'Jokes and their Relation to Social Reality', p. 290.

38 Isy Suttie, Interview, by email, 7 October 2008.

39 Critchley, *On Humour*, p. 11.
40 Eddie Izzard, *Glorious*. Ella Communications. 1997. VHS.
41 Isy Suttie, Interview.
42 Mintz, 'Standup Comedy as Social and Cultural Mediation', p. 77.
43 Dan Atkinson, Interview.
44 Lash, 'A Theory of the Comic as Insight', p. 119.
45 Josie Long, *Trying is Good*. Real Talent. 2008. DVD.
46 S. Freud, 'Humour', in *Freud: Collected Papers*, edited by J. Strachey, 5 vols (London: Hogarth Press, 1957), v, pp. 215–21 (p. 217).
47 Lash, 'A Theory of the Comic as Insight', p. 117.
48 Ibid., pp. 119–20. [Lash's italics].
49 P. Brooker, 'Key Words in Brecht's Theory and Practice of Theatre', in *The Cambridge Companion to Brecht*, edited by P. Thomson and G. Sacks (Cambridge: Cambridge University Press, 1994), pp. 185–200 (p. 191).
50 *Brecht on Theatre: The Development of an Aesthetic*, edited by J. Willett (London: Methuen, 2001), pp. 143–4.
51 Ibid., p. 125.

Chapter 2

1 S. Linstead, 'Jokers Wild: The Importance of Humour in the Maintenance of Organisational Culture', *Sociological Review* 33 (1985): 741–67 (p. 761).
2 Stewart Lee, Interview.
3 Ibid.
4 Richard Herring, Interview, by telephone, 9 March 2009.
5 Morreall, 'Humour and the Conduct of Politics', p. 70.
6 Ibid.
7 Ibid.
8 Critchley, *On Humour*, p. 88.
9 Eddie Izzard, *Definite Article*. Universal. 1996. VHS.
10 Stewart Lee, *90s Comedian*.
11 Double, *Getting the Joke*, 1st edn, pp. 136–7.
12 Ibid., p. 97.

13   T. Allen, *Attitude: Wanna Make Something of It?: The Secret of Stand-up Comedy* (Glastonbury: Gothic Image Publications, 2002), p. 28.

14   Dan Atkinson, Interview.

15   Rhod Gilbert, *Who's Eaten Gilbert's Grape*, Gulbenkian Theatre, Canterbury, 2 November 2007, 7:45pm.

16   Rhod Gilbert, *Rhod Gilbert and the Award-Winning Mince Pie*. Channel 4 DVD. 2009. DVD.

17   M. Burgess, 'Gilbert's Grape Expectations', *Manchester Evening News*, 25 January 2008.

18   Joe Wilkinson, Interview, by telephone, 29 September 2008.

19   Ibid.

20   Ibid.

21   Mark Thomas, *Dambusters: Live 2001 Tour*. Laughing Stock Productions. 2003. CD.

22   M. Thomas and YWGAV Limited, *Mark Thomas Info*, http://markthomasinfo.com [accessed 6 August 2009].

23   Mark Thomas, Interview, The Gulbenkian Theatre, Canterbury, 4 October 2008.

24   Ibid. [Thomas' emphasis].

25   Ibid.

26   O. Double, ' "That shit was funny *now!*": Emotion and Intense Personal Experience in Stand-Up Comedy', in Oliver Double, *Saint Pancreas* [DVD extra]. University of Kent. 2007. DVD, p. 8.

27   As Oliver Double has noted, the use of selective characterization to convey the performer's subjective opinion of his material has been theorized by Brecht: *Brecht on Theatre*, p. 123. Double, *Getting the Joke*, 1st edn, p. 218.

28   H. Bergson, *Laughter: An Essay on the Meaning of the Comic* (Rockville, MD: Arc Manor, 2008), p. 11.

29   Ibid., p. 10.

30   Morreall, 'Humour and the Conduct of Politics', p. 70.

31   Lash, 'A Theory of the Comic as Insight', p. 117. [Lash's italics].

32   Morreall, 'Humour and the Conduct of Politics', p. 70. [Morreall's italics].

33   Ibid., p. 71.

34 Jason Byrne, *The Jason Byrne Show*, Episode 2.

35 Tony Allen claims this as a common technique in stand-up performance: T. Allen, *Attitude*, p. 29.

36 Mintz, 'Standup Comedy as Social and Cultural Mediation', p. 75.

37 Morreall, 'Humour and the Conduct of Politics', p. 71.

38 R. de Sousa, 'When is it Wrong to Laugh?', in *The Philosophy of Laughter and Humor* (see Schopenhauer, above), pp. 226–49 (p. 240).

39 Douglas, 'Jokes', p. 152.

40 de Sousa, 'When is it wrong to laugh', p. 240. [De Sousa's italics].

41 Ibid., p. 241.

42 Ibid., p. 241. [De Sousa's italics].

43 Mark Thomas, *The Night War Broke Out*. Laughing Stock. 2004. CD.

44 Jack Dee, *Jack Dee Live*.

45 Linstead, 'Jokers Wild', p. 761.

46 Stewart Lee, Interview. [Lee's emphasis].

47 M. Billig, 'Humour and Hatred: The Racist Jokes of the Ku Klux Klan', *Discourse and Society* 12 (2001): 267–89 (p. 270).

48 D. Howitt and K. Owusu-Bempah, 'Race and Ethnicity in Popular Humour', in *Beyond a Joke* (see Lockyer and Pickering, above), pp. 45–62 (pp. 46–7).

49 Douglas, 'Jokes', p. 152.

50 Morreall, 'Humour and the Conduct of Politics', pp. 71–2.

51 Kevin Bloody Wilson, *Dilligaf Café 2009*, The Sovereign Hall, The Cresset, Peterborough, 8 November 2009, 7:30pm.

52 Performed by Kevin Bloody Wilson, *Dilligaf Café 2009*; lyrics transcribed from recording available at 'Kevin Bloody Wilson', *myspace*, http://www.myspace.com/kevinbloodywilson [accessed 15 September 2010].

53 Howitt and Owusu-Bempah, 'Race and Ethnicity in Popular Humour', p. 47.

54 K. Lorenz, *On Aggression* (London: Methuen, 1967), p. 253.

55 M. Philips, 'Racist Acts and Racist Humor', *Canadian Journal of Philosophy* 14 (1984): 75–96 (p. 81). [Philips' italics].

56 M. Philips, 'Racist Acts and Racist Humor', p. 80.

57 Howitt and Owusu-Bempah, 'Race and Ethnicity in Popular Humour', pp. 56–7.

58 R. de Sousa, quoted in Billig, 'Humour and Hatred', p. 277.

59 Howitt and Owusu-Bempah, 'Race and Ethnicity in Popular Humour', p. 49.

60 Philips, 'Racist Acts and Racist Humor', p. 92.

61 Howitt and Owusu-Bempah, 'Race and Ethnicity in Popular Humour', p. 48.

62 Allport, *The Nature of Prejudice*, p. 14.

63 Ibid., p. 15.

64 Robert Newman, *From Caliban to the Taliban: 500 Years of Humanitarian Intervention*. www.robnewman.com. 2003. CD.

65 Schopenhauer, 'The World as Will and Idea', p. 60.

66 Freud, *Jokes and their Relation to the Unconscious*, p. 103.

67 Philips, 'Racist Acts and Racist Humor', pp. 90–1.

Chapter 3

1 The material on stand-up venues has been re-worked from an article first published in *Participations: Journal of Audience and Reception Studies*: S. Quirk, 'Containing the Audience: The "Room" in Stand-up Comedy', *Participations Journal of Audience and Reception Studies* 8, no. 2 (November 2011).

2 Dave Bailey, Interview by email, 16 August 2008.

3 Matthew Crosby, Interview, The Duke of Cumberland, Whitstable, 31 October 2008.

4 Double, *Getting the Joke*, 1st edn, pp. 110–11.

5 Matthew Crosby, Interview.

6 P. Brook, *The Shifting Point: Forty years of theatrical exploration 1946-1987* (London: Methuen, 1988), p. 147.

7 I. Mackintosh, *Architecture, Actor and Audience* (London: Routledge, 1993), p. 172.

8 Double, *Getting the Joke*, 1st edn, p. 107.

9   Bergson, *Laughter*, p. 11.

10 Dan Atkinson, Interview.

11 Brook, *The Shifting Point*, p. 147.

12 Mackintosh, *Architecture, Actor and Audience*, p. 24.

13 Matthew Crosby, Interview.

14 Ibid.

15 Dan Atkinson, Interview.

16 Iain Mackintosh also notes that it is beneficial for a show to appear commercially successful; I. Mackintosh, *Architecture, Actor and Audience*, p. 128.

17 Matthew Crosby, Interview.

18 Ibid.

19 Richard Herring, Interview.

20 Dan Atkinson, Interview.

21 Stewart Lee, Interview.

22 Ibid.

23 J. McGrath, *A Good Night Out: Popular Theatre: Audience, Class and Form* (London: Nick Hern Books, 1996), pp. 5–7, 75–6.

24 Dan Atkinson, Interview.

25 Josie Long, Interview by telephone, 27 October 2008.

26 Isy Suttie, Interview.

27 J. Huizinga, *Homo Ludens: A Study of the Play Element in Culture* (London: Temple Smith, 1970), p. 28.

28 Ibid., pp. 28–9.

29 Ibid., p. 28. Huizinga drew a distinction between 'play' and 'the comic', yet Kaufman (1997) has demonstrated that much of Huzinga's analysis of play can be usefully and accurately applied to the work of comedians.

30 Mintz, 'Standup Comedy as Social and Cultural Meidation', p. 79.

31 O. Double, *Getting the Joke: The Inner Workings of Stand-up Comedy*, 2nd edn (London: Methuen, 2014), p. 53.

32 Josie Long, *Kindness and Exuberance*.

33 Dave Bailey, Interview.

34 Eric, *Eric's Tales of the Sea*, Horsebridge Arts and Community Centre, Whitstable, 25 June 2010, 8pm.

35 K. Fox, *Watching the English: The Hidden Rules of English Behaviour* (London: Hodder, 2004), pp. 88–9.

36 Douglas, 'Jokes'.

37 M. Roberts and T. Townshend, 'Young adults and the decline of the urban English pub: Issues for planning', *Planning Theory and Practice* 14, no. 4 (2013): 455–69.

38 Huzinga, *Homo Ludens*, p. 31.

39 S. Lockyer and L. Myers, ' "It's About Expecting the Unexpected": Live Stand-up Comedy from the Audiences' Perspective', *Participations: Journal of Audience and Reception Studies* 8, no. 2 (November 2011): 181–3.

40 Ibid., p. 175.

41 Joe Wilkinson, Interview.

42 B. Thompson, *Sunshine on Putty: The Golden Age of British Comedy, from Vic Reeves to The Office* (London: Harper Perennial, 2004), pp. 108–9.

43 Double, *Getting the Joke*, 1st edn, pp. 241–2.

44 Eddie Izzard, *Glorious*.

45 Eddie Izzard quoted in Thompson, *Sunshine on Putty*, p. 108.

46 Ibid.

47 Daniel Kitson, *The Impotent Fury of the Underprivileged*, Gulbenkian Theatre Canterbury, 31 May 2008, 7:45pm.

48 Eddie Izzard, *Glorious*.

49 Stewart Lee, *Stand-up Comedian*. 2 Entertain Video, Avalon Television. 2005. DVD.

50 Dan Atkinson, Interview.

51 While *Chortle* and *YouTube* cite this appearance as c.1986, Brand herself dates it at 1988 in an interview for *WhatsOnStage.com*; T. Atkins, '20 Questions with … Jo Brand', *WhatsOnStage.com*, 25 February 2008, http://www.whatsonstage.com/interviews/theatre/london/E8821203683 281/20+Questions+With+...+Jo+Brand.html [accessed 3 March 2010].

52 Jo Brand, 'Jo Brand on Friday Night Live', http://www.youtube.com/ watch?v=GTINPOKEOzQ&feature=related [accessed 3 March 2010].

53 Jo Brand, *A Big Slice of Jo Brand*. Stone Ranger Productions. 1994. VHS.

54 Jo Brand, quoted in Double, *Getting the Joke*, p. 211.

55 Double, *Getting the Joke*, 1st edn, p. 211.

56 J. Coates, *Women, Men and Language* (London: Longman, 1986), pp. 103–6.
57 O. Double, 'Not the Definitive Version: An Interview with Ross Noble', *Comedy Studies* 1 (2010): 5–19 (p. 6).
58 Double, *Getting the* Joke, 1st edn, p. 191.
59 Ross Noble, quoted in Double, 'Not the Definitive Version: An Interview with Ross Noble', *Comedy Studies* 1, no. 1 (2010): 5–19 (p. 16).
60 Morreall, *The Philosophy of Laughter and Humour*, p. 6.
61 Bruce Devlin, *The Stand: The Saturday Show*, The Stand, Edinburgh, 27 November 2005.
62 Bruce Devlin, *The Stand: The Saturday Show*, The Stand, Edinburgh, 25 November 2006.
63 Dan Atkinson, Interview.
64 Ibid.
65 Zijderveld, 'Jokes and their Relation to Social Reality', p. 287.
66 Dan Atkinson, Interview.
67 Zijderveld, 'Jokes and their Relation to Social Reality', p. 291.

Chapter 4

1 Dan Atkinson, *Edinburgh and Beyond 2008*, The Gulbenkian Theatre, Canterbury, 26 September 2008, 7:45pm.
2 Dan Atkinson, Interview.
3 Ibid.
4 M. Atkinson, *Our Master's Voices: The Language and Body Language of Politics* (London: Methuen, 1984).
5 Dan Atkinson, Interview.
6 Nick Helm, *Horsebridge Comedy*, Horsebridge Arts and Community Centre, Whitstable, 30 April 2010, 8pm.
7 J. Carr and L. Greeves, *The Naked Jape*, p. 3.
8 Mark Thomas, Interview.
9 Stewart Lee, Interview.

10 J. Limon, *Stand-up Comedy in Theory, or, Abjection in America* (London: Duke University Press, 2000), p. 12.

11 Josie Long, Interview.

12 Josie Long, *Kindness and Exuberance.*

13 Dan Atkinson, Interview.

14 M. Atkinson, *Our Master's Voices.*

15 Ibid., p. 13.

16 Ibid., pp. 25–31.

17 Ibid., p. 18.

18 Ibid., p. xvii.

19 Ibid., p. 48. The use of Atkinson's notion of calls to respond to political oratory in stand-up is established by Double (2005), p. 208.

20 Dylan Moran, *Monster.* Universal. 2004. DVD.

21 M. Atkinson, *Our Master's Voices*, pp. 55–6.

22 Dylan Moran, *Monster.*

23 Double, *Getting the Joke*, 1st edn, p. 207.

24 M. Atkinson, *Our Master's Voices*, p. 58.

25 Dylan Moran, *Monster.*

26 Lorenz, *On Aggression*, p. 253.

27 Double, *Stand-Up*, p. 132.

28 Philips, 'Racist Acts and Racist Humor', p. 91.

29 M. Atkinson, *Our Master's Voices*, pp. 57–8.

30 Richard Herring, Interview.

31 Ibid.

32 Stewart Lee, *90s Comedian.* Go Faster Stripe. 2006.

33 Ibid.

34 A. Koestler, *The Act of Creation* (London: Hutchinson, 1964), p. 35.

35 F. Ajaye, *Comic Insights: The Art of Stand-Up Comedy* (Los Angeles: Silman-James Press, 2002), p. 14.

36 Stewart Lee, *90s Comedian.*

37 Ibid.

38 Stewart Lee, Interview.

39 Ibid.

Chapter 5

1　Mintz, 'Standup Comedy as Social and Cultural Mediation', p. 77.

2　Ibid., p. 74.

3　Linstead, 'Jokers Wild'.

4　Mintz, 'Standup Comedy as Social and Cultural Mediation', p. 78.

5　Ibid., p. 79.

6　Mintz, 'Standup Comedy as Social and Cultural Mediation', p. 79.

7　Stewart Lee, *90s Comedian*.

8　Ibid.

9　Stewart Lee, Interview. [Lee's emphasis].

10　Stewart Lee, *90s Comedian*.

11　J. Levinson, *The Morality and Immorality of Jokes*, Research Seminar, University of Kent, 25 November 2008.

12　Stewart Lee, *90s Comedian*.

13　M. Atkinson, *Our Masters' Voices*, pp. 25, 33.

14　Stewart Lee, Interview.

15　Ibid.

16　Zijderveld, 'Jokes and their Relation to Social Reality', pp. 307–8.

17　Douglas, 'Jokes', p. 155.
　　Lash, 'A Theory of the Comic as Insight'.

18　Zijderveld, 'Jokes and their Relation to Social Reality', p. 299.

19　Ibid., p. 301.

20　Allport, *The Nature of Prejudice*, p. 21.
　　Freud, *Jokes and their Relation to the Unconscious*, p. 103.

21　W. Lippmann, *Public Opinion* (New York: The Free Press, 1922), p. 11.

22　Mark Thomas, *Serious Organised Criminal*. Phil McIntyre Television. 2007. DVD.
　　Mark Thomas, *The Night War Broke Out*.

23　Mark Thomas, *Serious Organised Criminal*.

24　Ibid. Brian Haw's protest took the form of a 'peace camp' in Parliament Square, London. His demonstration began in 2001 and lasted until his death from cancer in 2011.

25　Ibid.

26 Mark Thomas, *It's the Stupid Economy: The Manifesto*, Hazlitt Theatre, Hazlitt Arts Centre, Maidstone, 28 April 2009, 7:30pm.

27 M. Thomas, *The People's Manifesto* (United Kingdom: Ebury Press, 2010).

28 Ebury Press, publishers of *The People's Manifesto*, pledged the deposit money for one candidate who was chosen by national competition. Entrants were required to select their key policies from the manifesto and state how they would fund and publicise their campaign. The winner was Danny Kushlick who stood in the Bristol West constituency, winning 343 votes (0.6 per cent); BBC, 'Election 2010: Results, Bristol West', *BBC*, http://news.bbc.co.uk/1/shared/election2010/results/constituency/a73.stm [accessed 5 August 2010].

29 Mark Thomas, *It's the Stupid Economy*.

30 Mark Thomas, *Mark Thomas Live*. Laughing Stock. 1998. Cassette.

31 Mark Thomas, *The Night War Broke Out*.

32 Ibid.

33 Ibid.

34 Double, *Getting the Joke*, 1st edn, p. 225.

35 M. Atkinson, *Our Master's Voices*.

36 Joe Wilkinson, Interview.

37 Ibid.

38 Ibid.

39 Lippmann, *Public Opinion*, p. 11.

Chapter 6

1 Jenny Eclair, *Because I Forgot to Get a Pension*, Gulbenkian Theatre, Canterbury, 27 October 2007, 7:45pm.

2 C. Barker, 'The "Image" in Showbusiness', *Theatre Quarterly* 3 (1978): 7–11.

3 Dan Atkinson, Interview.

4 Barker, 'The "Image" in Showbusiness', p. 8.

5 Ibid., p. 7.

6 Ibid., p. 8.

7   Rob Brydon, *Rob Brydon's Identity Crisis*, BBC Four, 29 February 2008, 9pm. Television broadcast.

8   Ibid.

9   Ibid.

10 Ibid.

11 Ibid.

12 S. Bennett, 'Rob Brydon Live', *Chortle*, February 2009, http://www. chortle.co.uk/shows/tour/r/16027/rob_brydon_live/review?id_ review=16027 [accessed 27 June 2010].

13 Barker, 'The "Image" in Showbusiness', p. 8.

14 M. Gladwell, *The Tipping Point: How Little Things Can Make a Big Difference* (London: Abacus, 2000), p. 158.

15 Allport, *The Nature of Prejudice*, pp. 8–9. [Allport's italics].

16 Mark Watson, *Work in Progress*, Gulbenkian Theatre Café-Bar, Canterbury, 25 July 2008, 9pm.
    Mark Watson, *All the Thoughts I've Had Since I Was Born*, Gulbenkian Theatre, Canterbury, 31 January 2009, 7:45pm.

17 'Mark Watson: Comments Page', *Chortle*, http://www.chortle.co.uk/ comics/m/62/mark_watson [accessed 30 July 2007].

18 Double, *Getting the Joke*, 1st edn, pp. 73–81.

19 Josie Long, Interview.

20 Alexei Sayle, Research Seminar, University of Kent, 18 January 2006.

21 Double, *Getting the Joke*, 1st edn, pp. 97–8.

22 D. Maxwell, 'Why Al Murray is a Vintage Whine', *Sunday Times*, 27 October 2007.

23 A. Clayton, *The Layering of Intention: A New Theory of Comic Performance*, Research Seminar, The University of Kent, 20 February 2008.

24 In observing that character acts involve the dual presence of the performer and the character performed, I am drawing on Brecht's approach to acting. For example, in his 'Short Organum for the Theatre', Brecht describes actor Charles Laughton's performance as Galileo: 'Laughton is actually there, standing on stage and showing us what he imagines Galileo to have been' (Willett 2001: 194). His 'Street Scene' explains how the actor's judgement should inform the performance (Willett 2001: 121–9).

25 S. Lee, *How I Escaped My Certain Fate: The Life and Deaths of a Stand-Up Comedian* (London: Faber and Faber, 2010), p. 293.

26 Ibid., p. 294.

27 Maxwell, 'Why Al Murray is a Vintage Whine'.

28 O. Double, *Jo Brand in Conversation with Oliver Double,* University of Kent Open Lectures, 13 February 2008.

29 Allport, *The Nature of Prejudice*, p. 23.

30 Matthew Crosby, Interview.

31 Dan Atkinson, Interview.

32 E. Goffman, *The Presentation of Self in Everyday Life* (Harmodsworth: Pelican, 1959).

33 Ibid., p. 24.

34 Ibid., p. 28.

35 Ibid., p. 81. [Goffman's italics].

36 Joe Wilkinson, Interview.

37 Rhod Gilbert, *Rhod Gilbert and the Award-Winning Mince Pie,* Gulbenkian Theatre, Canterbury, 22 January 2009, 7:45pm.

38 Ibid.

39 Ibid.

40 Ibid.

41 Ibid.

42 Mintz, 'Standup Comedy as Social and Cultural Mediation', p. 74.

43 Ibid., p. 74.

44 Dylan Moran, *Monster.*

45 Lee Evans, *Wired and Wonderful: Live at Wembley*. Little Mo Films. 2002. DVD.

46 Freud, 'Humour'.

47 Lee Evans, in *World's Greatest Stand-up: Volume One*. Channel 4 DVD. 2006. DVD.

48 Dylan Moran, *Monster.*

49 Mark Thomas, Interview.

50 Mark Thomas, *The Night War Broke Out.*

51 Mark Thomas, Interview.

52 Josie Long, *Trying is Good.*
53 Josie Long, Interview.
54 Joe Wilkinson, Interview.
55 W. Cook, *Ha Bloody Ha: Comedians Talking* (London: Fourth Estate, 1994), p. 215.
56 C. Ritchie, *Performing Live Comedy* (London: Methuen, 2012), p. 177.
57 Robert Newman quoted in W. Cook, *Ha Bloody Ha*, p. 217.
58 Mark Thomas, Personal Communication, by email, 6 October 2008.
59 D. Atkinson, 'Is anything off-limits?', *Chortle*, http://www.chortle.co.uk/correspondents/2007/12/10/6142/is_anything_off-limits%3F [accessed 29 September 2008].
60 T. Allen, *A Summer in the Park: A Journal of Speakers' Corner* (London: Freedom Press, 2004).
61 Ibid., p. 32.
62 Ibid., p. 202.
63 William Cook, *Ha Bloody Ha*, p. 215.
64 Richard Herring, 'Sunday 30th March 2008', *RichardHerring.com*, http://www.richardherring.com/warmingup/30/3/2008/index.html [accessed 17 April 2014].
65 Richard Herring, *Richard Herring Slams a Heckler*, http://www.youtube.com/watch?v=H8IQYSp0EuE [accessed 17 April 2014].
66 Ibid.
67 Ibid.
68 J. Morreall, 'Funny Ha-Ha, Funny Strange, and Other Reactions to Incongruity', in *The Philosophy of Laughter and Humor* (see Schopenhauer, above), pp. 188–207.

Chapter 7

1 Lippmann, *Public Opinion*, p. 59.
2 E. M. Rogers, *Diffusion of Innovations*, 4th edn (New York: The Free Press, 1995), p. 164.

3 Lippmann, *Public Opinion*, p. 104.

4 Double, *Getting the Joke*, 2nd edn, pp. 53–5.

5 Stewart Lee, Interview.

6 Critchley, *On Humour*, p. 11.

7 S. Armstrong, 'Comic Relief', *Sunday Times*, 15 November 2009.

8 Ibid.

9 Robin Ince, 'Geoff Rowe and Robin Ince in Conversation', *Playing for Laughs*, Conference, De Montfort University, 6 February 2010.

10 Ibid.

11 Stewart Lee, Interview.

12 Ibid.

13 J. Fiske and J. Hartley, *Reading Television* (London: Methuen, 1978), pp. 85, 88–9.

14 Mark Thomas, Interview.

15 Stewart Lee, Interview.

16 Refers to *Stewart Lee's Comedy Vehicle*; Stewart Lee, *Stewart Lee's Comedy Vehicle*, BBC Two, 16 March–20 April 2009. Television Series.

17 Stewart Lee, Interview.

18 Ibid.

19 Huizinga, *Homo Ludens*, p. 28.

20 B. Kershaw, *The Politics of Performance: Radical Theatre as Cultural Intervention* (London: Routledge, 1992), p. 2.

21 *Brecht on Theatre*, p. 197.

22 A. Otchet, 'Mark Thomas: Method and Madness of a TV Comic', *The Unesco Courier*, http://www.unesco.org/courier/1999_05/uk/dires/txt1. htm [accessed 2 May 2009].

23 Stewart Lee, Interview.

24 J. Lahr, 'The Goat Boy Rises', *The New Yorker*, 1 November 1993, http://www.newyorker.com/archive/1993/11/01/1993_11_01_113_TNY_ CARDS_000365503?currentPage=all [accessed 5 September 2010].

25 Stewart Lee, Interview.

26 Ibid.

27 Mark Thomas, Interview.

28 Otchet, 'Mark Thomas'.

29 Ibid.

30 Robert Newman, *History of Oil*.

31 Lippmann, *Public Opinion*, p. 11.

32 Morreall, 'Humour and the Conduct of Politics', p. 75.

33 Mark Thomas, *It's the Stupid Economy*.

34 Critchley, *On Humour*, pp. 11–12.

35 Mintz, 'Standup Comedy as Social and Cultural Mediation'.

36 Ibid.

37 Ibid., p. 196.

38 Ibid., p. 196.

39 Hogg and Vaughan, quoted in R. Gross, *Psychology: The Science of Mind and Behaviour*, 3rd edn (London: Hodder, 1996), p. 452.

40 Gross, *Psychology*, p. 448.

41 Morreall, 'Funny Ha-Ha, Funny Strange', pp. 196–200.

42 Ibid., p. 197.

43 Stewart Lee, Interview.

44 Morreall, 'Humour and the Conduct of Politics', p. 70; Bergson, *Laughter*, p. 10.

45 Morreall, 'Humour and the Conduct of Politics', pp. 70–1.

46 Ibid., pp. 69–74.

47 Mark Thomas, *Dambusters*.

48 Ibid.

49 Zijderveld, 'Jokes and their Relation to Social Reality', p. 301.

50 Mark Thomas, Interview.

51 Zijderveld, 'Jokes and their Relation to Social Reality', pp. 306–7.

52 Ibid., p. 311.

53 Rame, in Fo, *Plays: Two*, p. xxi.

54 Ibid., pp. xxi–xxii.

55 Rame, in Fo, *Plays: Two*, p. xx.

56 A. Gumbel, 'Dario Fo Looks Back in Anger', *Independent*, 7 March 1998.

57 Zijderveld, 'Jokes and their Relation to Social Reality', p. 311.

Chapter 8

1 J. Oliver and A. Zaltzman, 'Close to the Edge', *The New Statesman Online*, 22 August 2005, http://www.newstatesman.com/200508220031 [accessed 11 March 2009].

2 L. Porter, 'The way I see it', *The New Statesman Online*, 5 March 2009, http://www.newstatesman.com/comedy/2009/03/comedy-art-politics-work [accessed 7 July 2014].

3 Stewart Lee, *90s Comedian*.
  Dan Atkinson, *Edinburgh and Beyond 2008*.

4 R. E. Lane and D. O. Sears, *Public Opinion* (New Jersey: Prentice-Hall, 1964), pp. 74–5.

5 Gross, *Psychology*, pp. 447–8.

6 Lane and Sears, *Public Opinion*, pp. 9, 53–4.

7 Ibid., pp. 70–5.

8 M. Oswald and S. Grosjean, 'Confirmation Bias', in *Cognitive Illusions: A Handbook on Fallacies and Biases in Thinking, Judgement and Memory*, edited by R. F. Phol (Hove: Psychology Press, 2004), pp. 79–96 (p. 89).

9 Lane and Sears, *Public Opinion*, p. 63.

10 M. Piattelli-Palmarini, *Inevitable Illusions: How Mistakes of Reason Rule our Minds* (Chichester: Wiley, 1994), pp. 19–20.

11 Lippmann, *Public Opinion*, pp. 63–4.

12 Gross, *Psychology*, pp. 447–9.

13 A. Campbell, 'Persuasive Speaking: Define Your Key Message', *The Speaker*, BBC, http://www.bbc.co.uk/speaker/improve/persuasion/ [accessed 17 May 2010].

14 Mark Thomas, *Dambusters*.

15 Ibid.

16 Double, *Getting the Joke*, 2nd edn, p. 290.

17 R. K. Merton, *Social Theory and Social Structure,* 1968 enlarged edn (New York: Free Press, 1968), p. 336.

18 Ibid., p. 336. [Merton's italics].

19 Lane and Sears, *Public Opinion*, p. 34. [Lane and Sears' italics].

20 J. Cooper, *Cognitive Dissonance: Fifty Years of a Classic Theory* (London: Sage, 2011), p. 119.

21 Mark Thomas, *The Night War Broke Out.*

22 Josie Long, *Romance and Adventure,* www.josielong.com [accessed 15 October 2014].

23 Double, *Getting the Joke,* 2nd edn, pp. 287–8.

24 B. D. V. Chow, 'Situations, Happenings, Gatherings, Laughter: Emergent British Stand-Up Comedy in Sociopolitical Context', in *Comedy Tonight!,* edited by J. Malarcher, Theatre Symposium Series, 16 (Tuscaloosa: University of Alabama Press, 2008), p. 127.

25 Ibid., p. 128.

26 B. Logan, 'Josie Long: Pleasance Upstairs, Edinburgh', *theguardian.com,* 13 August 2007, http://www.theguardian.com/culture/2007/aug/13/ edinburghfestival2007.edinburghfestival6 [accessed 15 October 2014].

27 Ibid.

28 Josie Long, *Kindness and Exuberance.*

29 Long created a 'Favorite Small Things' magazine from contributions, which is available on Josie Long, *Trying is Good* [DVD].

30 Josie Long, *Kindness and Exuberance.*

31 Ibid.

32 Josie Long, *Trying is Good.*

33 Merton, *Social Theory and Social Structure,* pp. 364–78.

34 Ibid., p. 366.

35 Cooper, *Cognitive Dissonance.*

36 Festinger, 'The Theory of Cognitive Dissonance' [lecture], *The Voice of America Forum Lecture Series* (USA, C.1960–9), p. 6.

37 Cooper, *Cognitive Dissonance,* p. 175.

38 Robert Newman, *History of Oil.*

39 Ibid.

40 Ibid.

41 Ibid.

42 Zijderveld, 'Jokes and their Relation to Social Reality', pp. 301–2.

43 Festinger, *The Theory of Cognitive Dissonance,* p. 6.

44 Cooper, *Cognitive Dissonance,* p. 73.

45 Howitt and Owusu-Bempah, 'Race and Ethnicity in Popular
    Humour', p. 47.

46 Lane and Sears, *Public Opinion*, p. 44. [Lane and Sears' italics].

47 The term 'message' is used as equivalent to the 'position' of the source in
    Lane and Sears' terminology.

48 Lane and Sears, *Public Opinion*, p. 47. [Lane and Sears' italics].

49 T. Backs and P. Robertshaw, 'Comments on Bruce Devlin', *Chortle*, http://
    www.chortle.co.uk/comics/b/614/bruce_devlin/comments/ [Consulted
    12 November 2008].

50 Double, *Getting the Joke*, 1st edn, pp. 60–3.

51 Josie Long, *Trying is Good*.

52 Douglas, 'Jokes', p. 158.
    Howitt and Owusu-Bempah, 'Race and Ethnicity in Popular
    Humour', p. 47.

53 Lane and Sears, *Public Opinion*, p. 51.

54 Philips, 'Racist Acts and Racist Humour', pp. 90–1.

55 Mark Steel, 'The French Revolution', *The Mark Steel Revolution*, BBC
    Radio 4, 30 June 1998, http://www.marksteelinfo.com/audiovideo/
    default.asp [accessed 1 March 2010].

56 Steel, 'The French Revolution'.

57 Ibid.

58 Lippmann, *Public Opinion*, pp. 63–4.

59 Robert Newman, *History of Oil*.

60 Lippmann, *Public Opinion*, p. 104.

61 Mark Steel, 'The French Revolution'.

62 Rogers, *Diffusion of Innovations*, p. 12.

63 Ibid., p. 366.

64 Ibid., p. 385. [Rogers' emphasis].

65 Ibid., p. 368.

66 Ibid., pp. 368–9.

67 Ibid., p. 385.

68 M. Watson, *Crap at the Environment: A Year in the Life of One Man
    Trying to Save the Planet* (London: Hodder, 2008), pp. 4–5.

69 Lucy Porter, *The Good Life*. Go Faster Stripe. 2008. DVD.

70 Mark Steel, 'Sexuality', *The Mark Steel Solution*, BBC Radio 4, 1995, http://www.marksteelifo.com/audiovideo/default.asp [accessed 24 May 2010]. [Steel's emphasis].

71 Ibid. [Steel's emphasis].

72 Guardian, 'Prejudice and the Police Constable: James Anderton's Comments on the Aids Epidemic', *Guardian*, 13 December 1986.

73 S. Rayment, 'Judges Back Forces' Ban on Gay Recruits', *Daily Mail*, 4 November 1995.

74 Ibid.

75 Mark Steel, 'Sexuality'.

76 J. Taylor and A. Grice, 'Clegg Lays Down Law to Cameron on Gay Rights', *Independent*, 13 January 2010.

Conclusion

1   Joe Wilkinson, Interview.

2   Dan Atkinson, Interview.

3   Mark Thomas, Interview.

4   Ibid.

5   C. Davies, 'The Right to Joke', *The Social Affairs Unit*, Research Report 7 (2004), http://socialaffairsunit.org.uk/digipub/content/view/11/ [accessed 23 July 2010], (p. 3).

6   Ibid., p. 3.

7   Stewart Lee, *41st Best Stand-up Ever*.

8   Morreall, 'Humour and the Conduct of Politics', p. 70.

9   Lippmann, *Public Opinion*, p. 10.

10 Mark Thomas, Interview.

11 Thomas, Mark, Personal Communication, by email, 5 October 2008. [Thomas' emphasis].

Bibliography

Books

Ajaye, F., *Comic Insights: The Art of Stand-Up Comedy* (Los Angeles: Silman-James Press, 2002).

Allen, T., *Attitude: Wanna Make Something of It?: The Secret of Stand-up Comedy* (Glastonbury: Gothic Image, 2002).

Allen, T., *A Summer in the Park: A Journal of Speakers' Corner* (London: Freedom Press, 2004).

Allport, G. W., *The Nature of Prejudice*, 25th Anniversary edn (Cambridge, MA: Addison-Wesley, 1954).

Atkinson, M., *Our Master's Voices: The Language and Body Language of Politics* (London: Methuen, 1984).

Bergson, H., *Laughter: An Essay on the Meaning of the Comic* (Rockville, MD: Arc Manor, 2008).

Brecht, B., *The Messingkauf Dialogues* (London: Methuen, 1965).

Brook, P., *The Shifting Point: Forty Years of Theatrical Exploration 1946-1987* (London: Methuen, 1988).

Brooker, P., 'Key Words in Brecht's Theory and Practice of Theatre', in *The Cambridge Companion to Brecht*, edited by P. Thomson and G. Sacks (Cambridge: Cambridge University Press, 1994), pp. 185–200.

Carr, J. and L. Greeves, *The Naked Jape: Uncovering the Hidden World of Jokes* (London: Penguin, 2007).

Chow, B. D. V., 'Situations, Happenings, Gatherings, Laughter: Emergent British Stand-Up Comedy in Sociopolitical Context', in *Comedy Tonight!*, edited by J. Malarcher, Theatre Symposium Series, 16 (Tuscaloosa: University of Alabama Press, 2008), pp. 121–33.

Coates, J., *Women, Men and Language* (London: Longman, 1986).

Cook, W., *The Comedy Store: The Club that Changed British Comedy* (London: Little, Brown, 2001).

Cook, W., *Ha Bloody Ha: Comedians Talking* (London: Fourth Estate, 1994).

Cooper, J., *Cognitive Dissonance: Fifty Years of a Classic Theory* (London: Sage, 2011).

Critchley, S., *On Humour* (London: Routledge, 2002).

Double, O., *Getting the Joke: The Inner Workings of Stand-Up Comedy*, 1st edn (London: Methuen, 2005).

Double, O., *Getting the Joke: The Inner Workings of Stand-up Comedy*, 2nd edn (London: Methuen, 2014).

Double, O., *Stand-Up!: On Being a Comedian* (London: Methuen, 1997).

Douglas, M., 'Jokes', in M. Douglas, *Implicit Meanings: Selected Essays in Anthropology*, 2nd edn (London: Routledge, 1999), pp. 146–64.

Freud, S., 'Humour', in *Freud: Collected Papers*, edited by J. Strachey, 5 vols (London: Hogarth Press, 1957), v, pp. 215–21.

Freud, S., *Jokes and their Relation to the Unconscious* (London: Routledge & Kegan Paul, 1960).

Fo, D., *Plays: Two* (London: Methuen, 1994).

Fox, K., *Watching the English: The Hidden Rules of English Behaviour* (London: Hodder, 2004).

Fiske, J. and J. Hartley, *Reading Television* (London: Methuen, 1978).

Gladwell, M., *The Tipping Point: How Little Things Can Make a Big Difference* (London: Abacus, 2000).

Goffman, E., *The Presentation of Self in Everyday Life* (Harmodsworth: Pelican, 1959).

Gross, R., *Psychology: The Science of Mind and Behaviour*, 3rd edn (London: Hodder, 1996).

Hobbes, T., 'Human Nature', in *The Philosophy of Laughter and Humor*, edited by J. Morreall (New York: State University of New York Press, 1987), pp. 19–20.

Howitt, D. and K. Owusu-Bempah, 'Race and Ethnicity in Popular Humour', in *Beyond a Joke: The Limits of Humour*, edited by S. Lockyer and M. Pickering (Basingstoke: Palgrave, 2005), pp. 45–62.

Huizinga, J., *Homo Ludens: A Study of the Play Element in Culture* (London: Temple Smith, 1970).

Kaufman, W., *The Comedian as Confidence Man: Studies in Irony Fatigue* (Detroit: Wayne State University Press, 1997).

Kershaw, B., *The Politics of Performance: Radical Theatre as Cultural Intervention* (London: Routledge, 1992).

Koestler, A., *The Act of Creation* (London: Hutchinson, 1964).

Lane, R. E. and D. O. Sears, *Public Opinion* (New Jersey: Prentice-Hall, 1964).

Lee, S., *How I Escaped my Certain Fate: The Life and Deaths of a Stand-up Comedian* (London: Faber and Faber, 2010).

Limon, J., *Stand-up Comedy in Theory, or, Abjection in America* (London: Duke University Press, 2000).

Lippmann, W., *Public Opinion* (New York: The Free Press, 1922).

Lockyer, S. and M. Pickering, eds, *Beyond a Joke: The Limits of Humour* (Basingstoke: Palgrave, 2005).

Lorenz, K., *On Aggression* (London: Methuen, 1967).

Mackintosh, I., *Architecture, Actor and Audience* (London: Routledge, 1993).

Merton, R. K., *Social Theory and Social Strucutre,* 1968 enlarged edn (London: Free Press, 1968).

McGrath, J., *A Good Night Out: Popular Theatre: Audience, Class and Form* (London: Nick Hern Books, 1996).

Morreall, J., 'Funny Ha-Ha, Funny Strange, and Other Reactions to Incongruity', in *The Philosophy of Laughter and Humor*, edited by J. Morreall (New York: State University of New York Press, 1987), pp. 188–207.

Morreall, J., 'Humour and the Conduct of Politics', in *Beyond a Joke: The Limits of Humour*, edited by S. Lockyer and M. Pickering (Basingstoke: Palgrave, 2005), pp. 63–78.

Morreall, J., ed., *The Philosophy of Laughter and Humor* (New York: State University of New York Press, 1987).

Oswald, M. and S. Grosjean, 'Confirmation Bias', in *Cognitive Illusions: A Handbook on Fallacies and Biases in Thinking, Judgement and Memory*, edited by R. F. Phol (Hove: Psychology Press, 2004), pp. 79–96.

The Paperback Oxford English Dictionary, edited by Catherine Soanes, 6th edn (Oxford: Oxford University Press, 2006).

Piattelli-Palmarini, M., *Inevitable Illusions: How Mistakes of Reason Rule our Minds* (Chichester: Wiley, 1994).

Pohl, R. F., ed., *Cognitive Illusions: A Handbook on Fallacies and Biases in Thinking, Judgement and Memory* (Hove: Psychology Press, 2004).

Ritchie, C., *Performing Live Comedy* (London: Methuen, 2012).

Rogers, E. M., *Diffusion of Innovations*, 4th edn (New York: The Free Press, 1995).

Schopenhauer, A., 'The World as Will and Idea', in *The Philosophy of Laughter and Humor*, edited by J. Morreall (New York: State University of New York Press, 1987), pp. 51–64.

de Sousa, R., 'When is it Wrong to Laugh?', in *The Philosophy of Laughter and Humor*, edited by J. Morreall (New York: State University of New York Press, 1987), pp. 226–49.

Spencer, H., 'The Physiology of Laughter', in *The Philosophy of Laughter and Humor*, edited by J. Morreall (New York: State University of New York Press, 1987), pp. 99–110.

Thomas, M., *The People's Manifesto* (United Kingom: Ebury Press, 2010).

Thompson, B., *Sunshine on Putty: The Golden Age of British Comedy, from Vic Reeves to The Office* (London: Harper Perennial, 2004).

Watson, M., *Crap at the Environment: A Year in the Life of One Man Trying to Save the Planet* (London: Hodder, 2008).

Wertheim, W. F., *East-West Parallels: Sociological Approaches to Modern Asia* (The Hauge: W. Van Hoeve, 1964).

Willett, J. ed., *Brecht on Theatre: The Development of an Aesthetic* (London: Methuen, 2001).

Academic articles

Barker, C., 'The "Image" in Showbusiness', *Theatre Quarterly* 3 (1978), 7–11.

Billig, M., 'Humour and Hatred: The Racist Jokes of the Ku Klux Klan', *Discourse and Society* 12 (2001), 267–89.

Davies, C., 'The Right to Joke', *The Social Affairs Unit*, Research Report 7 (2004), http://socialaffairsunit.org.uk/digipub/content/view/11/ [accessed 23 July 2010].

Double, O., 'Not the Definitive Version: An Interview with Ross Noble', *Comedy Studies* 1 (2010), 5–19.

Double, O., '"That shit was funny *now!*": Emotion and Intense Personal Experience in Stand-Up Comedy', in Oliver Double, *Saint Pancreas* [DVD extra]. University of Kent. 2007. DVD.

Lash, K., 'A Theory of the Comic as Insight', *The Journal of Philosophy* 45 (1948), 113–21.

Linstead, S., 'Jokers Wild: The Importance of Humour in the Maintenance of Organisational Culture', *Sociological Review* 33 (1985), 741–67.

Lockyer, S. and L. Myers, '"It's About Expecting the Unexpected": Live Stand-up Comedy from the Audiences' Perspective', *Participations: Journal of Audience and Reception Studies* 8, no. 2 (November 2011), 165–88, http://www.participations.org/Volume%208/Issue%202/2c%20Lockyer%20Myers.pdf [accessed 2 April 2015].

Mintz, L. E., 'Standup Comedy as Social and Cultural Mediation', *Amercian Quarterly* 37 (1985), 71–80.

Philips, M., 'Racist Acts and Racist Humor', *Canadian Journal of Philosophy* 14 (1984), 75–96.

Quirk, S., 'Containing the Audience: The "Room" in Stand-up Comedy', *Participations: Journal of Audience and Reception Studies* 8, no. 2 (November 2011), 219–38, http://www.participations.org/Volume%208/ Issue%202/2e%20Quirk.pdf [accessed 2 April 2015].

Roberts, M. and T. Townshend, 'Young Adults and the Decline of the Urban English Pub: Issues for Planning', *Planning Theory and Practice* 14, no. 4 (2013), 455–69.

Zijderveld, A. C., 'Jokes and their Relation to Social Reality', *Social Research* 36 (1968), 286–311.

Newspaper and magazine articles

Armstrong, S., 'Comic Relief', *Sunday Times*, 15 November 2009.

Brazil, D., 'How to Talk Dirty and Get Arrested', *The Leveller*, December 1979, p. 14.

Burgess, M., 'Gilbert's Grape Expectations', *Manchester Evening News*, 25 January 2008.

Guardian, 'Prejudice and the Police Constable: James Anderton's Comments on the Aids Epidemic', *Guardian*, 13 December 1986.

Gumbel, A., 'Dario Fo Looks Back in Anger', *Independent*, 7 March 1998.

Maxwell, D., 'Why Al Murray is a Vintage Whine', *The Sunday Times*, 27 October 2007.

Rayment, S., 'Judges Back Forces' Ban on Gay Recruits', *Daily Mail*, 4 November 1995.

Taylor, J. and A. Grice, 'Clegg Lays Down Law to Cameron on Gay Rights', *Independent*, 13 January 2010.

Live performance

Atkinson, Dan, *Edinburgh and Beyond 2008*, The Gulbenkian Theatre, Canterbury, 26 September 2008, 7:45pm.

Devlin, Bruce, *The Stand: The Saturday Show*, The Stand, Edinburgh, 27 November 2005.

Devlin, Bruce, *The Stand: The Saturday Show*, The Stand, Edinburgh, 25 November 2006.

Eclair, Jenny, *Because I Forgot to Get a Pension*, Gulbenkian Theatre, Canterbury, 27 October 2007, 7:45pm.

Eric, *Eric's Tales of the Sea*, Horsebridge Arts and Community Centre, Whitstable, 25 June 2010, 8pm.

Gilbert, Rhod, *Rhod Gilbert and the Award-Winning Mince Pie*, Gulbenkian Theatre, Canterbury, 22 January 2009, 7:45pm.

Gilbert, Rhod, *Who's Eaten Gilbert's Grape*, Gulbenkian Theatre, Canterbury, 2 November 2007, 7:45pm.

Helm, Nick, *Horsebridge Comedy*, Horsebridge Arts and Community Centre, Whitstable 30 April 2010, 8pm.

Kitson, Daniel, *The Impotent Fury of the Underprivileged*, Gulbenkian Theatre, Canterbury, 31 May 2008, 7:45pm.

Thomas, Mark, *It's the Stupid Economy: The Manifesto*, Hazlitt Theatre, Hazlitt Arts Centre, Maidstone, 28 April 2009, 7:30pm.

Thomas, Mark, *Mark Thomas*, Gulbenkian Theatre, Canterbury, 4 October 2008, 7:45pm.

Watson, Mark, *All the Thoughts I've Had Since I Was Born*, Gulbenkian Theatre, Canterbury, 31 January 2009, 7:45pm.

Watson, Mark, *Work in Progress*, Gulbenkian Theatre Café-Bar, Canterbury, 25 July 2008, 9pm.

Wilson, Kevin Bloody, *Dilligaf Café 2009*, The Sovereign Hall, The Cresset, Peterborough, 8 November 2009, 7:30pm.

Recorded performance

Brand, Jo, *A Big Slice of Jo Brand*. Stone Ranger Productions. 1994. VHS.

Brand, Jo, 'Jo Brand on Friday Night Live', http://www.youtube.com/watch?v=GTINPOKEOzQ&feature=relate [accessed 3 March 2010].

Byrne, Jason, *The Jason Byrne Show*, BBC Radio 2, Episode 2, 19 July 2008. Radio broadcast.

Byrne, Jason, *The Jason Byrne Show*, BBC Radio 2, Episode 3, 2 August 2008. Radio broadcast.

Carr, Jimmy, 'Royal Variety Stand-up Act 2008', *YouTube*, http://www.youtube.com/watch?v=0xSx0tibc0Q&feature=related [accessed 10 March 2010].

Dee, Jack, *Jack Dee Live*. WEA International/ Channel 4 Television. 1992. DVD.

Dunham, Jeff, *YouTube*, http://www.youtube.com/watch?v=1uwOL4rB-go [accessed 21 April 2010].

Evans, Lee, *Wired and Wonderful: Live at Wembley*. Little Mo Films. 2002. DVD.

Evans, Lee, *World's Greatest Stand-up: Volume One*. Channel 4 DVD. 2006. DVD.

Gilbert, Rhod, *Rhod Gilbert and the Award-Winning Mince Pie*. Channel 4 DVD. 2009. DVD.

Herring, Richard, *Richard Herring Slams a Heckler*, http://www.youtube.com/watch?v=H8IQYSp0EuE [accessed 17 April 2014].

Izzard, Eddie, *Definite Article*. Universal. 1996. VHS.

Izzard, Eddie, *Glorious*. Ella Communications. 1997. VHS.

Lee, Stewart, *Stand-up Comedian*. 2 Entertain Video, Avalon Television. 2005. DVD.

Lee, Stewart, *Stewart Lee's Comedy Vehicle*, BBC Two, 16 March–20 April 2009. Television series.

Lee, Stewart, *90s Comedian*. Go Faster Stripe. 2006. DVD.

Lee, Stewart, *41st Best Stand-up Ever*. Real Talent. 2008. DVD.

Long, Josie, 'Kindness and Exuberance', in Josie Long, *Trying is Good*. Real Talent. 2008. DVD.

Long, Josie, *Romance and Adventure*, www.josielong.com [accessed 15 October 2014].

Long, Josie, *Trying is Good*. Real Talent. 2008. DVD.

McIntyre, Michael, 'Michael McIntyre Live at the Apollo', *YouTube*, http://www.youtube.com/watch?v=Es2l4yUBY6M [accessed 11 February 2010].

Moran, Dylan, *Monster*. Universal. 2004. DVD.

Newman, Robert, *From Caliban to the Taliban: 500 Years of Humanitarian Intervention*. www.robnewman.com. 2003. CD.

Newman, Robert, *History of Oil*. Tiger Aspect Productions. 2006. DVD.

Porter, Lucy, *The Good Life*. Go Faster Stripe. 2008. DVD.

Steel, Mark, 'The French Revolution', *The Mark Steel Revolution*, BBC Radio 4, 30 June 1998, http://www.marksteelinfo.com/audiovideo/default.asp [accessed 1 March 2010].

Steel, Mark, 'Sexuality', *The Mark Steel Solution*, BBC Radio 4, 1995, http://
www.marksteelinfo.com/audiovideo/default.asp [accessed 24 May 2010].

Thomas, Mark, *Dambusters: Live 2001 Tour*. Laughing Stock. 2003. CD.

Thomas, Mark, *Mark Thomas Live*. Laughing Stock. 1998. Cassette.

Thomas, Mark, *Mark Thomas: The Manifesto*, BBC Radio 4, 18 February 2010.
Radio broadcast.

Thomas, Mark, *The Night War Broke Out*. Laughing Stock. 2004. CD.

Thomas, Mark, *Serious Organised Criminal*. Phil McIntyre Television.
2007. DVD.

Vine, Tim, *Live at the Apollo* [BBC]. *YouTube*, http://www.youtube.com/
watch?v=VPaZfeAYUyk [accessed 20 April 2010].

Internet

Atkins, T., '20 Questions with … Jo Brand', *WhatsOnStage.com*, 25 February
2008, http://www.whatsonstage.com/interviews/theatre/london/E8821203
683281/20+Questions+With+...+Jo+Brand.html [accessed 3 March 2010].

Atkinson, D., 'Is anything off-limits?', *Chortle*, http://www.chortle.co.uk/
correspondents/2007/12/10/6142/is_anything_off-limits%3F [accessed
29 September 2008].

Backs, T. and P. Robertshaw, 'Comments on Bruce Devlin', *Chortle*, http://
www.chortle.co.uk/comics/b/614/bruce_devlin/comments/ [Consulted
12 November 2008].

BBC, 'Election 2010: Results, Bristol West', *BBC*, http://news.bbc.co.uk/1/
shared/election2010/results/constituency/a73.stm [accessed 5 August
2010].

Bennett, S., 'Rob Brydon Live', *Chortle*, February 2009, http://www.chortle.
co.uk/shows/tour/r/16027/rob_brydon_live/review?id_review=16027
[accessed 27 June 2010].

Campbell, A., 'Persuasive Speaking: Define Your Key Message', *The Speaker*,
BBC, http://www.bbc.co.uk/speaker/improve/persuasion/ [accessed
17 May 2010].

Chortle, 'Did Johnny Vegas Go Too Far?', *Chortle*, http://www.chortle.co.uk/
news/2008/05/01/6719/did_johnny_vegas_go_too_far%3F [accessed
3 May 2009].

'Comments on Jeff Dunham Video', *YouTube*, http://www.youtube.com/
watch?v=1uwOL4rB-go [accessed 21 April 2010].

Evans, C., 'About Us', *Go Faster Stripe*, http://www.gofasterstripe.com/cgibin/
website.cgi?page=about [accessed 5 July 2010].

Hardwick, J., 'Al Murray is the LOWEST form of 'Humour', *Facebook*, http://
www.facebook.com/group.php?gid=2237201107 [accessed 28 June 2010].

Herring, Richard, 'Sunday 30th March 2008', *RichardHerring.com*, http://www.
richardherring.com/warmingup/30/3/2008/index.html [accessed 17 April
2014].

'Kevin Bloody Wilson', *myspace*, http://www.myspace.com/kevinbloodywilson
[accessed 15 September 2010].

Lahr, J., 'The Goat Boy Rises', *The New Yorker*, 1 November 1993, http://
www.newyorker.com/archive/1993/11/01/1993_11_01_113_TNY_
CARDS_000365503?currentPage=all [accessed 5 September 2010].

Lee, Stewart, 'The Trouble with Blasphemy', *StewartLee.co.uk*, http://www.
stewartlee.co.uk/youtube/youtubedontgetmestarted.htm [accessed
18 July 2009].

Logan, B., 'Josie Long: Pleasance Upstairs, Edinburgh', *theguardian.com*,
13 August 2007, http://www.theguardian.com/culture/2007/aug/13/
edinburghfestival2007.edinburghfestival6 [accessed 15 October 2014].

Logan, B., 'Laughing in the face of terror?', *Chortle*, 3 April 2009, http://www.
chortle.co.uk/interviews/2009/04/03/8675/laughing_in_the_face_of_
terror%3F [accessed 17 June 2009].

'Mark Watson: Comments Page', *Chortle*, http://www.chortle.co.uk/
comics/m/62/mark_watson [accessed 30 July 2007].

McDemos, www.mcdemos.com [accessed 3 October 2010].

Oliver, J. and A. Zaltzman, 'Close to the Edge', *The New Statesman Online*,
22 August 2005, http://www.newstatesman.com/200508220031 [accessed
11 March 2009].

Otchet, A., 'Mark Thomas: Method and Madness of a TV Comic', *The Unesco
Courier*, http://www.unesco.org/courier/1999_05/uk/dires/txt1.htm
[accessed 2 May 2009].

Porter, Lucy, 'The way I see it', *The New Statesman Online*, 5 March 2009,
http://www.newstatesman.com/comedy/2009/03/comedy-art-politics-
work [accessed 7 July 2014].

Spoonfedcomedy, 'Comic gives first aid to audience member', 12 April 2010,
Spoonfed, http://www.spoonfed.co.uk/spooners/spoonfedcomedy-8202/
comic-gives-first-aid-to-audience-member-2597/ [accessed 2 July 2010].

Thomas, M. and YWGAV Limited, *Mark Thomas Info*, http://markthomasinfo.
com [accessed 6 August 2009].

Interviews

Atkinson, Dan, by telephone, 29 September 2008.
Bailey, Dave, by email, 16 August 2008.
Crosby, Matthew, The Duke of Cumberland, Whitstable, 31 October 2008.
Herring, Richard, by telephone, 9 March 2009.
Lee, Stewart, The Leicester Square Theatre, London, 16 December 2009.
Long, Josie, by telephone, 27 October 2008.
Suttie, Isy, by email, 7 October 2008.
Thomas, Mark, The Gulbenkian Theatre, Canterbury, 4 October 2008.
Wilkinson, Joe, by telephone, 29 September 2008.

Miscellaneous

Brydon, Rob, *Rob Brydon's Identity Crisis*, BBC Four, 29 February 2008, 9pm.
Television broadcast.
Clayton, A., *The Layering of Intention: A New Theory of Comic Performance*,
Research Seminar, The University of Kent, 20 February 2008.
Double, O., *Jo Brand in Conversation with Oliver Double*, University of Kent
Open Lectures, 13 February 2008.
Festinger, L., 'The Theory of Cognitive Dissonance' [lecture], *The Voice of
America Forum Lecture Series* (USA, C.1960–9).
Ince, Robin, 'Geoff Rowe and Robin Ince in Conversation', *Playing for Laughs*,
Conference, De Montfort University, 6 February 2010.
Levinson, J., *The Morality and Immorality of Jokes*, Research Seminar,
University of Kent, 25 November 2008.
Sayle, Alexei, Research Seminar, University of Kent, 18 January 2006.
Thomas, Mark, Personal Communication, by email, 5 October 2008.
Thomas, Mark, Personal Communication, by email, 6 October 2008.

Index

About the Author

Dr Sophie Quirk is a lecturer in Drama and Theatre at the University of Kent, UK, where she teaches stand-up comedy and popular performance. Her previous publications explore the mechanisms and extent of manipulation in contemporary British stand-up comedy practice.

Lightning Source UK Ltd.
Milton Keynes UK
UKOW06n1626020216

267615UK00001B/2/P